Praise For

In This Lifetime

Magnificent! A novel that puts the human condition on full display. Christine Anderson gets it. Her brilliant character development masterfully reflects the whole spectrum of the highs and lows of ever human life.
—**Fr. Brain Sullivan,** Pastor, *Church of Christ the King*

***

For a person of faith, there is an ever-present challenge to connect to an unseen God. *In This Lifetime* gives us a realistic and imaginative opportunity to do just that. Christine Anderson invites the reader on a family journey with all the twists and turns of life, tragedy, forgiveness, and love. In the end, you realize that she is telling a deeper, faith-filled, universal story.
—**Dennis Corcoran,** *Corcoran Consulting. LLC*

***

As a medical professional, *In This Lifetime* resonates with me as it portrays an accurate account of the real-life struggles medical providers grapple with when caring for critical patients and their families and the role of faith in the healing process.
—**Melissa Gato**, MSN, RN, CEN Emergency Nurse

***

In This Lifetime is a profound story with a heart-racing conclusion that identifies our deepest human yearnings and answers some of life's most important questions. Authentic and relatable, the characters remain with you long after you turn the last page. It is a must read!

—**Pamela Abell**, Conference speaker, Bible teacher, marriage/family mentor

***

The writing details and descriptions totally allowed me to be there in the story and I was captivated from the first few lines. This beautiful story of love, forgiveness, acceptance, hope and letting go, helped me to realize that forgiveness is a journey and does not always come in the ways that you think it will. It reminded me that forgiveness is a choice and it is something we are always working on and striving to accept. *In This Lifetime* was truly a gift to read.

—**Erin Ranft**, Director of Religious Education, *Church of Christ the King*

***

Christine has a beautiful way of bringing us on a magic carpet ride towards forgiveness. She weaves her story together in such a way that it is very inviting and thought provoking! A must read!

—**Elizabeth Fitzpatrick**, Spiritual Director, Retired Guidance Counselor, *St Vincent de Paul Elementary School*

In This
Lifetime

CHRISTINE ANDERSON

Published by KHARIS PUBLISHING, an imprint of
KHARIS MEDIA LLC.

Copyright © 2024 Christine Anderson

ISBN-13: 978-1-63746-263-8

ISBN-10:1-63746-263-8

Library of Congress Control Number: 2024946496

Unless otherwise indicated, Scripture quotations are taken from:

Scripture taken from the NEW KING JAMES VERSION®. Copyright© 1982 by Thomas Nelson, Inc. Used by permission. All rights reserved.

All KHARIS PUBLISHING products are available at special quantity discounts for bulk purchase for sales promotions, premiums, fund-raising, and educational needs. For details, contact:
Kharis Media LLC
Tel: 1-630-909-3405
support@kharispublishing.com
www.kharispublishing.com

Christine Anderson

This book is dedicated to my children, Meredith, Kelly, and Michael, each one a gift from God, and to the two additional children God added to our family through marriage, Matthew and Allison. And to all the grandchildren, who have increased the size of our family and have filled our home with love and laughter: Josie, Camilla, Michael, Maxine, Patrick, and William. This book is for you.

Contents

Chapter One

"If you won't help him, he's going to die."

Cherie Hollister squelched the urge to spin from the stove and counter her mother's strident tone with one of her own. Instead, she inhaled sharply, biting back her instinctive response as she continued to stir the scrambled eggs for her daughters' breakfast. Through the thin walls of the toy strewn apartment, Cherie heard the pipes squeak and the toilet flush as the two older girls got ready for school. She glanced over at Carey, the youngest of the three, sitting in her booster seat at the table eating banana slices. Cherie kept her words even, the volume low. "Jake may be sick, Mom, but he's not dying."

"Not yet, but you haven't seen him lately." The galley kitchen suddenly became even smaller as Judith Ramsey approached the stove, her dark suit and overly highlighted hair making her look older than her sixty years.

Perhaps her gaunt appearance had more to do with worry about her youngest child, Cherie conceded as she spooned eggs onto three plates. "Mom, between work and the kids I haven't got time to drive to Long Island and see him. That's a two-hour trip from Jersey on a good day."

"You could call him."

The blatant attempt to make her feel guilty hung in the air as acrid as the fumes rising from the toaster. Cherie popped the toast up and then picked up two plates and squeezed past her mother. "He's as capable of making a call as I am." She placed the plates on the table and was about to retrieve the third, when her mother gently set it down beside the others.

Judith laid a hand on her arm. "But he won't. He still feels too guilty, you know that."

Cherie bit back an angry retort. She'd had all she could do to hold her own family together for the past three years since Paul died in a helicopter crash, leaving her a thirty-two-year-old widow. The irony of his safely having completed two tours in the Middle East and then coming home only to be killed in a training accident never failed to strike Cherie with a pain as deep as the act was random. Paul had been so honorable, a man who put country and family first in sharp contrast to her self-destructive brother. "Why are you here, Mom? You're usually at work by now." Cherie glanced at the clock, knowing this conversation was throwing off her mother's morning routine as well as Cherie's razor-thin timeline.

"Jake has been diagnosed with end-stage renal disease. They started him on dialysis last week."

Cherie froze, the butter knife poised over a slice of singed toast. Unbidden, the image of her brother as a fair-haired toddler stretching out his hands to his older sister assailed Cherie. But the baby who was always the center of attention grew up to be a teenager who craved it, his self-absorption leading to one crisis after another.

"He needs a kidney transplant. I came by this morning to ask if you would go and get tested to see if you are a match for your brother," Judith stated, delivering three glasses of orange juice to the table.

Cherie felt a sudden surge of acid reflux burn the back of her throat. She reached for the orange juice and swallowed a quick gulp, its sweetness playing over her tongue even as its acidity made her throat feel raw.

Cherie stared at her mother. "I can't believe you would ask me to do that."

Judith met her gaze squarely, any unease she felt at this request evident only in the hand that fluttered up to smooth her hair. "It's just a simple blood test. Dad and I were the first ones they tested but because we each contributed only half his DNA, his best hope for a match is a sibling."

"What about Amy?"

"She isn't a match."

"And you think I am?"

"We'll never know unless you get tested."

Cherie felt like a sacrificial lamb being led to the slaughter. Earlier in her life, she might have caved under the pressure of her mother's insistence, but the past three years of single parenthood had hardened her into a woman who would do anything to protect her children. "I have responsibilities here, Mom."

Giggles sounded from the hallway punctuating her words as backpacks slammed against the floor.

"We'll talk about this later," Cherie asserted, "because right now I have to get Molly and Sarah to school, Carey to daycare, and myself to work."

Judith glanced over her shoulder, her eyes softening at the playful antics of her two older granddaughters rifling through the pile of shoes under the bench by the front door. She turned back to Cherie, her words just above a whisper. "You still haven't forgiven him, have you?"

Cherie didn't want to talk about this, not again. "I told you I have, and I told Jake that, too."

"You said all the right words, but I think in your heart you never let it go." Judith shouldered her oversized purse as Molly and Sarah raced to the table. "Where does your Christian faith fit into how you treat your brother?"

Cherie gasped. The question hit its mark, digging deep into her conscience like a fishhook slicing through the flesh of a careless thumb. Judith knew just how to play on her guilt. Forgiveness had always been Cherie's stumbling block, as if by offering to forgive she somehow condoned the act. Anger roiled in her gut. Her mother never wanted to talk about her faith, which seemed limited to her dutiful attendance of weekly services, but she was certainly willing to use it to her advantage when it suited her purposes. Cherie bit her upper lip, using every ounce of self-control she possessed not to shout at her mother's retreating back as the apartment door closed with a firm thud.

"How come Grandy didn't stay for breakfast?" Sarah asked, upending the catsup, and covering her eggs. Her small hands slipped as she turned it upright, nearly dropping the bottle, and leaving a spray of red dots across her pink shirt and blonde bangs.

Molly grabbed the catsup before it careened into the glass of orange juice, her long dark hair, so like her mother's, shading the right side of her face. "Grandy has to go to work, and besides, she doesn't eat breakfast."

Sarah nodded, the eggs on her plate rapidly disappearing. "I forgot. She only drinks black coffee, right?"

Cherie wet a paper towel under the faucet and wiped Sarah's forehead, then gently blotted her shirt. Too late to change, it would have to do for today. "Eat up, you two. We're late."

"Ate, ate, ate," Carey squealed from her booster seat, making Cherie wonder if the toddler was still hungry or whether her own constant harping to keep them on schedule had made its way into Carey's language development. Below chubby cheeks, remnants of the scrambled eggs she had scooped from her own plate onto Carey's, clung to her lips and chin.

Cherie grabbed a few bites from her plate and smiled despite the mess on Carey's cherub face as an aching sadness tightened her throat. Paul had never gotten to meet his youngest child, born six months after the crash. If Cherie lingered on that thought, it would crush her, just as it had in the last months of her pregnancy when the only thing that kept her putting one foot in front of the other was her girls. She shook her head, pushing aside the sadness that still snuck up on her at random moments reminding her of all that Paul was missing.

A few minutes later, the hasty meal finished, she got everyone into their jackets and hoisted Carey onto her hip, wondering when spring on the calendar would equate to days warm enough to shed the outer layer. Clearly not yet. She herded the girls in front of her as they headed out for the day. They got as far as the door before Molly spun, a worried expression masking her face.

"I almost forgot. Ms. Richards said the money for the field trip is due today or I can't go." She peered up at Cherie, her dark hair falling behind her ear before she quickly shook her head, allowing the curtain of hair to fall back into place, obscuring the right side of her face.

Cherie's eyes stung at her daughter's self-protective gesture, now so automatic. She shifted Carey to her other hip and turned her handbag toward Molly. "Take the twenty that's in my wallet, Mol."

A flash of relief played across the eight-year-old's pretty features before she lifted the wallet and opened it. Her brow furrowed as she looked at Cherie. "But it's the last one."

"I'll stop at the ATM on the way home," Cherie said, knowing she wouldn't be going near the bank until the day after tomorrow when her paycheck was deposited into her account.

"We need to hurry. We're going to be late."

"Ate, ate, ate," Carey babbled as Cherie followed her older children to the car, a gust of biting wind making her wish she had taken the time to zip her own jacket.

* * *

Will Finnegan had started his shift in the emergency room at 6:00 a.m. At noon, he still hadn't eaten breakfast. And he still had two more patients to see before he had any chance of getting lunch. He pulled back the privacy curtain across the doorway to the ER bay, glancing down at the chart and then up at the panicked older woman holding a squirming toddler in her arms.

The woman began to chatter before Will even closed the curtain. "I certainly hope you're the doctor. Carey fell on the playground, tripped at the bottom of the slide and hit her head. I was watching her, but I had ten other children…"

Ten kids? Startled by the sudden outflow of information, Will interrupted her. "Can we start from the beginning, please? I'm Dr. Will Finnegan and you are…?"

"Dorothy Hansen," the woman replied. She cast a worried look at the little girl in her arms. "And this is Carey Hollister. I'm her teacher at Cedar Hills Day Care." Her words trailed off for a second as the little girl began to whimper. "I called her mother at work and asked her to meet us. She should be here shortly."

Will surveyed the blonde toddler making an initial assessment of the situation. She appeared to be a well-nourished child with a small gaping laceration of the forehead just above the eyebrow. She was moving all her extremities freely and didn't appear to be in a lot of pain, though she was clearly uneasy with the strange setting. "Well, let's take a look then."

He gently lifted the toddler from her teacher's arms, a bit surprised that at this age she would come to him so easily. "Hi Carey," Will said, addressing the child directly in a soothing tone as he laid her on the paper-covered exam table to begin his physical assessment. "Any loss of consciousness after the fall?"

"No, she screamed all the way here in the ambulance," Dorothy answered.

"Does she have any allergies to medications?"

"She's allergic to amoxicillin." A woman pulled back the curtain across the cubicle entrance. Her cheeks were flushed and her dark hair askew, and though she looked like she'd run from the parking lot, she wasn't winded.

"Mama," Carey squealed, reaching for her mother.

The woman bent and kissed her daughter softly before graciously dispensing with Dorothy Hansen's explanation and apologies.

Will continued his exam as she escorted Dorothy to the bay entrance and sent the teacher on her way with a thank you for riding in the ambulance with Carey.

"Does she have any medical or surgical history?" Will asked, suddenly acutely aware of the attractive woman at his side, though all her attention was focused on her child. She was what his grandmother would have called an Irish beauty. Pale skin. Long dark hair. Thick lashes rimmed her eyes, eyes the color of the Caribbean Sea during a storm, somewhere between a green and a gray. He shook his head to clear it of these irrelevant observations and returned his gaze to his patient. "Any history of prior head injury?"

"No surgical history or head injuries," the woman said, never glancing up from her daughter. Her words were brief to the point of curt, yet he sensed an undercurrent of anxiety that didn't match her clinical tone.

"Has she ever been hospitalized?" Will asked.

The woman shook her head. "No."

"Has she received regular medical care, including all her vaccinations?"

"Yes."

Will straightened, wondering what it was going to take to get more than the briefest of answers from this clearly loving mother. Perhaps he should go back and start over. Will extended his hand. "I'm sorry, I should have introduced myself. I'm Dr. Will Finnegan, chief ER resident."

"Cherie Hollister," she replied, quickly shaking his hand, and then returning her attention to her daughter. "And yes, Carey has had all her shots and check-ups. Have you had a chance to do a neurological exam?"

Will noted the firm set of her jaw as well as the defensive edge to her tone. "Yes, all within normal limits."

"And her vision?"

"She is tracking objects as I would expect for a child her age."

"What about a concussion?"

Will's eyes narrowed, wondering if Cherie Hollister had any medical training. Her questions were focused and appropriate for the injury her child had sustained.

"It's a possibility," Will responded. Her concern for her child was natural though her tone bordered on accusatory rather than questioning. "The injury to her forehead will need to be sutured, and then we'll discuss what you should look for in terms of symptoms after you take Carey home."

"Nausea and vomiting, difficulty rousing from sleep."

"Are you a nurse?" Will asked.

"No, a teacher," Cherie responded.

Will noted the way her lips pressed together as if she'd started to say more and then thought better of it. "Considering the location of Carey's injury would you like a plastic surgeon to do the closure?"

He assumed, given the wariness of her tone, she would readily agree, but she surprised him when she met his gaze and asked, "How long will it take to get a plastic surgeon to see Carey?"

"To be honest with you, it could be anywhere from an hour to several hours. The plastic surgeon on call takes cases in order of severity, and we have several patients here who are in more urgent need of her care. I don't want to downplay Carey's injury..." Will continued, wondering why he felt the need to justify a logical process like patient triage, "but it could be a little while."

Cherie Hollister glanced around the ER bay as she scooped Carey up. "She'll never last in here that long. I assume as a chief resident you've done this kind of suturing before, Dr. Finnegan?"

"Yes, of course, many times."

"And when you're finished, we can go?"

"Yes..."

"Then let's get started," Cherie said, not giving him the chance to finish speaking as she boosted the toddler up on her hip.

Will left the cubicle to gather the necessary supplies wondering where Cherie Hollister had developed such a clear aversion to hospitals. Almost everyone who came through the ER doors wanted to go home as quickly as possible. But he sensed something more, an undertone of panic tightly controlled, like she couldn't draw a full breath until she and her child had put the ER behind them.

He returned to the cubicle moments later with one of the ER techs. Taking Carey from Cherie, he swaddled the child using a sheet and a blanket so that when he finished her arms and legs were immobile and her head protruded from the medically fashioned cocoon.

The ER tech stepped up to the exam table and was about to stabilize Carey's head when Cherie spoke up. "I can hold her."

The tech glanced at Will who nodded, knowing how busy they were today. Why waste a pair of hands when Cherie was determined to participate in the care of her child. Will had decided to do a multilayer closure. It would leave a scar that would be less visible in the long term and since the injury was to Carey's face, it seemed an appropriate choice though it would take a bit longer.

Cherie held her daughter's head firmly between her palms as Will administered the local anesthetic. After a brief yelp at the injection, Carey was silent, her mother's calm voice speaking softly into her ear.

Will listened as he sutured, enjoying the monologue and the rare glimpse into their lives. Cherie didn't speak to her daughter with baby talk but simply kept up a verbal flow that required no response from her child. She spoke about Molly and Sarah, who Will assumed must be the toddler's siblings, about preschool and favorite toys and a grandmother who Will sensed was a source of some irritation to Cherie from her tone. Through it all, Will wondered why Cherie never mentioned the child's father. He chided himself on the instant wave of interest that had him wondering if she was divorced or a single parent by choice.

When he released the toddler from the makeshift cocoon, Carey wrapped her arms around her mother's neck, looking like a child who needed a good nap. Will went over the discharge instructions with Cherie. Usually, a nurse took care of this last task before sending the patient home, but he found himself surprisingly reluctant to see them go. How many families did he see in a shift with every imaginable type of injury, and yet here he sat, his stomach growling, prolonging an encounter with this pretty mother and her child.

"Any last questions for me?"

Cherie shook her head.

"Perhaps your husband can help you keep an eye on Carey tonight," Will said.

Cherie's chin shot up, but she voiced no reply, simply shook her head and hoisted Carey up onto her hip. Clearly, she was ready to leave but before she turned to go, she glanced up at him, meeting his gaze.

"Thank you," she said simply. "When I raced over here, all I could think was…" She bit her lower lip and then shook her head. "Thank you for making this visit as easy as it could be given the circumstances. I appreciate it more than you know."

And with that, she pushed the curtain open and was gone, leaving Will wishing he could stare into those green eyes just a moment longer.

Chapter Two

Cherie came through the apartment door with Carey on one hip and the girls on her heels. Backpacks hit the floor, shoes flew across the carpeted entryway before Molly and Sarah ran for the kitchen, starving as usual after a day of school and an afternoon of dance class.

"Save some room for pizza," Cherie called after them, setting Carey down and watching as the toddler ran after her sisters, seemingly none the worse for her ER visit this morning. "Aunt Amy will be here any minute."

Wednesday was pizza night and had been every week since Paul died. At first it was Amy's way of checking in on her older sister, but for Cherie the weekly dinners proved to be a lifeline of normalcy in a world that had suddenly lost all sense of reason and hope. Cherie looked forward to Wednesdays with Amy, and the girls were always eager to see their cousin, Mark, a shy eight-year-old with his mother's gentle smile and his father's notable height. In the second grade, Mark towered over all his peers, which could have made him a bully but instead made him a gentle giant.

In the first few months after Paul died in what was later determined to be pilot error during a routine training exercise, Wednesday nights were sometimes solemn and silent, and at other times tearful and angry. Amy had been there every week, a steady grounding presence in a world suddenly spinning on the wrong axis. And while their parents, Judith and Joe, had gently urged Cherie to move on with her life after the first anniversary of Paul's death, Amy had allowed her the space and time to heal. She let Cherie talk about Paul endlessly one week and then mourn in silence the next. Perhaps Amy's instinctive ability to just be present came from being married to a cop, and she unknowingly gave what she would have wanted had the roles been reversed, but whatever the reason, Cherie thanked God for her sister every day.

A loud chime from her coat pocket made Cherie reach for her phone, hoping Amy wasn't canceling their dinner. She groaned inwardly scanning the text from her mother as Molly handed small bags of Goldfish to her sisters.

> **Cherie, I know what you said this morning, but I also know the girl your father and I raised would never deny her brother the help he needs. I've made an appointment for you at the hospital lab. They'll draw a blood sample and send it to Hopewell Atlantic for testing. Saturday at 10:00. I'll even watch the girls for you. Please Cherie, call me.**

Cherie fumed, heat flooding her face as a knock sounded on the front door. The girls raced over, throwing the door open without asking who was there as Cherie had taught them to do. The aroma of freshly baked dough and crispy pepperoni wafted into the apartment as Amy held the pizza aloft and negotiated around the children hugging in the doorway. The girls quickly flanked their cousin and whisked him away for a little playtime before dinner. Carey tried to keep up with them, trailing the older kids to the corner of the living room still covered in toys as Cherie greeted her fair-haired sister.

"Just in time, you saved me from a phone call I'll regret later."

Amy placed the pizza boxes on the counter separating the galley kitchen from the living room, glancing over her shoulder at Cherie. "Okay, what's Mom done now?"

Cherie hesitated, knowing Amy had stepped up to be tested without being asked. "She wants me to get tested."

"As a possible donor for Jake?" Amy dropped her pink jacket on one of the stools by the counter, sitting down on the other and lifting the lid of the pizza box with one glittered fingernail. "I understand why you think Mom's asking a lot after what Jake's done."

"I think I hear a BUT coming …"

Amy glanced up from the pizza, a sad smile touching her full lips. "I wasn't a match, and maybe you won't be either …"

The sound of a church bell rang as Cherie's cell phone lit up on the counter. Distracted by the interrupted conversation, she picked it up automatically.

"Cherie Hollister, please," a male voice said. "This is Dr. Will Finnegan from Mercy Medical Center. I just wanted to follow up and see how Carey is doing."

"She's fine, thank you," Cherie replied, smiling as she watched Carey imitating the dance moves her sisters were showing their cousin.

"No headaches or dizziness?"

"No, she's acting very much like her usual self."

"Eating and drinking, okay?"

"She had a small meal after we got home from the ER."

"No nausea or vomiting?"

Very clinical, Cherie mused, but he would be, that's why he was calling. "None."

"Good to hear. Any questions for me about the follow up care?"

"No, I just need to see her pediatrician in a week, right?"

"Exactly." He paused. "We like to touch base with our patients after they get home. We find that sometimes in the commotion of the ER experience they don't always recall all we've told them."

"Even with the printed instructions you send home with them?"

Dr. Finnegan laughed. "Most often left in the car and never read."

Cherie smiled, thinking she had done the same thing, tossing them on the dashboard after buckling Carey into her car seat. "I appreciate the call. The hospital must be very concerned about their survey results. I've never gotten one of these before."

"A new initiative. End of my shift and I wanted to check in before I head home. Anyway, if you have any concerns, you can call me. My card was in your discharge packet."

Really, a doctor giving out his cell number? "Thanks."

"Take care then, Ms. Hollister."

The call ended, and Cherie was left staring at the home screen.

"Who was that?" Amy asked, having poured drinks for the kids and opened the salad in the middle of the table.

"The ER doctor who stitched up Carey's forehead after she fell on the playground."

"Sounded very thorough. I like that kind of care for my niece."

"Me, too."

"Kids, time to eat," Amy shouted.

Thundering feet were followed by chants of 'Pizza, Pizza' as the kids swarmed the table for their Wednesday feast.

Will Finnegan massaged his forehead with one hand as an embarrassed chuckle escaped his lips. Could he have been more obvious? Not that anything he'd said was untrue. Yes, the hospital did want them to follow up with their patients to make sure they understood their discharge instructions, but he had been looking forward to making this call all afternoon. In fact, he'd deliberately placed it last just in case a more in-depth conversation was needed, and he'd used his personal cell phone instead of his dedicated work phone. He was nearly forty and left feeling like a twelve-year-old with a crush who had called just to hear the girl's voice.

Okay, shake it off, he told himself. Clearly, his lack of recent dating experience was showing, he thought as he exited the ER. He had been so focused on his career change and just getting through medical school that he hadn't paid much attention to dating. So why did he suddenly find Cherie Hollister so intriguing? He'd been thinking about her all day. Beyond the beautiful, but prickly, exterior, he sensed a vulnerability and an instinctive suspicion of the medical establishment he had worked so hard to join. He recalled her definite dodge when he mentioned her husband, just the faintest glimpse of sadness and steel as she had avoided answering his question.

His phone rang as he crossed the parking lot. Grabbing it from his pocket, he hoped to see the number he had just called. He hit accept before processing that he was out of luck on that one.

"Hello, Will?"

Startled at a voice he hadn't heard in a very long time, he swallowed hard. This couldn't be good news.

"Maddie, how are you?"

"I'm well, very well actually. How about you?"

"Fine. We haven't talked in a while," Will said, wondering why his sister was calling.

"A bit of an understatement, but yes, it's been a few years," she said, her tone light, with just a hint of uncertainty.

So, not bad news, Will thought, but figured he'd ask anyway. "Mom and Dad alright?"

"Yep, both doing fine last time I checked."

"When was that?" Will asked, unlocking his Porsche Boxster with a touch to the key fob. He pulled open the door to the one remnant of his former life he had never been able to give up.

"I talked to them a week ago. Saw them at Christmas. Scott and I took the kids to see them."

"New Hampshire to North Carolina is a long drive. I thought your one summer visit was all you could handle?"

"You have a good memory, little brother."

Will flinched. He hated it when she called him that.

"I know you must be very busy in the last weeks of your residency, but ..." She paused and Will could hear the hesitancy in her tone. "Scott and I are coming to New York for a conference on small business start-ups and I was hoping we could get together while I'm in the area."

Startled, Will blinked. He couldn't remember the last time his sister had sought him out. "When's the conference?"

"First week in May."

"Send me the dates. I can shuffle the schedule to make it work. The only benefit of being a chief resident, I get to make the schedule. Everything alright?"

"Is now," Maddie said, her tone undeniably upbeat but then Maddie always was one to put a good face on things. "I'm sending you the dates. Try and make it work if you can. I'd love to see you."

"Okay, I will," he responded, baffled by the sudden invite as they said goodbye. He tried to recall the last time he had talked to Maddie and couldn't come up with one. A few Christmas cards and a note of congratulations on his graduation from med school, the only communication he could remember.

When he first heard Maddie's voice, he'd thought she was calling to tell him that one of their parents had died, the only plausible reason he could see her reaching out. Relieved that was not the case, he was left curious at the sudden interest in getting together from the oldest of the five siblings.

They had never been a close family, each leaving the family home in North Carolina right after graduation from college and finding new lives across the country. Tyler in Colorado. Jeremy in California. Mitch in Florida.

Maddie in New Hampshire. And himself in New York at first and then, after his residency match, in New Jersey. Different job opportunities had put miles between them, and none of them had tried to bridge the gap created by busy lives and busier jobs.

Will wondered whether their lack of connection had more to do with the home in which they were raised, a strict household filled with silence and impossible expectations. His father, Caleb, had been elected a Superior Court judge probably due in large part to his old money connections. His distinction in the community and the size of his bank account could have made him benevolent, but instead made him superior and distant, consumed by his work and his reputation. Which led to expectations of perfection in his offspring no child could ever hope to meet. And on the occasion when they acted like kids, trespassing on their neighbor's property and eagerly scaling their 200-year-old oak tree or skipping out on school to watch the set-up for the county fair, their punishment had been severe. After a stone-cold reprimand by the judge, a sentence was passed, a period when no one in the house was allowed to speak to them, including their mother. His father's version of solitary confinement had isolated them from each other and was supposed to deter future infractions. It had worked, but at the cost of separating them from each other and from their mother, a beautiful but mentally troubled woman who had been unable or unwilling to stand up for herself or her children. Will had never known which it was. When he had left for Columbia University in New York, fully paid for by his father, he had followed Maddie's example and never looked back, spending breaks with his friends' families and working whatever summer job he could find until school began again in the fall.

Still in his hand, his phone chimed a new text. He glanced down and saw three dates in early May from Maddie's number, followed by a series of smiling emojis. Really? He wouldn't have thought her the emoji type. He saved the dates to his calendar, shrugging off a feeling of disquiet, sensing there had to be more of a reason for Maddie to reach out than just a sibling reunion.

Starting the car, Will registered the satisfying roar and then the steady hum of the powerful engine. He loved this car. It cost a fortune to maintain, and, with his current salary, he could barely afford the monthly insurance premiums, but he wasn't trading it in for a more practical car. He shifted into reverse and eyed the backup camera before returning to his earlier musings.

He would make one of those dates work with Maddie. He wondered if his brother-in-law had finally decided to branch out on his own and start his own architectural firm which would explain the trip to New York for the conference. Will could certainly understand Scott wanting to get out of the Boston corporate world. He had been doing that commute into the city for nearly two decades ever since he and Maddie had built their dream home on the lake in New Hampshire. Will had been there just once, many years ago when his niece and nephew were small. The tranquility of the stately colonial with its wrap-around porch and green lawn rolling down to the lake's shallows had been soothing, though Will had wondered if it was worth the commute. Two hours one way. Every day. And the hassle of working for a corporate firm. If Scott was finally getting out, that was a good thing. Will had done the same thing himself.

Chapter Three

What was she doing here? Cherie glanced at the intake booths in the hospital registration area. After a lengthy discussion with Amy on Wednesday night about whether to do the blood test, Cherie had decided to keep the appointment her mother had made to avoid yet another argument. In the last few years her relationship with Judith had taken such a downward turn that avoiding a confrontation came at the expense of literally drawing blood. Sitting here, Cherie was beginning to question that decision.

What Judith had neglected to mention was that in making the appointment she had set off a chain of events which included a phone call from the transplant coordinator on Long Island to complete a brief intake form prior to the blood test. The woman from Hopewell Atlantic was professional and very enthusiastic about her job of which this initial contact was only a small part. Cherie had gone online after the conversation ended to find out just what a transplant coordinator does and was astounded at the breadth of responsibilities, from pre-operative scheduling and testing for potential donors to coordinating dates for surgery and post-operative care. For Cherie though, it would all be a moot point when she, like Amy, tested negative and being a donor for Jake was no longer an issue.

That sounded so heartless, Cherie thought, opening her bag to retrieve her driver's license and insurance card. Several times this week she had reached for her phone to call Jake but then the image of Molly being loaded into the ambulance would assail her, making her stomach roil and her pulse race. Was everyone deserving of a second chance? She had wrestled with that question for years. Her faith told her to forgive, and yet every maternal bone in her body couldn't let go of the sheer fury at what her brother had done.

"Ms. Hollister?"

Cherie glanced toward the registration desk and then realized the words had come from the other direction. She shifted her gaze and saw Carey's doctor from the ER walking toward her.

"How is Carey feeling?" he asked, coming to a stop in front of her.

She wished she could recall his name, but it was escaping her. Looking up at him strained her neck and Cherie got to her feet. She didn't remember him being so tall.

Clearly her expression must have been as blank as her brain because he supplied the missing information voluntarily. "Will Finnegan, we met in the ER."

"Dr. Finnegan, yes, of course," Cherie managed. "Carey is totally back to normal."

"Kids rebound quickly," he responded. "I'm glad she's doing well."

He looked weary, his eyes bloodshot and hair askew as if he'd just taken off a hat. "Just getting off shift and I spotted you and thought I'd check in."

"You must have worked all night."

A slight smile tweaked the corners of his mouth. "Do I look that bad? Don't answer that, I'm sure I do. I grabbed a protein bar from the vending machine around 8:00 p.m. last night and I've been moving ever since."

"Sounds like a busy Friday night."

"And Saturday morning. Some shifts the patients never stop coming."

He ran a hand through his light brown hair, trying to restore some order and making it worse. "Sometimes I miss my old job, but not too often. At least I got to sleep through the night with that one."

"You had another career before becoming a doctor?" Cherie asked, recalculating his age up a decade. He looked young despite the tired exterior.

"I did." He waved a hand at the chair beside her. "Mind if I sit?"

She shook her head and watched as he melted into the vinyl upholstery with a barely audible sigh. Feeling awkward still standing, she sat down as well. "So, what did you do?"

"I was a defense attorney for a major New York firm."

Intrigued, Cherie turned toward him. "You gave up a career as a lawyer to go to medical school?" From a prince to a pauper, she thought. What made a man do that? The question came out of her mouth before she could stop it. "Why?"

He extended his legs out in front of him, crossing them at the ankles. "Crazy, right? Everyone thought so. My buddies at work. My girlfriend, I guess I should say ex-girlfriend."

"Why did you do it then?"

He turned his head to look at her. "Because I couldn't stand watching people with more money than morals using the legal system to dodge the fall out of their own greed. And get away with it. Our firm was really good at what we did."

"That had to be a hard decision to make. There must be more to it than that," Cherie said, relaxing back into her seat and hoping he would finish the story.

"Next!" The registration clerk called over the speaker system.

Startled, Cherie glanced over at the desk and realized it was her turn.

"You'd better go," Will said, unfolding himself from the chair and gaining his feet. "I'm going to try and stay awake long enough to get a quick run in before crashing. Hope all goes well with whatever you're here for today. Something routine, I hope."

Cherie shifted to her feet, reminded of why she was here. "Just a little blood work."

"Well, you picked a good day. The wait time on Saturday is much less than the rest of the week. Have a good day. And again, I'm glad Carey is doing well."

And with that Cherie was left staring at his back as he exited the registration area. She gathered her bag and coat, hoping he was right, and she would be out of here in time to get Molly to lacrosse practice.

* * *

Will pulled his running gear from his locker, tossing his scrubs in the laundry basket by the locker room door. Still thinking about the chance encounter with Cherie Hollister, he pulled a navy T-shirt over his head.

What were the odds the woman he'd been thinking about since their first meeting Wednesday would cross his path this morning? Had to be high, he thought, catching a glimpse of his tired eyes and disheveled hair in the mirror on the inside of his locker door. That mirror came in handy when he needed a quick shave, but today it reminded him that his fortieth birthday was right around the corner. He looked exhausted and felt every one of those years. Cherie Hollister wasn't going to be left thinking about him that much was certain.

He was pushing himself to go for a run before he gave into the fatigue. As easy as it would have been during his residency to let regular workouts fall by the wayside in favor of more sleep, he knew the long-term damage of that decision. He saw it every day in the ER. The heart attacks, strokes and obesity caused by a sedentary lifestyle with too much food and too much stress. Running had always been his stress reduction. It had gotten him through high-profile trials with arrogant defendants as well as four academic years of medical school. He wasn't giving up on it now.

Tugging on his running shorts, he pivoted and grabbed his well-worn sneakers returning his thoughts to the young mother in the registration area. When he'd spotted her, he thought she looked nervous, almost afraid, an emotion he had not seen in the ER when he had sutured Carey's forehead. He'd debated just moving on, but something in her expression made him cover the distance between them. He sensed a vulnerability there, had come to recognize it over and over again in his ER patients and their families.

Easing the awkward moment by giving her his name, she had quickly shuttered her personal feelings behind a pleasant facade as she answered his questions about Carey. She was easy to talk to and Will noted her curiosity when he shared his unusual career path. It made for a good story but one he seldom shared, making him wonder why he had chosen to do so with a woman he hardly knew. But the obvious answer was the right one. He just wanted to keep her talking.

When she mentioned the blood work, a haunted expression flashed across her features making Will wonder what tests they were doing. But as intriguing as he found Cherie Hollister, when he walked away, he resolved to push her from his thoughts. He'd seen the ring on her finger which in Will's book made her off-limits. Even in a town the size of Darby he was unlikely to see her again anyway. It was time he got a life beyond his work and found an available woman to date.

He closed his locker with a thud and resolved to try one of the dating apps he had been avoiding for years, wondering if he would find anyone as intriguing as the young mother he had just left behind.

Fridays were brutal. The kids were tired from a week of learning and ready for the weekend. Cherie was looking forward to it every bit as much as her students. Fortunately, Fridays also included a physical education class that gave her fourth graders a chance to direct all that energy in a positive direction. After walking the kids over to the gym and leaving them in the capable hands of Coach Reston, Cherie headed back to the classroom. She had to finish the lesson plan for the week after next and assemble the supplies they would need for the science experiment they were doing after lunch. A 45-minute gym class was barely enough time to get it all done.

Spring sunlight filtered through the window behind her as she settled at her desk and reached for the lesson plan. Her phone vibrated in her pocket and Cherie pulled it out, always worried that a mid-morning call was from the girl's school or Carey's day care. Recognizing the number from last week, Cherie's finger froze over the green icon. The results couldn't be back yet, could they? She had been so sure when she did the test, she would be negative, but the unease she felt in this moment suggested a subconscious awareness the outcome was still in doubt. She placed the phone on her desk and answered the call, her tone tentative. "Hello."

"Good morning, Ms. Hollister. This is Brook Sheraton, the transplant coordinator at Hopewell Atlantic." Her tone was pleasant, the words lifting lightly at the end of each phrase, leaving an impression of excitement. "I received your test results this morning and wanted to get back to you as soon as possible. I am happy to tell you, you are a match for your brother, Jake. In fact, your HLA typing showed a six-point match. That's as good as it gets."

Cherie sat in stunned silence, sunlight warming her back even as an icy chill coursed through her limbs, making it hard to move and even harder to speak.

Brook Sheraton seemed to intuitively sense this conversation was different than others she had with eager family members. Her tone was softer, her words measured. "We have seen many different reactions to the news of a tissue match. No two people are alike in how they receive these results."

"I'm surprised," Cherie finally managed, pushing the words out but with little breath behind them, making them sound wispy and uncertain. "I had assumed I would be negative like my sister."

"This may take a little time to process," Ms. Sheraton assured her. "The abstract idea of donation may be different than how you feel now that you know you are a match. Take some time. Talk to your family. Talk to Jake."

Startled, Cherie sat up straighter. Talk to Jake! She clutched the phone in her hand. "Did you call and tell him?"

"No, we can't do that. HIPPA privacy laws apply to all patients. These are your medical results, and we can't tell anyone without your consent."

A wave of relief washed over Cherie like standing under a warm shower on a winter morning, driving the tension from her shoulders. "I do need to speak with my family. When do you need to hear back from me?" Cherie asked, suddenly realizing how little she knew about this whole process. She had been more worried about getting her mother to stop asking her to be tested than she had about the outcome. Now, that seemed a bit short-sighted.

Brook Sheraton's tone was reassuring, "Take all the time you need. No one is going to pressure you into making a decision about donation."

Cherie frowned. Clearly, Ms. Sheraton had never met Judith Ramsay.

"If you have any questions feel free to contact me. Sometimes more information about the donation process makes the decision easier," the transplant coordinator continued. "If you decide to move forward, there would be additional testing we would need to ensure you are a qualified donor. The HLA typing is just the first step in the process."

All Cherie wanted to do was get off the phone and put this conversation out of her mind long enough to get through the rest of the school day. Then she could think about it and decide who she needed to talk to. "Thank you, if I have any questions, I will give you a call."

"Any time. We have a team of 4 coordinators, and someone is always available. Your safety and peace of mind are our top priority."

"Thank you," Cherie said, even as she wondered if that were true.

Alone in the staff lounge two hours later, Cherie opened the refrigerator and reached for her lunch bag. She had managed to make it through the rest of the morning with a class of Friday-crazed 10-year-olds by abandoning the lesson plan and opting to play a game they loved. A takeoff on Jeopardy she divided the class into three teams to answer an integrated board of questions, in math, science, English, and current events. The reindeer bells from their Christmas decorations, stashed in the bottom drawer of her desk, worked well as buzzers filling the classroom with the sound of their merry jingle.

Cherie settled into her favorite seat by the window, surprised the day beyond wasn't as stormy as her emotions. Finally able to give the call with Brook Sheraton more considered thought, Cherie sat back in her chair, her food untouched. One thought loomed. She would have to tell her mother. Stalling would only work for so long, and by the time she did tell Judith, she needed to know what she was comfortable doing. Unbidden, a mental image formed in her mind of Judith sitting with Molly and Sarah on the couch in her apartment reading them a bedtime story. Paul had begun his second deployment just weeks after Sarah was born, and Cherie remembered standing in the bathroom doorway feeling exhausted and lonely and watching her mother snuggle with the baby and her sister. Cherie knew she never would have made it through those months alone without Judith.

What she really needed now was to talk to someone about the unexpected match. Pastor Michaels might be a good choice, though with her weekend schedule of services and events that probably wasn't possible until at least Sunday afternoon. Which left a weekend of shuffling children to birthday parties and sports practices as well as the 10k fundraiser she had signed up to run to benefit the Burn Center at Mercy Medical Center. Amy had generously agreed to take the kids when they had seen each other on Wednesday, knowing the cause was dear to Cherie's heart. And all of that with the news of a perfect tissue match hanging over her head and a mother who would not be put off for much longer.

She needed more information about end stage renal disease and transplants. She could start with the Internet, of course, but a medical opinion might be helpful. Her primary doctor had office hours on Monday; she could give her a call then and beg for an appointment. And with that thought Cherie felt like she'd been granted a 48-hour reprieve. Not that she wouldn't think about it, but there would be no decision making without more information. Taking a deep breath, she felt the tightness ebb from her chest and drew in her first full breath since mid-morning. Eyeing her lunch sitting open on the table, she reached for her sandwich. Taking on a Friday afternoon class on an empty stomach seemed unwise.

Chapter Four

Saturday dawned with a cloudless sky and low humidity. By 10:00 a.m. the temperature had risen into the high fifties. A perfect day for a run. The hospital's annual fundraiser for the Burn Center was going to break a few records today, judging by the crowd in line at the registration table, a mixture of runners, walkers, and families with strollers.

Will spotted her across the parking lot, bent down tying her sneaker. Cherie Hollister. He'd finally managed to stop thinking about her, and here she was. Will crossed the asphalt toward her. She wore a mint green jacket and 3/4 length workout pants with bright pink sneakers. Her dark hair was pulled back in a tight ponytail, her cheek bones prominent as she stood and reached for her backpack. She was attractive, but her appearance wasn't the draw. He sensed a vulnerability beyond that confident exterior, and he found that all he wanted to do was make her smile.

"Cherie?" he said, stepping up next to her as she rummaged around in her backpack.

She glanced up, a water bottle in her hand. "Dr. Finnegan."

At least she'd remembered his name this time. "You could call me, Will. I'm off duty this weekend, a rare and welcome event." Will shook his head briefly, trying not to babble.

"And yet here you are, running in a hospital fundraiser." She slipped her arms out of the jacket, revealing the numbered bib they had all been handed when they signed in. "That's dedication to your employer."

"The burn center is a good cause. The ER is where they start their recovery, but the burn unit does all the hard work." He noted a subtle shift in her expression, a clenching at the jawline and the very smallest nod of her head. Curious, he asked, "What brings you out here this early on a Saturday morning?"

"I've been a runner since high school," she replied. "Sometimes it feels good to compete against other people and not just the time on my watch."

"Okay, now I have to ask, how fast are you?"

"I'm hoping to finish in 50 minutes. That's the goal anyway." She reached up and tightened her ponytail with a quick tug.

A little faster than he'd been planning. He'd been out for a more casual run, but he could step it up a notch. "Since you enjoy a bit of competition, how about we run together?"

Cherie looked skeptical, clearly wondering if he could keep up.

"I wouldn't want to slow you down," he said, giving her an easy out, but then making an appeal to her competitive nature. "Although I did finish in 48 minutes last year."

She rolled up her jacket and stuffed it in her backpack, the slightest lift of the corner of her mouth letting him know he had won the day. "Sure, we could try it, but if you can't keep up, I might have to leave you behind."

Not quite a smile, he thought, studying her uplifted face but he'd take it. "No worries about that."

"I'll be right back then." She took a final sip from the water bottle, stowing it in the backpack's outside pocket before jogging over to the registration table. She exchanged a few quick words with the heavy-set blonde woman signing in the runners who laughed then pointed over her shoulder. Cherie skirted around the table and left her backpack on the far side.

Interesting, Will thought. The event was staffed by hospital employees, and the woman Cherie was talking to was one of the RNs on the same-day surgery unit. He watched Cherie moving back toward him, her expression as serious as her stride was easy.

"You ready?" she asked, stepping up beside him.

He nodded, letting her lead the way to the starting line where moments later the starter's horn sounded. Will and Cherie quickly distanced themselves from the pack, finding a steady pace. The course was clearly labeled, a 6.2-mile loop that would end back at the hospital, with volunteers situated at regular intervals with tables covered in water bottles and portable snacks.

They ran in silence, side by side, neither wanting to waste breath on conversation. Cherie was keeping a good pace and Will found that after the first two miles he had to mentally recalculate to keep up with her. If he had been running alone, he might have pulled back a bit and enjoyed the beautiful morning, but Cherie seemed not to notice, her mind clearly fixed on the clock as she occasionally checked her watch. Her breathing wasn't labored, and her stride remained even. She kept pace with him as if she had been running with a partner for years. Perhaps so, he thought, wondering about the father of her children and where he fit into her life.

At the five-mile mark, she seemed to falter a bit. Will found himself glad of the reprieve for a block or two before she picked up the pace again and pushed the final mile, kicking into a sprint down the final stretch to the finish line. Clearly, Cherie had a reserve to use on the last hundred yards as the clock at the line gave her one final challenge. They crossed the finish line at 48:43.

Will slowed to a jog and finally to a walk, each of them breathing heavily. They made an easy circuit around the parking lot before Cherie stopped and looked up at him, her face shiny with sweat, but her eyes alight with appreciation.

"Thanks, that was fun. I never would have made that time without you pacing me," she admitted, wiping the sweat from her face with the palm of her hand.

"I don't think I was the one doing the pacing, but I was happy to oblige. It's nice to have someone to run with who makes me work a bit harder."

Hands on hips, Will felt his breath returning to normal. The light breeze in the morning air felt good on his skin, though the damp shirt he wore would need an exchange with the dry one in his car for the ride home.

The scent of rose and jasmine wafted upward as Will watched Cherie sink to a squat to retie her sneaker, a look of thoughtful concentration on her face. She rose to her feet, paused a moment, and then stole the words from his mouth.

"Do you have time for a late breakfast?"

* * *

Clearly, she had taken him by surprise with the question, Cherie thought, watching his eyes widen, but his response was immediate, and his grin made the whole scene she had envisioned in her head far less awkward.

"Sure, I worked up an appetite," Will responded. "Got some place in mind?"

"I was thinking of the diner just off Elm Street."

"Ah, a classic. Best breakfast sandwiches in town."

"And the best coffee," Cherie added. "I'm going to grab my bag. How about we meet there in 15 minutes."

"Sounds like a plan."

Cherie could feel his gaze on her back as she jogged over to the registration table. She had been thinking about it for most of the run, debating whether it was a good idea to involve this man she barely knew in the hardest decision of her life. Since talking to the transplant coordinator yesterday, she had scoured the Internet looking for answers to her questions. She knew she could call Brook Sheraton for more information, but she found she wanted an uninvolved but still knowledgeable opinion about the living donor transplant process. She needed facts, and this very nice doctor might be able to help her with that.

Having retrieved her backpack, and thanked Marilyn for watching it for her, she found her car in the parking lot and reached into the backseat for the dry shirt she had tossed back there amidst the car seats and toys. She stripped off the sweat-drenched top, the air chilling her skin before dragging the clean T-shirt over her head. She glanced in the rearview mirror, noting the flush on her cheeks, a post-workout glow that erased all the lines from around her eyes and made her look five years younger. She considered redoing her hair and then tugged the ponytail a bit tighter and started the engine. What did it matter what she looked like? This wasn't a date, just a quick meal. Briefly, she felt a bit guilty about her motive in asking Will to join her but brushed it aside. She was just gathering information, she thought, even as she realized she hadn't eaten a meal with a man who wasn't a family member since Paul died.

She found Will seated in the corner booth when she came through the diner's front door. He raised a hand and then shrugged with a grin as if realizing the gesture was unnecessary in a place as small as the Trailway Diner.

The diner was a mainstay of the Darby downtown. The rail-car style eatery sat across from the train station and did steady business from 6 a.m. to

3 p.m. Counter service allowed five to sit, and the half dozen tables on the aisle were always full. Will was lucky to have gotten one, she thought, covering the distance in a few strides. She slipped onto the bench seat across from him as the waiter approached with a pot of coffee.

Will turned over both their cups, letting them settle with a clink back into their saucers before nodding at him. "Fill 'em up, please."

The waiter, a gangly teenage boy with hair pulled back in a low-slung ponytail, grinned and complied, before taking their order.

Cherie didn't need the menu. "A spinach omelet with home fries."

Will didn't either. "A number 3 with bacon, eggs over easy, and an extra stack of pancakes. I worked up an appetite."

"That you did." Cherie paused, studying her coffee cup as the waiter departed to place their order. "I think I need to tell you I had an ulterior motive for asking you to breakfast."

"Ah, the truth comes out," Will said, his face set in a pseudo-serious frown he couldn't quite pull off. "So, it wasn't my running skills and my charm that has you sitting across from me in my favorite restaurant."

Clearly, he wasn't put off by her admission. "Not exactly, though your running skills are significant. I can't speak to the charm part."

Will smiled. "A discussion for another time, the charm part I mean. What can I help you with?"

"I need you to tell me about living donor transplant surgery."

Instantly, his eyes narrowed, his former light-hearted banter gone. "That's a big topic. Which organ transplant are we talking about?"

Cherie reached for her coffee, holding the cup in both hands, the porcelain warming her palms. "Kidney."

"You're the donor?"

"Maybe, I don't know yet. That's why I need more information."

"Was that the blood work you were having done last Saturday when I saw you at the hospital?"

She had opened the discussion and, no doubt, piqued his curiosity; there was no going back now. "Yes, I heard from the transplant coordinator yesterday. I'm a match."

"How many points?"

"A six-point tissue match."

Will opened his mouth to speak and then shut it abruptly, choosing to take a gulp of coffee. "That's a significant match. Who is the recipient?"

"Possible recipient, my brother."

She watched him digest this information, awaiting the inevitable questions about Jake and the reason he needed a transplant. But Will didn't ask the obvious question. He paused, then leaned forward. "What do you really want to know, Cherie? I'm sensing you've got one question that has us sitting here today."

Setting down the cup in her hand, she met Will's gaze squarely, finally giving voice to her biggest fear.

"Could I die from this surgery?"

* * *

The waiter's sudden appearance startled them both. Will took a moment to collect his thoughts as two steaming plates were set in front of them. What had started as a casual meal had taken an abrupt turn as Cherie's question hung in the air between them. From a purely medical point of view, living kidney donors eased the pressure in a system where the need for donation far exceeded the number of available organs. With so many end-stage renal patients waiting for a kidney from a deceased donor, every living donor helped remove a name from the United Network Organ Sharing (UNOS) database. But this was more than just a medical decision, and he wanted to be as truthful with Cherie as possible.

Will shook his head as the waiter asked if they needed more coffee, then he leaned forward pushing his plate aside. "Bottom line, Cherie, is it likely you could die as a result of this surgery, no. But has it happened, yes."

Cherie nodded, picking up her fork though she appeared to have little appetite for the food in front of her. "Please eat, all this information will go down better on a full stomach."

Her words were at odds with her demeanor, but Will complied, pulling the plate back toward him. "What else can I tell you? Fire away."

He wanted to help Cherie get the information she needed to make an informed decision. The rotation he had done to the transplant service during his intern year put him on solid ground for this discussion.

"How long is the surgery?"

"2-3 hours."

"And it's a laparoscopic procedure, right?" Cherie started in on her omelet.

"Yes, with three small abdominal incisions and one slightly larger incision in the lower abdomen for the retrieval of the kidney." Will followed her lead and dug into the sizable breakfast in front of him.

"What about the recovery? How long will it take to get back to the way I feel today where I can take care of my kids and exercise without any pain?"

"All in, about two months. With the laparoscopic approach the recovery is quicker, but a full recovery to unlimited activities and the high level of exercise you seem to be used to would be several months."

"How long until I can lift Carey up?"

"Six weeks. You would need some help at home to take care of your children." Will paused, wondering whether to ask the question he had wanted the answer to since they had first met, but now for a totally different reason. "What does your husband think about you being a donor for your brother?"

Cherie flinched. Setting her fork down, she met his gaze. "My husband, Paul, died three years ago."

"I'm so sorry," Will said, startled at a scenario he hadn't even considered.

She nodded automatically, and Will knew she must have responded to condolences many times in the past three years. "Thank you. As you can see that makes this decision more difficult. The girls are my priority, always have been, but now even more so since I'm the only parent they have."

"I think anyone in your situation would want to think carefully about donation. From a medical standpoint, donation is quite safe, but it is not without risks." Will paused, wondering how much she understood about her brother's condition. "End stage renal disease can be managed with dialysis, but your brother's only chance to return to a normal life is a kidney transplant either from a deceased donor or a living donor like the one you are considering."

"How long can someone live on dialysis?" Cherie asked, returning her attention to her plate.

"Dialysis isn't a cure; it's a chronic management technique to keep the patient alive until a donation can be found. And it takes a toll on the body, on the vascular system, the heart, even the skin and hair."

"I hadn't really thought about the dialysis," Cherie said. "Jake just started needing it, and I thought he could be on it for a long time."

"And he can, but the patients who do well long-term are the ones who follow the dietary restrictions carefully. A high-protein, low-sodium diet and no more than 32 ounces of fluid a day." Will glanced at the cup of coffee in front of him. "Since the patient produces little or no urine, any fluid they drink remains in their system increasing their circulating volume and taxing the heart."

"32 ounces isn't a lot for a whole day."

"It's not. Feeling thirsty is a real issue for these patients. Your brother must be fairly young, how did he end up in kidney failure?"

Cherie paused, pushing aside the home fries on her plate. "My brother is a recovering drug addict, at least I think he's in recovery according to my mother."

"When was the last time you spoke to him?" Will asked, suddenly not sure donation was the best plan.

She vacillated for a moment before laying her fork down and looking up at him. "I haven't talked to Jake in four years."

"And you are seriously thinking about being his donor?"

"Like I said, I'm just gathering the facts."

"Might be a good idea to talk with him, don't you think?" Will countered, trying to keep the skepticism from his tone.

The waiter returned and slipped a check under the napkin dispenser. It was in Will's hand before Cherie had a chance to move.

"I asked you, remember? Let me get the check," she insisted.

"Next time," Will answered. In any other situation, he would have been planning for next time already, but his thoughts were preoccupied with the medical dilemma confronting him here. Cherie hadn't asked for a recommendation as to what she should do, and he was glad. He wasn't sure what to tell her.

Leaving the check on the table with an ample tip, Will stood as Cherie did likewise.

Out on the street a moment later, Will asked, "Can I walk you to your car?"

"Sure, and thanks for breakfast." She turned toward the train station parking lot, sparsely used on Saturday morning.

"Can we circle back for a minute to your brother?" Will said, as they crossed the street to the metered lot. "I'm assuming there were no other matches?"

"I'm the only one. My sister wasn't a match."

"Are you feeling some pressure to make a decision then?"

Cherie reached into her pocket, retrieving her keys before stopping in front of an old Jeep. "Yes, mostly from my mother, and I haven't even told her I'm a match yet." She leaned back against the driver's side door and turned her face to the cloudless sky. "I like to think as a mom myself, I wouldn't do that to my kids, but the thought of losing a child makes you take extreme measures. I get that."

Will noted the subtle clench of her jaw at these last words. "You should take all the time you need to think this through, to make sure it's the right thing for you and your family."

Cherie glanced over at him. "There was a time in my life when I could have been talked into this from an altruistic point of view, but since Paul died, I've changed. I'm tougher because I have to be."

"Because your kids are counting on you."

She nodded. "I got used to single parenting when Paul was deployed overseas. Two tours in the Middle East. But knowing he was coming home, even if it's months away, is totally different than knowing he's never coming home at all."

"Did he die during his deployment?"

"No, in a training accident right here in the states. I lost my husband and my home. We had to move out of our base housing which is how we ended up back here in Darby."

Will did the mental math. "And you were pregnant with Carey."

Cherie turned her head away from him, her eyes gleaming with unshed tears. "Yes, she was born a few months after we made the move here. She's the last piece of our life together. Hanging on until she was born was what got me through."

"I am so sorry, Cherie," Will said, wanting to reach out and touch her but holding back.

She pushed herself off the car and turned to unlock the door. "Thank you for taking the time to answer all my questions."

"You'll likely think of a few more in the coming days; you can always call me. You have my number, unless you tossed it with the discharge instructions from Carey's hospital visit," Will said, trying to lighten the moment in what suddenly felt like an awkward goodbye.

"I do still have them since I'm a bit of a hoarder when it comes to medical records." Cherie smiled. "And thanks for listening."

"Anytime," Will responded as she slipped into the driver's seat.

He stood rooted to the ground until she had made the turn onto Elm Street and accelerated through the green light. Now he knew why she was always so serious. Cherie Hollister was carrying a huge load on her shoulders. The loss of a husband. A single parent of three girls. A full-time job. All of that was enough to manage but add to that a brother in renal failure and a parent with weighty expectations and the burden seemed too big for one person to carry. He hoped he had helped her gain some clarity, though truth be told he had found her candor captivating.

Will shook his head. She needed good counsel and perhaps a shoulder to lean on. Not some guy who couldn't stop thinking about her green eyes, Will thought. Their relationship had started out as a professional one since she was the parent of a young patient, and now it felt like that would still be the boundary between them. He shrugged, not happy about it, but resigned. She needed the kind of help he was more than willing to give, and if that was the extent of their relationship, so be it. This was exactly why he had gone back to medical school in the first place. He would do what he could to help if she would let him.

Chapter Five

Cherie herded the girls into the last pew just as the opening hymn ended. She sank onto the cushioned seat, holding Carey on her lap as she reached into her bag for a book to keep the toddler occupied long enough for the rest of the family to listen to Pastor Michaels.

Cherie found it hard to concentrate on the readings as the girls squirmed and hummed and poked each other. Sarah leaned forward and started blowing on the lacquered hairdo of the older woman in front of them who had clearly just been to the hairdresser for a perm. Cherie quickly pulled her away, trying not to laugh as she recalled doing the same thing with Amy as little girls. Handing her daughters each a pad and a few crayons, she sat back, her thoughts returning, as they had all weekend, to the decision before her.

Last night she had considered calling Will with a few additional questions about the transplant process until concluding her indecision had more to do with her attitude toward her brother than with the details of the surgery. For that discussion she needed, not a doctor, but a voice of Christian reason.

Pastor Michaels stood in front of the altar giving her sermon, with no notes, her smooth southern drawl easy on the ears. Her six-foot frame radiated sincerity and purpose, her white robe contrasting with the warmth of her dark skin. She loved a good story, and used them liberally throughout her sermon, the fervor of her words and her spot-on analogies leaving the congregants nodding in agreement.

At the end of the service, Cherie funneled the girls into the line waiting to speak with the pastor. They were just a few families away from the pastor's outstretched hand when Cherie felt a light touch on her shoulder.

"Can I talk to you for a moment?"

Recognizing the voice, Cherie squared her shoulders and turned. Judith stood in the center aisle, her cream-colored pants and floral blouse mirroring the flowers on the altar.

"I was wondering if you'd heard from the transplant coordinator about your test results?" Judith stepped closer to Cherie and gently pulled her out of the way of other parishioners waiting to speak with Pastor Michaels. She glanced down at her granddaughters and quickly gave each one a hug.

"Don't you all look so pretty this morning." Judith kissed Carey on the cheek and then returned her attention to her daughter. "So, any news?"

Cherie glanced over her shoulder at the pastor, unwilling to lie in the presence of this woman she very much admired. "Can we talk about this later today. I need to get the girls home for lunch."

"Oh, of course, they must be hungry," Judith responded, with a smile. "I used to bring snacks for the ride home. The three of you were always starving after church. Maybe I could stop by later? I wanted to let Jake know as soon as possible about …"

"You told Jake I was getting tested?" Cherie's voice rose in pitch even as she tried to keep the volume low.

"Of course," Judith said as if that had always been a given. "You may be his best chance for a …"

Cherie cut her off. "I wanted to wait until we knew something before talking to Jake."

"I didn't realize it was a secret," Judith responded. "I'm sorry, I thought when you agreed to the test …"

"Mommy had to take a test?" Sarah piped up, her eyes darting from her mother to her grandmother. "I thought only kids took tests, right, Mommy?"

"Yes, that's right," Cherie answered, patting Sarah's shoulder even as her maternal gaze went immediately to Molly who was listening to the exchange with wide-eyed concentration and little creases in her brow.

Cherie mentally berated herself for what now seemed obvious. All she had wanted to do was get through the weekend, having gathered some information about the transplant process before talking to her mother, a goal that now seemed incredibly short-sighted. Of course, they were going to see Judith in church and, of course, she wouldn't be able to resist asking about the test results. Cherie stifled a groan and then offered up a desperate prayer. She needed to get the girls home before Judith laid bare the very adult issues Cherie had been trying to hide from her children.

A shadow appeared on the floor as Pastor Michaels stepped into the family circle, her tall frame sinking to eye level with the three girls as she asked a question. "Were you three coloring during my sermon?" She looked serious for just an instant before breaking into a wide grin. "I wish I'd had a few crayons to make my points more colorful. I especially like the green ones."

"Pink. I like pink," Carey said as Sarah started to giggle.

"You mean you don't mind if we color while you talk?" Molly asked.

"Not a bit. Your ears are open, right?"

The girls nodded in unison.

"Then I figure you're going to take home exactly what God wants you to hear. So, color away!" She rose gracefully to her full height. "Now I might be expecting a bit more from you two though."

Judith looked bewildered at this, but Cherie had worked with Gabby Michaels on enough fundraisers for military families to know that teasing tone.

"I can't say what the girls are going to take away from this morning," Cherie responded, her tone light, "but I thought the sermon was inspired."

"Always is," Pastor Michaels said, raising her hand and pointing upward. "Now what was your favorite part?"

Cherie smiled, knowing it was a trick question. It wasn't a test to see if she'd been listening but rather an opportunity for her to express the one thought she was going to take out into her week. Gabby called it the "nugget of truth". For each person listening it might be something different as they filtered the sermon through their own life lens, so it didn't matter what she said as long as it was real. "I was reminded how tired Jesus must have been, healing all the sick and then feeding them as well. I only have three little girls and I know how tired I get. Jesus must have been exhausted after a day like that."

Gabby Michaels smiled, an ear-splitting grin. "Fully God and yet living in a body just like ours. I bet he needed a good night's sleep after that one."

The girls were starting to wander down the aisle toward the door and Cherie took a step to follow. She hadn't gotten a chance to ask the pastor for a few minutes of her time, but she could make a phone call and set up an appointment.

As if reading her mind, Pastor Michaels called after her. "Would it be alright if I called you later this afternoon? I have a new project I wanted to get your input on."

"Yes, of course, any time," Cherie said over her shoulder, increasing her pace as Carey neared the stairs.

Behind her she could hear Gabby engaging Judith in a conversation about the annual Christmas in July bazaar. Gabby Michaels was incredibly observant; she had sensed the tension between mother and daughter and defused it as only she could. Cherie offered up a quick thank you for the answered prayer as she scooped Carey up and headed across the parking lot with Molly and Sarah at her side.

* * *

Driving into New York City on a Sunday morning was a more pleasant experience than the commute he used to make from Brooklyn in his days at Boyle, Mendelson, and Cobb. Exiting the Lincoln Tunnel, he navigated his way to the restaurant having done so many times before. He and Maddie had agreed via text on the time, and he had recommended the restaurant, one he and Jen had frequented when they were first dating. Will was eager to try it again.

The late morning air was cool and breezy as he stepped from the parking garage into a cascade of sunlight that promised a warmer end to the day. He would have to make time for a run later when he got home. Waiting at the corner for the light to change, he eyed the restaurant, its large bay window and striped awning just as welcoming as he remembered.

Pulling open the door to the restaurant, Will immediately spotted Maddie and Scott sitting at a table by the window. She looked thinner than he remembered, her blonde hair shorter but still with those unruly curls. Of the four brothers, he was closest in age to Maddie, but none of them had paid much attention to their older sister's looks. Will did remember her as rounder though and always worried about her weight. Didn't look like that was a problem anymore.

Maddie spotted him as he came through the door. She quickly stood and met him halfway, a wide smile increasing the tiny lines around her eyes that hadn't been there a decade ago.

"I am so glad to see you," she said, looking a bit uncertain and then enfolding him in a hug.

Will had been prepared for something more formal. Awkward handshakes and stilted conversation. More like the home in which they were raised where anything more than a hand on the shoulder was considered excessive physical contact. But Maddie defied all his expectations with her warm embrace and eager words. "It has been way too long, Will."

He hugged his sister, reminded of how all the brothers had a good eight inches on her. He pulled back to meet her upturned gaze, surprised by the wave of longing that welled up in him like a kid coming home from summer camp. "Good to see you, Maddie. Thanks for reaching out."

She smiled then turned, one arm still around his waist. "You remember Scott."

"Of course." Will stepped closer to the table holding out a hand to his brother-in-law. At just over six feet with broad shoulders, Scott was a bit thicker through the torso and sported a few gray hairs to mark the passage of a decade since they had last seen each other.

Scott's grip was firm, his smile welcoming. "Glad you could make it."

"We just arrived this morning," Maddie added as they settled into their seats. "The conference starts tomorrow."

"Have you left the corporate world in Boston?" Will asked Scott.

"Yes, I started my own architecture firm a little over a year ago," Scott reached over and covered Maddie's hand with his own.

"I run the office, and he does the design. We're a good team," Maddie responded, glancing over at her husband with a smile.

They seemed happy as if they had been finishing each other's sentences for years. From what Will could remember though, they had been well on their way to repeating the silent distance of his own parents, a marriage in name only. Clearly something had changed, and Will found himself a bit envious of their easy camaraderie.

"How is the final year of your residency going?" Maddie asked as a waitress approached the table and took their drink order.

"Hectic with the additional responsibilities of supervising the other residents, but I graduate from the program in six weeks."

"And will you stay on at Mercy?" Scott asked.

Will nodded. "They offered me a job and I accepted. I'm hoping to get a bit more sleep as a staff physician, but that remains to be seen."

Maddie leaned forward. "I never told you how much I admired your decision to follow your heart and start over. It took a lot of courage to walk away from a well-established career."

Her words of praise made him feel self-conscious, a mixture of embarrassment and pleasure.

He'd been 30 years old the day he decided to start studying for the MCATS, the standardized test needed for medical school admission. He figured he'd take the test and the score would tell the tale of whether he could even get in. If he'd gotten a poor score, he might still be working at Boyle, Mendelson, and Cobb, but he'd scored in the top percentile, likely because his competitive nature had him studying most of his non-working hours. Which had started the downturn in his relationship with Jen.

"Being any attorney is the right profession for some, just not for me." Will shrugged, as the waitress placed three mugs of coffee on the table. "I'm glad I figured it out when I did."

"It took guts," Scott said. "Actually, your example was one of the reasons I chose to go out on my own, that and a few others." Scott clasped Maddie's hand. A subtle look of encouragement passed between them, and she nodded.

"I do have something to tell you. It isn't the only reason I reached out to you. I've been meaning to for quite a while," Maddie said, lifting her eyes and meeting his gaze. She quickly continued as if wanting to get the whole story out before he said anything. "Eighteen months ago, I was diagnosed with lung cancer, what they called an incidental finding, after I had a car accident, and the first responders brought me to the ER."

Startled by the diagnosis, Will registered the pain on Scott's face. So many questions came to mind, but he held his tongue sensing that Maddie wasn't finished yet.

"It was remarkable, really. Truly a God sent that accident," Maddie continued, her voice wavering as she turned to her husband, her eyes shiny with tears before giving Will her full attention again. "They never would have found it otherwise. I had no symptoms and thought I was in perfect health.

Later that week, they removed a lobe of my left lung and then followed up with several months of chemotherapy."

Shaken, Will found his voice, asking the only question that mattered. "How are you now?"

"Doing well. My last scan was clean. No cancer anywhere."

Will felt his shoulders relax. She wasn't dying. Her doctors had found the cancer early, making her chances for long-term survival much higher. Still, the diagnosis shook him to his core. Cancer. She was 42 years old.

As if reading his thoughts. Maddie reached across the table and squeezed his hand. "I know I'm not out of the woods yet, but one-year post-treatment with no cancer in sight feels like a mountain I've been waiting to scale. I've got my eyes fixed on the five-year mark now."

Will felt torn, wishing he had known about all Maddie was going through and yet understanding why she had not reached out sooner. Their family never talked about real struggles. You were expected to bury the emotions and find a way to deal with it on your own.

"I'm sorry you had to go through that."

"Okay, and here's the strange part," Maddie said. "I'm not sorry. Having cancer saved my life, the rest of my life."

"Not the typical response to having cancer."

Maddie chuckled. "Not usually, no." She nodded at Scott who took up the explanation.

"Maddie and I were in a bad place in our marriage right before the accident. I spent all my time either at work or at home thinking about it and Maddie devoted all her attention to the kids." Scott shook his head. "We were living in the same house for years without connecting with each other or caring if we did."

This was what Will remembered. The silence between them. "Like Mom and Dad."

Maddie flinched. "Yes, and we weren't doing anything to fix it, until the accident."

Scott put his arm around Maddie's shoulders. "The truth is, we had a terrible fight that night, said a lot of things we'd been holding onto for too many years. Maddie ran to her car and drove away before I could stop her. She was furious with me and distracted, and when a deer stepped into the road, she swerved and hit a tree. According to the first responders, she was unconscious when they came on scene."

Working in the ER, Will knew what came next. A full work-up when she came through the door. Airway management. Blood work. Abdominal ultrasound. A chest x-ray and a CAT scan. "And they found the cancer?"

"I was terrified when they told us," Maddie said, her eyes wide as if recalling the moment. "I still am sometimes, but that diagnosis saved our marriage and our family."

"It made us work together, all of us, to really start talking to each other again," Scott said. "Taking care of Maddie and the kids during those months of chemotherapy was the hardest thing I have ever done and the most important."

"And watching him work and struggle," Maddie nudged Scott with her elbow, "I fell in love with him all over again. God gave a us a second chance to get it right."

"Could just be a coincidence the accident revealing the cancer," Will suggested, having set aside the Christian upbringing that had been such a part of their childhood. "So, you found each other, and you found God?"

"More like He found us," Scott replied, picking up his menu. "What made you choose this place?"

Grateful for the change of subject, Will opened his menu as well. "I used to come here a lot with Jen. We'd meet here for dinner because it was close to both our jobs. Hope the food is still as good as I remember."

"What ever happened with you and Jen?" Scott asked.

Another uncomfortable subject. First God and now Jen, Will thought, but in keeping with their honesty he responded in kind. "We'd been dating for a few years, talking about getting engaged, when I started the med school application process. But a fulltime job as an attorney working over 60 hours a week and studying for the MCAT was tough on our relationship. And when I got accepted to med school and quit my job, it got worse."

"Not what she'd signed up for?" Maddie asked.

"Something like that, yes. I don't think I realized how much Jen liked dating a guy with a secure future and a sizable back account. Without that income, I had to downsize to a studio apartment in a different part of town, and shortly after, I knew she wasn't in it for the long haul anymore." Will winced at the memory of how close he had come to marrying a girl who bailed at the first sign of hardship. How had he so badly misjudged this woman he claimed to love? It still baffled him.

"Are you dating anyone now?" Maddie asked.

An image of Cherie Hollister dripping with sweat as she ran by his side flashed through Will's mind before he forcefully pushed it aside. "No time for dating," he responded. "Working staggered shifts in the ER doesn't work well with starting a new relationship or at least it hasn't so far." Another image of Cherie leaning against her car and sharing with him the loss of her husband made Will drop the levity. "Relationships are complicated."

"I know that look," Maddie said. "That's the same look you used to get when your heart was pulling you in one direction and your brain was trying to stop you. Like the time you found that stray puppy and were trying to decide if it was worth the fight with dad to try and keep her."

Intrigued, Scott looked up. "How did that one turn out?"

"Won the argument. Kept the dog."

"Only because Dad thought it made us look like a regular family when he was up for reelection to the bench," Will added.

"So, who is she?" Maddie persisted.

"This is her relentless side as I remember," Will said, glancing at Scott.

"Don't I know it. You should just 'fess up now and save yourself the interrogation," Scott joked, flashing a smile at his wife who was giving him the stink eye.

Will agreed, recalling his sister's determination. "She's not a girlfriend. Just the mother of a young patient who needed some information about transplant surgery."

"But you like her?" Maddie asked.

Will nodded. "More than I should."

"Is she married?"

"No, she's a widow with three young kids, and we're going to leave this conversation right there. I don't want to violate any HIPPA laws or anything," Will said, dodging any further questions with a change of subject. "Tell me how the kids are doing? Kylie must be thinking about college, right?"

Maddie lit up at the mention of her children and Will knew he was out of the woods on the girlfriend discussion.

The meal passed in easy conversation. Outside on the sidewalk an hour later. Maddie hooked her arm through Will's glancing up at him. "Thank you for meeting us today. And forgive me for not getting in touch earlier when I was sick. I should have told you sooner."

"I'm just glad you told me now," Will said, pulling her into a hug. "Let's not let a whole decade go by without doing this again."

"Not a chance," Scott responded. "We were thinking you might like to join us July 4th. We do have a home right on the lake and a perfect view of the county fireworks from our deck."

"Throw in a few beers and I'll have to take you up on that, but first I have to escape working the holiday. Let me get back to you on that one," Will added.

"Okay, I know this is going to sound stupid after the last ten years but I'm going to miss you," Maddie said, her brow furrowed and her eyes shiny. "We've lost a lot of time …"

"Not out of anger or malice," Will interrupted. "More like apathy. We just drifted apart and not one of us cared enough to try and pull us back together as a family. Thanks for being the one brave enough to start it off. Can I assume you're doing the same with Tyler, Mitch, and Jeremy?"

"Not yet, but I intend to. I wanted to start with you first."

Will looked down at his sister, a wave of warmth spreading through his chest at her words. "Maybe we can try reaching out together."

Maddie beamed. "What a great idea. Let's talk about it in July."

"Enjoy the conference," Will said, shaking hands with Scott.

"I'm planning on it. And three dinners alone with my wife just might be the best part." Scott said, as the two joined hands.

Will watched them walk away, Maddie's shoulder bumping into her husband's arm, a couple clearly in sync with one another. From what he had seen, both personally and professionally, that was a rare happening in a world filled with infidelity and divorce, making him wonder if it was possible for lightning to strike twice in one family.

* * *

Will cleared the Lincoln Tunnel and settled in for the drive home. He set the cruise control at 70 and hit the button on the steering wheel which picked up the podcast where he had left off. The drive would take an hour, plenty of time to get in a run before he was due back to work.

The podcast abruptly cut out as a phone number flashed across the console. He'd only called it once, but he recognized it instantly. He hit the icon on the wheel and answered the call.

"Hi, Will, it's Cherie Hollister. I hope I'm not getting you at a bad time."

"No, not at all." Will smiled, glad she had taken him up on his offer. "Just finished having brunch with my sister and I'm headed home. Did you have more questions after our discussion yesterday?"

"Yes, I mean … no," she answered.

"Now you're confusing me," Will laughed, wondering how this woman who was usually so assertive could sound so unsure.

"You really helped me understand what's involved with living donor transplants and I was hoping you could do it again." She paused, clearly choosing her words. "The truth is, I need your help."

Will heard the uncertainty and exasperation in her tone. This wasn't a woman used to asking for help. "What can I do?"

"I'm about to get the world's biggest pressure campaign from my mother when I tell her I'm a match."

"And you need some back up," Will said. "Someone to help her understand the process."

"Yes," Cherie answered, sounding relieved.

"When and where?" Will asked.

"Could you possibly come by my place in an hour? I feel bad asking since this may be your only day off."

"It's all good. I'm doing a short shift tonight to cover for one of the interns who is about to get engaged, but I'm not due in until 6:00."

She gave him the address in Darby, and Will realized she didn't live far from where they'd had breakfast together yesterday.

"My mother is coming at 3:00, and my sister is going to keep the kids out of earshot."

"Sounds like a plan," Will said. "I told you yesterday you could call me anytime. I'm glad you did."

"You may not say that after you meet my mother."

Clearly there was a history between mother and daughter. Good to know going in. Will chose his next words carefully. "From what I can see you are a woman who loves her children fiercely. I'm thinking your mother might be a good bit like you."

She didn't reply. Perhaps he had said too much, but he liked to keep an open mind about people. Too often he found, especially in his work, that prejudging people led to the wrong diagnosis.

"Thanks for doing this, Will."

"Anytime, Cherie. I'll see you in an hour," Will said. Dropping out of cruise control, he hit the gas and headed home.

Chapter Six

Cherie stood at the screen door watching her sister escort the kids to the park down the street. The girls were clamoring for their cousin's attention as Amy herded them onto the sidewalk. What would she have done in the last three years without Amy's help, Cherie thought, watching them turn the corner. And without her mother as well, Cherie had to admit. Will's words rang in her head, "I bet she's a good bit like you." Probably more truth in that than she was willing to admit. Still, she wasn't looking forward to telling Judith about her test results.

A sleek black convertible with the top up pulled to a slow stop in front. Cherie wasn't much of a car lover but even she could appreciate the high-end features and clean lines of the Porsche roadster. She and Paul used to go to the car show when it came to the Meadowlands. They would push Molly around in her stroller and admire all the luxury cars they would never own. Who could possibly be driving that car in this neighborhood, Cherie wondered before the driver's door opened and Will emerged from the car. He reached back in for his jacket and shrugged into it before turning toward the apartment complex.

She had only seen him in scrubs and then dripping wet yesterday in his running gear, but the man who strode up the walk to her apartment wearing khakis, a plaid shirt, and a blue blazer was undeniably handsome, leaving Cherie flustered and a bit annoyed with herself for noticing.

She tried to move past that thought by pushing open the door and meeting him on the top step.

"Thanks for coming."

"Of course," Will responded, mounting the two steps with an easy stride to stand beside her. "Is your mother here yet?"

Cherie shook her head, looking up at him. "Should be here any minute."

She preceded him into the apartment, suddenly very aware of its size. Usually, she gave it little thought, though often she did wish for just one more bedroom. After Paul's death, she had moved back to Darby to be closer to her family and found the rental prices in New Jersey much higher than she expected. This two-bedroom was a stretch even with her salary and the survivor benefits from the government. She led him through the tiny entryway where a wooden bench was home to four backpacks. A myriad of girl's shoes rested beneath. Plastic hooks on the wall provided a home for raincoats, sweatshirts, and sports apparel.

"Can I get you something to drink?" she asked as she waved him to a stool on the living room side of the pass through. "I just made some lemonade." She retrieved a pitcher from the refrigerator, before reaching for a glass from the laminated cabinets above the sink.

"Sounds good," Will said, sitting on the bar stool and taking the glass from her outstretched hand. "Do you have a plan for how you want to handle this?"

Cherie shook her head. "With my mother you need to just roll with the punches."

"Got it. Just let me know when you want me to clarify something."

"Is it okay if I introduce you as Carey's doctor? If I tell her you and I are friends it will set her head spinning. A professional relationship just seems safer."

"Of course," Will said, and Cherie thought she detected just a touch of a smile.

He seemed incredibly comfortable here in her apartment among the bins of toys, her kitchen table just a few feet away strewn with stencils, coloring books, and markers. She had thought about cleaning up a bit, but the effort wasn't worth the result.

"That is a very serious car you have there," Cherie said, pouring herself a glass of lemonade.

"A remnant of my former life. I probably should have traded it in for a more practical car, but I just couldn't part with it." Will shrugged. "On a resident's salary, it's the insurance that gets you."

Outside a car door closed and Cherie grimaced. "Someday I would like to hear the end of that story about the move from trial law to medicine."

"Anytime," Will said, getting to his feet.

High heels clicked on the cement walkway. Judith was still wearing the pants and blouse she had worn to church as her voice carried through the screen door. "Cherie, did you see that car at the curb? I wonder who owns it?" She pulled the door open and then stopped abruptly as she realized they were not alone.

"That would be me," Will said, covering the distance between them.

Cherie stepped in to make the introductions. "Mom, this is Dr. Will Finnegan, Carey's doctor. And Will, this is my mother, Judith Ramsey."

Judith looked surprised but covered with a dazzling smile and an outstretched hand. "It's very nice to meet you."

"You as well, Mrs. Ramsey."

"Why don't we sit down. Can I get you some lemonade, Mom?" Cherie asked.

Judith shook her head. "No, thank you."

Clearly, she wanted the information she had come for. Cherie settled on the navy sectional next to her mother while Will took the chair across from them.

Judith cast a glance first at Will and then at Cherie. "Is Carey ill?"

"No, Mom. I asked Will here to give us a medical perspective for our discussion."

Judith leaned forward; her eyes expectant. "You heard from the transplant coordinator?"

Cherie reached for her glass. Taking a sip, she then folded her hands in her lap. "Yes, she called me on Friday. I am a match for Jake."

Cherie had been expecting her mother to rejoice at the test results, but Judith's eyes were wet with tears, her lower lip trembling. "Really? Did you call Jake and tell him?"

"Not yet, I wanted to talk with you first before making a decision."

"A decision, I don't understand," Judith said. "You're a match, what kind of decision would there be?"

Cherie glanced over at Will, knowing he was getting an inkling of what she was up against here. For Judith the match was the only important part, the rest was a given.

Will leaned forward and clasped his hands together between his knees. "Judith, being a kidney transplant donor is a complicated process. There are many steps between a positive match and a transplant surgery, and a number of tests that need to be done to ensure the donor is a viable candidate medically. What's important is to protect the health of the donor, so they don't suffer any ill effects from the surgery."

"But if the donor is young and healthy, like Cherie, none of that should be a problem."

"For the most part that's true, but sometimes the anatomy of the kidney or the vessels providing its blood supply may be compromised. That would disqualify the donor."

"Mom, I'm still adjusting to the fact I'm a match, and I need to take some time and think this over before going forward," Cherie said, getting to her feet and turning to face her mother.

"But surely you could go ahead and get the testing done so we would be one step closer when you do decide to do it." Judith looked at Cherie, her eyes pleading.

"Do you even know what you're asking?" Cherie said, trying not to lose her temper in front of Will. "I have three little girls with only one parent, and you want me to agree to this surgery without even thinking about it."

Judith got to her feet. "Your girls will be fine and so will you."

"You don't know that!"

"You still haven't forgiven him. That's it, isn't it?"

"And what if it is?" Cherie tried to modulate her volume, her words crisp and angry. "He's an addict, Mom."

"Not anymore."

"For how long?" Cherie asked.

"It's been more than two years," Judith asserted. "But you wouldn't know that because you refuse to even talk with him."

Her words only fueled Cherie's mounting fury. "How many times has he relapsed? Five? Six?"

"He never meant to hurt Molly," Judith insisted, taking a step toward her daughter.

"He relapsed in my house while he was supposed to be watching Molly. He set the house on fire! I don't think I can ever forgive him for that. My little girl is going to be scarred for the rest of her life because of him." Cherie drew in a shuddering breath, trying to reign in her anger. "You always take his side! When are you ever going to side with us, with Molly? With me?" Tears stung her eyes, and she shook her head, trying to clear her vision.

Will stood and reached out a hand, touching Cherie's shoulder before letting his hand fall to his side. "Ladies, one thing you both need to know is that every potential donor is required to undergo a psychological evaluation. And at this point with all the unresolved issues you have spoken about here, you wouldn't pass that part of the pre-op work-up, Cherie."

"So, you're telling me it's over then," Judith said, looking at Will.

"No, Mrs. Ramsey, Jake will remain on the transplant list and can still be matched with a deceased donor organ."

"But that could take years," Judith pleaded.

"Yes, it could," Will admitted. "Or it could be much sooner. There is no way to tell."

In the distance, the sound of children laughing spilled through the open door.

"Mom, I need you to promise me something?" Cherie insisted, her tone urgent.

"And what would that be?" Judith wiped her cheeks with the tips of her fingers.

"I need you to promise you won't tell Jake about the match. I need to be the one to tell him."

"Certainly, why would I get his hopes up for no reason," Judith said, lifting her handbag from the couch. "I'm going to go out the back. My granddaughters don't need to see me like this."

She strode down the hallway, stepping out onto the side patio just as the screen door opened and a jumble of sweaty bodies engulfed Cherie's lower legs.

"So sorry, I know you said an hour, but Sarah had to go to the bathroom and then Mark did too," Amy said, the last one through the door, her eyes widening as she spotted Will.

Cherie stepped into the commotion. "Will, this is my sister, Amy, and her son, Mark. That was Sarah who just flew through here to find the bathroom. And this is Molly."

Cherie rested a hand on Molly's shoulder and watched as her daughter instinctively tilted her head, letting her hair fall over her face before glancing upward to acknowledge the introduction. Just beyond the curtain of long dark hair, the scars from the burn were clearly visible. The side of her cheek had an irregular texture, while evidence of a skin graft ran upward from her neck past her reconstructed ear. It was better than it had been five years ago, but it was still a source of embarrassment and anxiety for Molly.

"Molly, this is Dr. Finnegan. He took care of Carey in the emergency room after she fell."

Molly held out her hand and Will engulfed her small fingers in his. She said nothing, just nodded and met his gaze which was an improvement from the years immediately following the burn when she used to run from the room rather than face anyone new.

"And you remember Carey?" Cherie said.

Carey stared up at Will, then broke into a grin. "Dr. Fin. You made my head not hurt. See!" She pointed at her forehead where the stitches had recently been removed.

Will dropped to a squat in front of Carey. "You have a good memory. I'm glad you're feeling better."

Amy took in the discussion then raised her eyebrows in an unvoiced question that was going to remain unanswered, at least for now.

"Can you stay for a few minutes while I walk Will out to his car," Cherie asked.

"Sure, I'll just grab a snack for everyone, and we can watch a movie."

The kids ran for the kitchen at the mention of a snack as Cherie and Will stepped out of the apartment. Sunlight filtered through the trees to create a dappled pattern of shadow and light on the grass on either side of the walkway. A warm breeze lifted the leaves changing the pattern as Cherie inhaled deeply, her first easy breath since this morning.

"Thank you for coming on such short notice," Cherie said as they walked toward his car. "I can't tell you how much I appreciate you being here today. Doing that by myself would have been a nightmare. We would still be yelling at each other if you hadn't stepped in."

"I'm glad you called. And yes, I was trying to help you, but everything I said was true. With your history with your brother, most reputable transplant programs would disqualify you as a donor unless you had truly been able to put the past behind you. Sounds like you're not quite ready to do that yet." Will pulled his key fob from his pocket.

Cherie sensed his concern and turned to face him as they reached the car. "You just learned more about me than I'm sure you ever wanted to know."

"Not even close," Will said, meeting her upturned gaze.

She'd been joking, trying to lighten the moment, but Will's expression was serious, his eyes sincere. Cherie paused, her next words spilling from her mouth. "I keep asking you for help and you keep saying yes. Why is that?"

"Because you are a strong woman with a complicated family and more responsibilities than anyone should have to shoulder alone," Will said. "And I want to help you."

"Because you're a doctor and that's what you do," Cherie said, her tone questioning.

"No, because we're friends." Will smiled. "I'm sure I heard you say that earlier."

Cherie laughed. "Yes, we're friends."

"And that's what friends do for each other. Who knows, I might need to call and ask for your help and you would do that, right?"

"Of course, I kind of owe you after yesterday and today."

Will paused, clearly weighing a thought before saying it. "Do you think it might be time to talk to your brother?"

Cherie nodded. "On my list of things to do tonight."

"Will you let me know how it goes?"

"Sure." Cherie started walking backward up the path. "I'll call you tomorrow?"

"You can call me anytime," Will said, opening the passenger door and tossing his jacket on the seat.

"You may live to regret that statement," Cherie called.

"Not in this lifetime." He rounded the car and opened the door, ducking into the coupe.

Cherie stood on the steps and watched him pull away. It could have been a casual throwaway line but from what she knew of Will Finnegan so far, he was a serious guy with a penchant for helping people. Not likely to say something he didn't mean. Which left only one conclusion.

And much as she wanted to have a friend, and be a friend, to have someone in her life besides Amy to really talk to, she didn't know if she was ready for the admiration she had seen in Will's eyes.

* * *

Will hit the gas hard then realized he was in a residential neighborhood and punched the brakes. Not exactly a man of mystery, Will chided himself, palming the steering wheel and making the turn for home.

He hadn't intended on doing anything but running a bit of interference so Cherie could get through the meeting with her mother. But the story about Jake's relapse, the fire, and then meeting Molly had laid bare his emotions, and he found himself wanting to protect Cherie and Molly. The professional separation he maintained between his emotions and his patients had served him well throughout his medical training, allowing him to give good care and not get lost in their tragedies. Until now. That inner wall had evaporated like frost in the sun when he saw Molly's scars. He had felt a protectiveness and a longing for a deeper connection as he and Cherie stood together on the sidewalk. What came out of his mouth in the moments that followed was simply the unvarnished truth. Well, she wouldn't have any doubts about how he felt about her now, Will thought, pulling into the driveway of his condo. He glanced at the dashboard. He still had time for a run before he was due in the ER.

If he had scared her away with his candor, if she wasn't ready to have a male friend after her husband's death, then better to know now. He pulled his running gear from the stacked washer and dryer in the bathroom and put it on. He'd invested in relationships before, most notable with Jen, and gotten burned enough times to know that people brought their own expectations into any new relationship. Better to be clear about his up front.

He grabbed his sneakers and sat on the tile floor to put them on, then tucked his house key into his shorts and opened the door. He set off at a fast pace, quicker than usual as he tried to outrun one disquieting thought.

He wouldn't be happy if he never heard from Cherie Hollister again. He admired her strength, her devotion to her kids, even the little chip on her shoulder he'd noticed the first time he met her. And he liked the fact she wasn't afraid to ask him for help.

He hoped today wasn't the last time that happened.

✳ ✳ ✳

The kids settled in front of the latest Toy Story sequel. Amy cornered Cherie in the kitchen. "How did it go with Mom?" Amy asked, leaning up against the counter.

Cherie glanced into the living room, the kids enthralled with the movie, the music loud enough to prevent any eavesdropping, before giving Amy a pared down version of the argument with Judith. "Will ended up stepping in and explaining that I would likely be disqualified as a donor unless I was able to put the past behind me about the fire and Molly's injury."

"And you aren't ready to do that?" Amy asked.

"I thought maybe I was, but clearly, I'm still angry with Jake. The weird part is I hadn't decided about being a donor until Mom backed me into a corner. I know I'm his best chance at a life free of dialysis — which I hear is awful by the way — but I just wanted more time to consider the consequences, for me and the girls."

"Understandable." Amy's tone was reflective. "I remember the day Paul got home to see Molly on the Burn Unit. He was furious!"

Cherie winced at the memory, recalling the searing anger that poured from her husband's soul. "In all the time I knew him I'd never seen him that mad. I think without his military training, he might have gone after Jake. But being a father was his life blood, and he would never have risked being separated from the girls by an act of vengeance. The girls were everything to him …"

"So were you."

Cherie bowed her head, feeling the sting in her eyes as the tears began to form. It had been three years and still she cried when she remembered just how much they had loved each other. "Maybe, that's a part of it, too. I feel like I'd be betraying my husband if I agree to risk my life to help Jake."

On the counter, her cell phone began to vibrate still in silent mode from church this morning. Cherie glanced at the number. "Okay, if I take this?"

Amy nodded, heading into the living room where she plopped down on the floor to watch with the kids as Cherie answered the call.

"What kind of project are we working on this time, Gabby?" Cherie asked, stepping outside and sitting on the stoop to take the call.

Pastor Michael's chuckle was warm and lilting, her rich contralto like an oboe swaying from note to note in a smooth fluid melody. Cherie could picture her in her office behind her massive desk, the mahogany surface eclipsed by an abundance of paperwork. Sermons, committee reports, bake sales, and teen nights. And she could lay her hand on any one of those in an instant.

"That was just a cover," Gabby replied. "You looked like you needed a little rescuing."

"You were definitely the answer to prayer," Cherie admitted.

"That would be me. One of God's largest earthbound emissaries," Gabby replied. "I had a feeling you wanted to talk when I saw you in line after the service. Usually, you're slipping out the side door herding a gaggle of girls to the car. Is my ministerial radar still intact?"

"Right on target. Do you have a few minutes to talk?"

"How about I listen, and you talk." The squeak of her desk chair let Cherie know she was getting comfortable. "Is this about Jake?"

"Yes, how did you know?"

"The only thing that seems to make you and your mother frown at the same time is a discussion about your brother. Just an observation, go on."

After Paul's death, Cherie had returned to Darby determined to make a fresh start in her hometown. A young pregnant widow with two small children, she had started attending Lakeview Baptist and Gabby Michaels, its new pastor, had taken the whole family under her wing. She'd encouraged Cherie to join *We Mourn Together*, a group of parishioners of all ages who had lost a spouse. She was by far the youngest one there, but she quickly realized grief had no age limit. She took as much solace from the widow on her third marriage as she did from the gentleman who had been married to his wife for over sixty years. And in the months that followed as she became a part of this generous and loving community, Cherie had shared with Pastor Michaels the trauma of Molly's injury and Jake's part in it.

Cherie brought the pastor up to date on Jake's need for a transplant, saving until the end the revelation that she was a perfect match.

Through it all, Gabby listened quietly, and when Cherie fell silent, Gabby said only, "I think you have a question for me."

"I do, and I think you may be the only one I know with the answer." Cherie inhaled deeply. "Is everyone worthy of a second chance?"

Gabby paused for a moment, never one to just give a superficial answer. Her voice when she spoke was soft and serious. "Let's turn that around and ask it differently. Is anyone worthy?"

Cherie knew the answer to that one. "I don't remember what book it's in, but I remember the scripture. 'For all have sinned and fall short of the glory of God'."

"So, is anyone worthy?"

"No, we're all a mess."

Gabby chuckled at the phrasing. "Exactly. It isn't really a question about second chances at all. It's a question of forgiveness."

"Is anyone worthy of forgiveness," Cherie said, rephrasing the earlier inquiry, her tone resigned because she knew the answer.

"Forgiveness isn't earned, Cherie." The rich truth seemed to flow from the pastor right through the phone. "It's a gift given to those who don't deserve it by someone who is ready to move on from the past. Not to forget, but to move on."

"I don't know how to do that."

"I think you do, but you don't want to. You're still holding on to that anger like an anchor, a tether that keeps you tied to a time and place where your husband was still alive, and your beautiful Molly had the face of an angel."

Cherie inhaled sharply, then clamped her mouth shut, biting her cheek in the process. Hadn't she just said as much to Amy not five minutes ago, that it would be a betrayal of Paul to forgive Jake.

Gabby didn't need a response, her words unhurried and soothing. "God offers His forgiveness out of a place of pure love but that would be a lot to ask of us mere mortals. But we can choose to move beyond a past that can't be changed and to offer a gift of grace. You know what grace literally means, don't you?"

Cherie nodded, the phone bumping up against her ear. "Grace is God's unmerited favor."

"Freely given ..."

"To those who don't deserve it," Cherie said, completing the phrase.

"You've been listening to me!" Gabby thumped the desk with her hand, and Cherie could hear a cascade of paper hit the floor.

"I always do. You're a wise woman."

"As are you, my friend. Can I just add one thing? If you choose to forgive your brother that doesn't mean you have to be his donor. The two issues seem linked right now like a magnet finding metal, but they're two separate decisions and should be treated that way."

At her words a wave of relief washed over Cherie like a baptism from above.

"You can forgive Jake and still not be his donor, but you can't be his donor and not forgive him. It won't work that way."

"So, I've heard."

"From someone as smart as me?" Gabby blustered, feigning indignation.

"Very close, but maybe not quite," Cherie replied, feeling again the brush of Will's hand on her shoulder as he ended the argument with her mother. She had felt like he was defending her, relieving her of the weight that had settled on her shoulders since Friday.

"I think I feel a prayer coming on," Gabby said.

"Go for it," Cherie responded as she pictured the pastor lifting her hand in the air.

"Oh Lord, we thank you for guiding our words here today. My friend, this beautiful young mother has two important decisions to make in these coming days. We bring this whole situation before you, knowing you already know all the details, and ask you to guide her in the process of forgiving her brother. We know it is your will that we should forgive as you have forgiveness us, but we need your help to do it. We also ask that you guide Cherie in deciding whether to be a donor for her brother. She's going to talk to you about all of this, and we ask you to show her the clear path that is your will for her life. In Jesus name we pray, Amen!"

"Amen." Cherie echoed.

"Are you good?"

"I am now, how can I thank you …"

"You know where I live. Stop by anytime and bring some of that lemonade," Gabby said. "God bless you, my friend."

Cherie smiled, holding the phone in both hands like a treasure, feeling on this day she was indeed rich in friends.

* * *

The girls tucked into bed Cherie knew what she had to do. She pulled up the contacts on her phone as she settled on the bar stool at the counter. She knew she had to do this tonight. Judith's promise not to tell Jake about the match, likely had an expiration date, she thought as she steeled herself for the next few minutes. Then remembering Pastor Michaels heart-felt prayer earlier, Cherie offered up one of her own.

"Lord, help me see the truth, not through my lens but through yours." She touched the screen and waited as the phone rang.

"Cherie? Hold on." Jake's face filled the screen as he adjusted his cell phone. He carried the phone a few feet and propped it against the open screen of a laptop before taking a seat in front of it. "It's good to see you."

She hadn't seen him in more than four years but at 24, he looked a decade older. His blond hair, once shoulder length, was now cut short with a military feel to the close-cropped crew cut. His skin was tan as if he spent a lot of time outdoors though an underlying note of pallor made him look weary. Unsure now they were face to face, just how to start this conversation, Jake beat her to it.

"I'm sure Mom has filled you in on all the health-related details," Jake said.

"How is the dialysis going?" Cherie asked, noting the oddly shaped window behind him on the screen. It looked like a barn door and above it the apex of a roof line.

"Takes a little getting used to, and the time involved messes with my job."

Having never known Jake to be able to hold down a job, she asked, "What are you doing for work?"

"I'm a custodian and groundskeeper for a local church. They've been very accommodating about my need to flex my hours for the dialysis."

Jake sat back in his chair, and Cherie could see he had filled out in the years since they had last seen each other. His shoulders were broader, his arms muscular, the distinct shadow of a day's growth of beard framing his jawline.

"When I first came out of rehab," Jake continued, "I worked bussing tables until the owner helped me find this job. It's a good fit. I get to spend a lot of time outside, a little cold in the winter with all the shoveling and salting, but it's good work." He smiled revealing straight teeth still with that slight gap between the two front ones, and Cherie was reminded of the day he had lost his first tooth and tried to wait up all night to see if the tooth fairy was the real deal.

"And you can't beat the perks," Jake added. "The church grounds have a small caretaker's unit. A studio apartment over the garage, just one big room but it's warm, and comfortable and makes getting to work on time easy."

"I'm glad you are doing okay. Mom made it sound like …"

"Like I was dying?"

"Something like that, yes," Cherie said, feeling herself start to relax until she remembered what she had called to say. "Jake, actually I called to tell you something."

"Okay, shoot."

Cherie forged ahead before she lost her nerve. "You knew Amy was tested to see if she was a match for you. I was recently tested as well and I just found out, you and I are a match."

Jake leaned forward, his expression surprised, his tone firm. "I don't want your kidney, Cherie."

Startled by his words and the sincerity, bordering on frustration, in his tone, Cherie found herself literally speechless.

Jake sank back in his chair, rubbing the top of his head with one hand, the way he always had when he was agitated. "Mom made you do it, didn't she? I told her I didn't want you involved in this."

Cherie found her voice. "Have you ever known Mom to listen when she thinks she can fix things for one of her kids."

"Never, you're right," Jake admitted. "My mistake was thinking she would respect my request."

"Were you going to tell me?" Cherie asked, feeling relieved at the direction the conversation had taken and curious as to his reasoning.

"I was still working that out. Besides I knew Amy would tell you, and I wasn't sure how you felt about hearing from me."

Cherie didn't know how she would have reacted to a call from Jake after more than four years.

"Listen Cher, contrary to what Mom is filling your head with, I'm doing fine. I don't need your help, and I don't deserve it. So, let's just leave it alone."

Pastor Michaels words from earlier in the day filled her head. Is anyone worthy? She had known the answer then, and she knew it now. Cherie tried to refocus on her brother who was still speaking.

"I am glad you called, but also sorry Mom browbeat you into it," Jake continued. "I know these last few years have put a massive weight on your shoulders and for my part in contributing to all you have to deal with, I am incredibly sorry."

Jake fell silent, and Cherie was left holding an apology she had not sought and wasn't sure she wanted.

"I'm glad you're doing okay," Cherie said, dodging the subject entirely.

"Before you go, there is one thing you could do for me if you would."

Cherie stilled. Here it comes. "And what would that be?"

"Could you pray for me? You were always much better at that than I was," Jake said.

Cherie studied his expression, just the right balance of sincerity and uncertainty. It was a simple request that would cost her nothing, yet why did it feel so contrived. She hesitated and then answered. "I could do that. We could all use more prayer in our lives."

"I agree," Jake replied and then smiled. "Good night, Cherie."

With a brief touch of the screen, he was gone, leaving Cherie to wonder what to make of a brother she had never understood.

Chapter Seven

Throughout the next day as she dropped the kids at school and then hurried to work, her mind kept returning to the conversation with Jake. He had seemed so sincere and appeared to truly be building a new life, though her more cynical side did wonder if she was being manipulated by a brother who had known how to get his way with each member of the family using his charm and good looks. Stopping at the supermarket before picking the girls up, her thoughts turned to his odd request for prayer. Jake had always hated going to church. He sulked in silence each Sunday morning as Judith and Joe funneled them all into a pew. How ironic that now he was earning his livelihood as a church employee.

By the time she and the girls came through the apartment door, she felt relieved; the transplant decision no longer hung around her neck like an anchor waiting to drown her, though relief felt like the easy way out of a situation that was far more complicated. Jake had let her off the hook but was that merely a ploy to gain her sympathy when a few months from now he needed her help.

She set Molly up at the table to start her homework, gave Sarah an alphabet workbook and a box of crayons to share with Carey who quickly opened her Disney princess coloring book. Cherie knew she had about ten minutes to unpack the groceries and start the ground turkey tacos she'd planned for dinner.

The phone at her elbow began to chime as she added the taco seasoning to the cast iron skillet. The spicy aroma of chili powder and cumin filled the kitchen as it hit the hot pan. Cherie reached over and put the call on speaker, recognizing the number from yesterday.

"I was going to call you," Cherie said, bypassing the usual hellos.

Will's voice came through the speaker. "Never doubted you would, but I had a few minutes between patients and thought I'd check in and see if you wanted to talk later. I could stop by after my shift ends if you're not too tired. Say 8:30?"

"I think I could keep my eyes open until then, but just barely." Cherie reached for a tomato and began to cut it into small cubes for a topping.

At the table, the decibel level increased as the girls started to argue over the single box of crayons they were supposed to be sharing.

"I need the blue one," Sarah shouted.

"You can use another color," Molly said, evenly.

"I'm doing the "B" page and blueberries are always blue."

"I have to referee," Cherie said.

"I can hear that," Will chuckled. "I'll see you later."

Will pulled up in front of Cherie's apartment for the second time in as many days. Starting up the darkening walkway, he straightened the collar of his navy golf shirt, noting it was more wrinkled than he remembered when he grabbed it from the dryer this morning. Usually, he just changed into a clean pair of scrubs before heading home, but this morning on the off chance he might see Cherie he'd grabbed some clothes before heading to work. Then since he was prepared to see her, he decided to make it happen. After all, she'd called him yesterday and he figured it was his turn to do the reaching out.

He winced at that transparent logic, knowing he was already getting in over his head with Cherie. Which was absurd when he thought about it logically. He had known Cherie less than two weeks from their first encounter in the ER until tonight when he had literally invited himself over to her home.

74

Cherie appeared in the doorway. She wore faded jeans and a white zippered sweatshirt, the bright white contrasting with her dark hair, which hung loose around her shoulders. In the receding twilight with only the light from the entryway spilling out onto the stoop, she stood for a moment framed in the brightness. If he'd thought he was in over his head before, one look at her confirmed that conclusion.

Cherie opened the screen door with her hip and stepped outside, holding two glasses. She extended one to Will as he approached.

"I thought maybe we could sit out here," Cherie said. "Sometimes the girls are light sleepers."

She sat down on the top step, and Will followed her lead, the crisp evening air filled with the sounds of distant traffic. "Remember the story you promised to tell me?" Cherie asked. "I believe you said anytime. How about now? Before we get into the whole phone call with Jake."

"Sure," Will nodded, wrapping his hands around the cold glass. He had been prepared to listen tonight, not talk, and he wasn't always easy with sharing his story.

"Tell me how it felt to start over," she said softly, angling her body to face him and leaning back against the wrought iron railing.

Mentally, he had been preparing for a recitation of the facts, but clearly, she was looking for more. Shifting gears, he thought for a moment, not about the facts but the feelings. "I think the hardest part was going from knowing the answer to any question to knowing nothing at all," Will said. "I was really good at what I did."

"I guessed that much," Cherie said with a laugh gesturing at the car by the curb almost invisible in the darkness.

"It was more than just the money. I was recruited right out of law school by one of the top firms in New York City, and after seven years I knew what to expect. And when I left it felt like I stepped off a cliff because when it came to medicine, I knew nothing, and everyone treated me that way."

"So, why did you do it?"

Will glanced over at her, knowing his usual superficial answer wasn't going to cut it here in the darkness, and he found he wanted to give her the honesty she had allowed him to see yesterday. "Because I hated it. Kind of ironic, right? I was good at something I hated, and I couldn't imagine spending the rest of my life defending corporate hot shots trying to drag legitimated claimants through the court system. And all so they could stall year after year and not have to pay for the harm they'd knowingly caused. I saved my clients from paying millions in damages to people who had been harmed by their greed. Made me sick to my stomach most days, watching them just walk away, but I told myself that everyone deserves a vigorous defense. It's how our system works." Will bowed his head, feeling disgusted with himself again before looking up expecting to see the same from Cherie. "I couldn't do it anymore, so I walked away."

Cherie turned the glass in her hands. Her eyes held no judgement, just a quiet resignation. "It's one thing to recognize the injustice and a whole other thing to do something about it. Most people aren't brave enough to act on their principles."

"Brave or desperate, I still wonder sometimes, but I have never regretted that decision. My bank account feels the hit, especially after paying for med school but it was the only thing for me to do and be able to live with myself." Will raised his glass and swallowed, feeling the tightness in his throat that always accompanied the strong emotions he usually kept buried deep. "I'll never make the kind of money I was making back then, but I wake up every morning knowing that I'm going to get a chance to help people, not hurt them."

Cherie sipped her drink. "So, what happened to the ex-girlfriend?"

Startled, Will recalled their encounter before her blood draw. "Whoa, you were listening to me babble that day. I was so tired I'm surprised it made any sense."

"You don't have to answer. Sorry, I was just being nosey."

"No, it's okay," Will said. "But as it turns out, Jen wanted the guy who knew it all and got paid for it. It was my first serious relationship since law school, and I guess I didn't see what was right in front of me. Jen had a life plan and my going back to school was messing with the timing and the finances."

"I'm sorry, that must have been a rough break-up."

"Actually, it was more sad than tough. I blamed myself for not putting the pieces together. She'd never made any secret of the fact she wanted to be married and a mom by the time she was 35. We parted amicably and moved on. Last I heard, she's married to some hedge fund guy, living in Westchester, the mother of two kids. You can accomplish a lot in eight years when you have a plan." Will rested his back against the railing, facing her. "Are we ready to talk about your call with Jake?"

Cherie drew her legs up and wrapped her arms around her knees. "That is why we're here, right? So, spoiler alert, it doesn't end the way you might think."

Intrigued, Will settled in, watching a series of emotions play across Cherie's face as the darkness grew deeper. It didn't take a genius to recognize the defensive posture she maintained, hugging her knees to her chest. He let her deliver the virtual blow by blow without interruption, hearing the words but learning far more from her demeanor. He registered her determination and her unease before making the call, her surprise at Jake's appearance and his job working for a church. Her eyes grew wide at her brother's declaration he did not want her to be his donor and finally, Cherie's disbelief at his final request for prayer.

Her words faded into the darkness before she stretched her arms out in front of her, easing the tension in her neck by tilting her head from side to side. "Not what I'd expected. He's more together and less needy than I've ever seen him."

"Which leaves you feeling what?" Will asked.

"Relieved, mostly. If I take him at his word, I'm off the hook completely."

"I'm sensing there might be more to it than that."

"Shouldn't be, right? It's over now."

"It certainly could be," Will said, pivoting to sit facing the road and giving her a moment free of scrutiny to think. Tonight, he was her sounding board, the person you talk to out loud so you can understand how you are feeling yourself. That she trusted him enough to give him that insight into her life stole his breath away. "Can you tell me about the fire, Cherie?"

Out of the corner of his eye, he saw her flinch.

"You don't have to," Will said, echoing her earlier words.

She turned to sit beside him, her face in shadow as a curtain of dark hair obscured her features in much the same way Molly had done yesterday. "No, I think you're right, for you to understand I think you need to know. It's the whole reason this is even a decision and not a given like my mother wants it to be."

Their shoulders just inches apart, Will sensed her fear before her words broke into the night.

"Paul was due to be deployed on his second tour to the Middle East when he suffered a severe concussion during a training exercise. He wasn't fully recovered in time to leave with his unit, and he got to be home to see Sarah's birth."

"That's how you knew so much about concussions."

Cherie nodded. "He was pretty messed up, and it took a while for him to get cleared to return to duty, but a month after Sarah was born, they sent him back to rejoin his unit." Cherie sighed, her breath seeming to come a bit faster. "About a month later Jake was staying with us overnight because he had a job interview near the base where we were stationed. He'd been clean for more than a year by then but was still having a hard time finding work."

Cherie's shoulders rounded forward; her hands clasped between her knees. "I put Molly and Sarah down for the night and was watching TV with Jake when I heard Sarah coughing. I had never heard that kind of a cough from a child before. It was more like a bark, and it terrified me."

"Croup," Will said, quietly.

Cherie nodded. "I snatched her out of the crib and then, remembering what my mom used to do, I took her into the bathroom and ran the shower until the room filled with steam. But she just kept coughing. I should have called 911 but the response time on the base was going to be long and, I couldn't wait. I bundled her up and put her in her car seat and, for a minute, I thought about getting Molly up and taking her with us. I swear to this day it haunts me, I thought about it and I didn't do it. I was so scared, and I just wanted to get Sarah to the hospital. So, I asked Jake to keep an ear out for Molly, and I ran for the car with Sarah coughing the whole way."

Will heard the break in her voice, the desperation that even now made her shoulders shake. "Sarah was already starting to breathe easier by the time we got there, but she still had the cough, and they took us right away in the ER. They did the usual exam and tests, and it all took time, too much time. Sarah was acting and sounding normal by the time they discharged us in the middle of the night."

Cherie paused drawing in a deep breath before she continued. "I saw the glow in the sky first and then heard the sirens wailing. It didn't make any sense that of all the houses on the base it would be my house that was lighting up the sky, but I knew in my soul it was my house, and that Molly was still in there." Her voice broke, her hands clenched in tight fists.

Will listened, helpless to do anything but watch this play out to its conclusion. He should never have asked. He knew the story had to be traumatic for her. He should have left it alone.

"When I made the turn onto our street and saw the flames literally shooting from the windows, I couldn't breathe. All I could think about was Molly."

Without thinking, Will reached over and covered her fist with his hand. She opened her fingers, and he could feel the slick sweat of her palm as her fingers wrapped around his.

"I saw Jake first. He was sitting in the back of the ambulance breathing oxygen through a mask. I just kept screaming at him, at everyone, "Where's Molly". But Jake seemed dazed, and he didn't answer. I started to run for the door but tripped over a fire hose and fell to my knees. And when I looked up this big burly fireman stepped from the house with Molly in his arms. Half her hair was gone and the side of her head I could see was raw tissue and smoky soot, but she was breathing, I could see her chest rising and falling. and I knew she was alive."

Will could hear the relief in her voice as she leaned into his shoulder as if this solid touch in the present moment could drive the terrifying memories back into the dark. Will wrapped his arm around her and held on tight. "I'm so sorry, Cherie. No mother should ever have to live through that."

"I didn't find out until later what had happened. Jake's injuries were very mild, some smoke inhalation and burned fingers, which should have been the first clue, but I wasn't putting the pieces together then. The firemen said Jake was out on the lawn when they arrived. When they asked him if anyone was in the house, he couldn't give them a straight answer, so they did a room by room search and they found Molly."

"There's a part of me that still can't believe he didn't try to help her, because apparently he didn't remember she was in there." The sarcasm in her tone was sharp. "The fire investigator told us the fire started in the living room when something ignited the newspapers on the floor by the couch. Jake was smoking a joint apparently, and he either fell asleep or dropped it when he got up to use the bathroom, and when he came back the room was on fire. And he ran. He could have saved Molly, but he ran."

Will could hear the thickness in her words and knew that the tears she had managed to hold back had finally won the battle. He had no words, nothing to offer in the face of such a terrifying memory except his solid presence at her side. They sat in silence, his arm around her, each with their own thoughts about that night. Against his shoulder he could feel the moment when her breathing began to return to a normal cadence.

Her words when she finally spoke were soft, almost reverent. "God was there with Molly that night. The firemen who came to check on Molly at the hospital told me it was a miracle she wasn't more badly burned. When they saw the room engulfed in flame, they thought no one could survive in there, and then they heard a sound, something between a cough and a cry, and they found her under the bed."

Cherie reached up and wiped the tears from her cheeks. She turned to look at him, her eyes shining in the halo of light behind them. "Sometimes, even now, when I smell wood burning in a fireplace, my heart starts to race, and I am back on that front lawn on my knees looking up at the men brave enough to go into that house and save Molly."

Will lifted his hand, his thumb wiping away the last remnants of her tears. "You are the strongest woman I have ever met."

Cherie shook her head. "Not me, Molly's the strong one. The road to recovery has been long and painful. She's the brave one."

"She gets it from you," Will said, meeting her upturned gaze. Looking into her eyes, still shiny with tears, he felt a deep longing like nothing he had ever experienced before, a visceral yearning to protect this woman. His hands trembled, and it was all he could do to restraint the impulse to kiss her. Instead with great reluctance, he slowly released her, his arm returning to his side. "Thank you for telling me."

Cherie sat up, her arm still touching his. "I wanted you to understand. You have been so generous in helping me. I didn't want you to think I was being selfish."

Will turned to her. "It never crossed my mind you were."

Cherie's lips lifted in a hint of a smile. "Feels like you always have my back."

"I do, we're friends, right? Although after tonight with all your transplant concerns put to rest, you aren't going to need me anymore," Will teased, trying to lighten the mood of a very somber evening.

Cherie stared at him a moment. "I don't think that's true," she whispered before getting to her feet.

Will stood up, her words settling into his consciousness and sparking a glimmer of hope. Maybe he wasn't the only one in over his head here.

"Thank you again," Cherie said. "I do always seem to be thanking you for something." She stepped back, reaching for the door and then stopped turning back to face him. "My life is complicated as you've seen, the girls, my job, and a past I'm still dealing with. You might want to rethink that offer of friendship. We're kind of a mess over here."

"Going in with eyes wide open," Will said.

He could sense the shift in her tone before the words left her mouth.

"But this is all I have the bandwidth to give right now. I think you're looking for more. I can see it in your eyes." She paused, lifting her gaze to meet his across the dimly lit stoop. "You are a good man, Will Finnegan. You have given me your time and your help, and you deserve the truth. I can't do more, not now, maybe not ever, I don't know. You should think about that before we see each other again. Might be better to walk away now before we both get hurt."

She was right, of course, Will thought, admiring her ability to put it all out there. She was protecting herself and her family, and she was protecting him. He chose his next words carefully. "I think over the past few days we've made a connection, and those are rare in this world. I could use someone to talk to and I'm thinking you could, too. Now we know the boundaries, let's just take it from here. What do you say?"

He sensed she was as reluctant to let this go as he was despite her words of warning. Having said his piece, he waited to see if this was true. He would respect whatever she decided and move on if that was what she wanted, though he fervently hoped it was not.

Cherie stared at him. "This could be a big mistake for both of us …"

"I'll take that chance," Will replied. "How about you?"

"Okay," she said softly then paused leaning against the door. "You may regret this."

Will started walking backward down the walkway before she could change her mind. "Good night, Cherie."

* * *

Closing the door behind her, Cherie heard the soft purr of Will's car turning over. It idled for a moment before the sound receded into the night. Pushing off the door with both hands, she started the nightly ritual of checking the doors and window locks before unplugging the appliances in the kitchen. Even after five years she found her hypervigilance about fire safety had not receded.

She had no regrets about telling Will the terrifying story of the night Molly was burned, though it had taken a momentous effort to get the words out without dissolving into fear again. What she had not mentioned was the desperate trans-Atlantic call to Paul while she waited in the hospital with Sarah. Paul had promised to wrangle an emergency leave, his words filled with anguish, anger, and a rare hint of helplessness from a man who was usually so in control of any situation. Cherie had followed that call with one to Judith who had immediately offered to take care of Sarah, so Cherie could stay at the hospital with Molly. Her mom had arrived in the waiting area an hour later, clearly having blown through the speed limit on the Jersey Turnpike to have arrived so quickly.

"How's our girl?" Judith asked, her arms encircling Cherie in a fierce hug. And though her tone was purposefully calm, Cherie could feel the tension in Judith's shoulders. She was putting on a good show for her daughter, and at the realization someone who loved her was there to share the load of this impossible situation, Cherie burst into tears. Judith had been there that night and so many of the nights that followed.

Paul had arrived home late the next day looking ragged and worried, their phone updates during his journey having only marginally abated his paternal panic. Judith had quietly taken care of Sarah in the small emergency housing unit allocated by the base after the fire, while Cherie and Paul spent every waking minute on the burn unit with Molly. And when a week later Paul had reluctantly returned to complete his tour of duty, Judith had moved in with Cherie and stayed with them until Molly was discharged from the hospital.

Turning off the lights in the living room. Cherie knew she would never have made it through those days and weeks without her mom. She opened the door to the second bedroom to check on the girls. Molly lay on her stomach in the twin bed closest to the door, her hair obscuring the scars resulting from that terrible night. She had needed several surgeries to debride the burned area and apply a skin graft to her cheek and neck. After the burn had healed, they began a separate series of surgeries here in Darby to reconstruct her ear. She still had hearing loss on that side, but she was alive and thriving despite the trauma. Cherie's eyes welled with tears of gratitude for God's deliverance that night. Sarah stirred in the other twin bed positioned at ninety degrees to maximize the space in the small room. Cherie loved that they slept with their heads so close together, which made for many whispered words and giggles after the lights were out. She smiled and closed the door softly.

So how had Judith, the woman who had saved her family and her sanity become the thorn in her side? Cherie flinched, knowing the answer. In the weeks following the fire Judith had been as outraged as Cherie and Paul at the relapse into drug use Jake had managed to hide from their family. But in the months that followed, Judith's ire had morphed into a determination to help her youngest child kick the drugs that had been his go-to vice since high school. That determination to help Jake severed the connection between Paul and his mother-in-law, their relationship deteriorating in direct proportion to the amount of time and money Judith spent trying to get Jake clean. Cherie found herself naturally siding with her husband, and though she had maintained a relationship with her mother, she had done so mostly for her father. But the tenor of her bond with Judith had taken on a perfunctory tone, marked by Cherie's tendency in her thoughts, if not her words, to call her mother by her given name. Mentally, she had separated the mom of her youth from the woman who devoted all her energy to her youngest child. If Paul had lived, it might still be so. But in the days and months after his death, Judith and Joe had been there. Day after day. Helping with the girls, giving her time to mourn and grieve, and in the light of their earnest, unflappable love, a new way forward began to form.

Quietly, Cherie switched on the bathroom light, shedding just enough light into the bedroom for her to change without waking Carey. The two had shared a room since the day Carey was born, though probably not for much longer. She stared down at the toddler sleeping deeply with her arm wrapped around her favorite elephant. Carey was the last tangible link to Paul, all the girls were, but Carey looked like her father, her lighter coloring, her more angular face and the two prominent dimples that appeared whenever she smiled.

Stepping into the bathroom, Cherie splashed water on her face before adding a foaming cleanser to remove the days grime. She reached for a towel and studied her face washed clean of what little make-up she usually wore. She looked pale and tired, making Cherie wonder what Will Finnegan saw when he looked at her. A flash of guilt had her wondering how she could be thinking about Paul one minute and Will the next. It seemed wrong, even after all this time. And yet still her thoughts returned to the man who had just left here, having listened with such care to all she had to say.

He had to be crazy to want to be a part of her life. What single man would want to start a relationship, a friendship, she corrected, with a woman who had almost no time to give him. And then Will stood there tonight offering something she very much wanted, a lifeline to adult conversation, some time to just be herself again. More than a mom, more than a teacher or a sister. A woman with a future that seemed unknowable right now. Talking to Will was easy, making her consider what she wanted her life to look like in a few years when the girls were a bit more independent. She hadn't spent any time in the last three years thinking about her future. Instead, she had put one foot in front of the other and just kept going.

Walking by the crib, Cherie rested a hand on Carey's back, feeling the gentle rise and fall of her breathing, before slipping under the covers and closing her eyes. Her alarm would go off soon enough and the whole routine would begin again. Had she been wrong to agree to seeing Will again? Her mind gently shifted into that pre-sleep state where thoughts were hard to hold onto and floated away before you could catch them. In the moment before sleep drew her in, one thought rose to the surface, how good it had felt to rest in his arms. She smiled drifting off into a dreamless sleep.

Chapter Eight

William stepped through the sliding doors, nodding to the security guard outside the ER. It had been a brutal week. He had worked four shifts in as many days, each of them beginning at 6 a.m. and finishing well after 8 p.m. And the patients never stopped coming.

The evening air felt cool and smelled better, a whiff of pine with a hint of tar from the parking lot renovations, but with no undertone of any body fluids. He inhaled deeply, feeling grateful for a healthy body, something he never took for granted any more, though he had for many years before starting his residency. At least he'd managed to find a clean pair of scrubs to change into for the ride home.

Driving home, his thoughts turned to Cherie. He'd hoped to hear from her by now, having made the decision to leave the reaching out up to her after their conversation on Monday. If this relationship was going to work on any level, she had to want it too, and he was giving her the space to work that out. That had been a better thought on Tuesday morning than it was on Thursday evening, when all he wanted to do was call her and see how her week was going.

Unlocking the door to his condo, he wandered into the kitchen, considered making dinner and decided it was too much work. And while he'd intended to do nothing more than change into his sweatpants and then watch a ballgame, when he sat down on his bed, he couldn't resist the urge to close his eyes for just a few minutes.

He awoke to a dark room and the sound of his phone blaring somewhere near his ear. Confused for a moment as to whether he was in the call room at work or at home, he grabbed the phone, hitting the screen to stop the noise as he sat up abruptly and came to the bleary realization, he was home. "Hello?"

"Will, I'm so sorry. I didn't mean to wake you. Go back to sleep," Cherie said, regret tinging her tone.

"Well, I'm awake now, so don't hang up," Will said quickly, his face breaking into a grin as he tried to shake off the remnants of sleep.

"Must have been a rough day if you're asleep before 9:00 p.m."

"More like a long week so I take my sleep where I can get it. I was thinking about you earlier today. How is your week going?" The headboard squeaked as he settled back against it, propping a pillow behind him and putting the phone on speaker.

"Not as exciting as yours I think but just as exhausting. Can you share a story without violating any HIPPA laws?"

Will's smile widened. So, she hadn't had a reason for calling, which meant she just wanted to talk. "I can. Sad, silly or glad? My job comes with all kinds."

"Tonight, I choose glad. Next time I'll choose something else."

"Well, that sounds hopeful. Are we planning on doing this on a regular basis? I could use a nightly debrief."

"Depends on how good a storyteller you are," Cherie responded in a teasing tone.

"Then I'll make it good," Will replied, feeling his exhaustion lift. "Today the choice of a happy ending is an easy one since I started my shift by delivering a baby in the parking lot."

"You're kidding!"

"Nope, a car pulled up to the ER entrance and the security guard took one look at the size of the patient and the strain on her face and called for help. I grabbed a pair of gloves and ran outside. Her husband was holding her up, trying to hurry her inside as she tried to blow through the contractions and not push. But that sensation, so they tell me, is an irresistible urge."

"You got that right," Cherie said with certainty.

"All she did was stop that forceful exhale and I knew what was coming next. I caught her baby girl making a quick entrance into the world."

"Will, you saved that little girl's life," Cherie exclaimed, her voice filled with wonder.

"I was just glad I grabbed the gloves. Newborns are slippery." Will recalled his relief as he placed the tiny newborn on her mom's stomach and they whisked the pair off to the nearest bay, where he had clamped the cord, done a quick assessment of mother and infant, and sent them up to labor and delivery to deliver the placenta.

"What a great start to your day. I can't say as I do anything quite so momentous in my work," Cherie said with a touch of envy.

"Hold on, you teach little kids to read and write. I'd say that's right up there in terms of making a serious impact on the world." Will countered.

"I don't think I have any future senators or presidents in my class, but I do have one little boy very serious about saving the ice caps from melting."

"We could use more good minds on that problem." Enjoying the light-hearted conversation, Will debated the merits of asking a more serious question but then plunged ahead. "So, have you heard from your mother since Sunday?"

"No, radio silence on that front, which is very unlike her. I know I need to touch base with her, but her obvious disappointment with me makes that a conversation I'm not looking forward to having. I'm putting it off for a few more days. Does that make me a coward?" Cherie asked, and though her tone was joking, he sensed she needed an answer.

"More like a woman with a complicated relationship with her mother."

"I was thinking after we talked on Monday, about all the times she's helped me, saved my sanity, by jumping in to help with the kids."

"Maybe you can find your way back to that."

"Maybe."

Encouraged by her having reached out to him, Will ventured. "Any chance we can fit in a run this weekend?"

Cherie laughed, the sound warm and inviting even through the phone's speaker. "Reading my mind now, are you?"

"I'm glad we're thinking the same thing," Will responded, unsure how with his crazy work schedule and her kids and job they were ever going to make this work, though he was eager to try. "I'm working Saturday, off on Sunday."

"I'm taking the kids to church Sunday morning. No plans for the afternoon though."

"What would you think about taking the girls on a picnic?" Will asked.

"Three little girls freed from the confines of a church pew? It could be mayhem."

"I'll take that chance."

"You're a brave man."

"Okay, now you're scaring me," Will laughed. "How bad could it be?"

"Depends on the day, their moods, and how many snacks we bring," Cherie chuckled. "Try it once, and you may not do it again."

"Not a chance," Will said, suddenly serious, the words leaving his mouth before he could stop them. "You're stuck with me now, if you want to be."

She paused, taking in that bold statement, her response quiet. "Go back to sleep, Will. I'll see you, Sunday."

* * *

Cherie exited the school into a cloudy afternoon of light spring rain and wished she'd remembered a jacket this morning. Feeling the weight of the week fall from her shoulders, she turned her face up to the metallic sky, the steady drizzle misting her skin as she savored the freedom of the weekend ahead, and the plans for Sunday she and Will had set in motion via text.

She unlocked the Jeep with her key, tossing the canvas work bag on the passenger seat, and glancing at her phone before starting the engine. A single voice mail caught her attention. Cherie knew she must have missed it in the flurry of activity before the final bell rang releasing the kids for the weekend.

She slid the phone into its holder and played the message.

"Good afternoon, this is Brook Sheraton from Hopewell Atlantic. I wanted to follow up on our discussion last week and see if you had any further questions about the transplant process. If you could give me a call at your earliest convenience."

Cherie frowned. Since the discussion with Jake last Sunday, she felt the transplant question had been settled, but she supposed she did owe the coordinator a call to explain the conclusion she and Jake had come to. Cherie connected the call.

"Brook Sheraton, Hopewell Atlantic, how can I help you?

"Ms. Sheraton, it's Cherie Hollister returning your call."

"Thanks for getting back to me. I wanted to touch base with you about the transplant for your brother."

Gone was the lilting tone Cherie remembered from their previous call. Clearly it was the end of a long week for Ms. Sheraton as well.

"I probably should have gotten back to you sooner, but to be perfectly candid, my brother, Jake, and I have some unresolved personal issues and after talking to him last weekend, he told me he doesn't want me to be his donor." Cherie stared through the windshield as the rain increased from a steady drizzle to a constant pelting.

"I see, and when did you speak to him?"

"Last Sunday night. Why?"

"A lot can change in a few days," Brook Sheraton replied.

"Has something happened to Jake?"

"I can't disclose any of your brother's medical information. HIPPA guidelines were put in place to protect our patient's privacy ..." Her voice trailed off.

Cherie had a feeling the incomplete sentence was a purposeful event. "But something has changed."

"I am on call this weekend if you have any questions. Please feel free to call me anytime," Ms. Sheraton concluded.

Cherie shivered as the screen went dark, the damp shoulders of her cotton shirt suddenly cold against her skin. The tenor of that brief conversation was markedly different from their discussion a week ago. She started the car, switching on the heater, wondering what could have happened to Jake that had Ms. Sheraton so worried she had brushed right up against the HIPPA mandates. Not quite a violation, but close. Cherie knew she could call Jake and ask him, but she wanted more information before she did, and she could think of only one man who might know the answer.

Ten minutes later, she pulled up in front of her parents' home. Pale yellow siding and windows with bright blue shutters flanked a matching door. Purple and yellow pansies sprouted from window boxes on the first floor giving the house a colorful and welcoming appeal. Judith and Joe had moved from the four-bedroom colonial where Cherie was raised to this more compact home after one floor living became a necessity.

Cherie parked on the street, knowing her mother would still be at work. Judith's job as an administrative assistant to the superintendent of schools, almost never got her home before 6:00 p.m. Tiny white petals littered the slate pathway and adjacent lawn brought down by the heavy rain which had blown through as quickly as it came. The air felt damp and close, tinged with the subtle sweetness of apple blossoms. Cherie bypassed the ramp, climbing the steps to the porch and letting herself in.

"Dad?"

"In the kitchen. This is a nice surprise. Your mom forgot to mention you were stopping by." His baritone was welcoming despite her unexpected arrival.

"That's because she didn't know. I came to see you." Cherie hung her bag on the hooks by the door, knowing her mother disliked them on the counters.

"To what do I owe the pleasure?"

Cherie stepped through the archway into a spacious kitchen with a large family room beyond.

"I'm making coffee. Do you want some?" Joe said, rolling his wheelchair around the oval island with its bilevel counters. Three quarters of the island was at the standard height while the remaining end of the oval was six inches lower.

Cherie marveled at the ease with which he maneuvered the chair. That feat had seemed impossible in the months after a drunk driver side-swiped his Acura sedan, causing the car to careen over a guard rail, crushing the roof. Ten years ago, now. Joe had never walked again.

"I would love a little caffeine."

Joe pulled the coffee maker closer to the counter's edge and then reached for the coffee and filters on the open shelving beneath. "So, what brings you by? I'm thinking it's about Jake, am I right?" Deftly, he filled the coffee canister with water from the bar sink and made quick work of getting the coffee brewing.

Cherie nodded. "I got a call from the transplant coordinator today, and I got the sense that something had changed in Jake's condition. I thought you might know what it is."

"Mom and I talked to Jake last night. Apparently, he hasn't been completely forthcoming about how the dialysis is going."

"So, there is a problem?" Cherie said, opening the refrigerator and pulling out the half and half. Joe liked his coffee very strong with a generous amount of cream and sugar.

"He's been hospitalized twice since they started the dialysis a few weeks ago. Something called Disequilibrium Syndrome."

"But he must have known about this when we talked last Sunday?"

Joe nodded. Reaching for two mugs from the shelf, he poured the coffee and handed one to her. "He did. The first incident was two weeks ago. The symptoms then were mild, a headache and blurred vision, but during yesterday's treatment he had a seizure."

Startled, Cherie put the mug down, the porcelain impacting the granite with a crisp clink. "A seizure?"

"Caused by some kind of brain swelling, apparently. They kept him overnight, ran a bunch of tests and then discharged him this morning." Joe stirred his coffee after making it the color of sand on a summer morning. "I did some reading on it last night. It's a lot of medical jargon, but from what I could gather it happens during or immediately after the dialysis."

"Could it happen again?"

"Yes, it could."

"How is he doing?"

"Making light of it, putting on a good face for your mom. You know how she gets."

Cherie nodded, knowing Judith's affinity for a child in trouble must have been in overdrive. "She drove out to Long Island, didn't she?"

"First thing this morning. She wants to be there for the treatment tomorrow."

"Did Jake try and talk her out of it?"

"He did, gave it a good shot too, but I think in the end when he knew she was coming anyway, he sounded a little relieved."

Cherie settled on the bar stool by the counter, her hands wrapped around the warm cup. "Mom told you what we talked about last weekend?"

"You know she did. Secrets were never your mother's style," Joe responded, leaning one arm against the lower counter, and lifting his gaze to meet hers. "She assumed when you agreed to be tested it meant you were agreeing to the transplant. I tried to tell her she might be off base on that one, but she wasn't hearing it."

Cherie faltered under his steady scrutiny. As a teenager, she had never understood why her father put up with Judith's bossy ways. What she had come to understand after the accident was the quiet determination and strength of this man who chose to let his wife be out in front while he remained in the background, supporting her and all his children. Judith and Joe had a relationship that worked. The accident had tested its bounds and strength but had not broken what decades together had built.

"So, what do you think about the transplant?" Cherie asked. "Mom was so upset with me. Is that how you feel, too?"

Joe didn't hesitate. "Absolutely not. I think with those three beautiful girls to raise by yourself your mom was wrong to put any pressure on you to help Jake. It has to be your decision, and I respect whatever choice you make."

"I appreciate that, Dad, more than I can tell you." She slid off the stool and bent down to hug the man who had been her steadfast supporter all her life. She sank to her knees, sitting back on her heels and holding onto his hands, feeling thankful the accident had not stolen him away from his family.

"Here's my problem, Dad," she said, her words just above a whisper. "If it were Amy, I wouldn't think twice. I would put it all in God's hands and give her the gift I know she would give me. And I can't do it for Jake."

"So, when he said he didn't want you to be his donor, he bailed you out," Joe said, squeezing her hand.

"Yes, and all I felt was relief. That sounds so selfish, I know."

"The bottom line is you still don't trust Jake not to throw away this chance like he has all the others in his life, am I right?"

Cherie nodded, hearing out loud what she had been thinking. "We've all been trying to save him for years, how many chances do we have to give him? And at what cost?"

Joe leaned forward, meeting her gaze. "But you came here this afternoon. Why?"

"Because I was worried about him after talking to the transplant coordinator."

"More than just curious then, worried, right? So, what does that tell you?"

"I don't know," Cherie admitted as she got to her feet.

"Food for thought, maybe." The tenor of his tone changed as if, having made his point, he was content to let her sort it out. "I will say your mother was also very interested in the young doctor she met at your house, though that did take second place to the transplant discussion."

Cherie winced. "She mentioned Will."

"I believe she called him Dr. Finnegan. Like I said, no secrets here."

"He's a friend who's been helping me figure it out."

In This Lifetime

"And does he have an opinion about the transplant?"

"You would think as a doctor, he would, but he's carefully navigating the neutral waters just like you."

"Sounds like a good man." Joe glanced at the clock. "Don't you have to pick up the girls?"

"I've got a few minutes, yet. Don't worry, I won't be racing to get over there."

"I always worry. Comes with the parental territory," Joe said with a smile.

"Don't I know it." She kissed his cheek. "Thanks, Dad."

"Anytime, my sweet girl. You can stop by even if you don't have a reason," Joe added.

Coming from her father, it wasn't a reprimand but a reminder, making her feel glad she had come today and determined to do it more often.

"Sounds like a good idea." She gave him a final hug. "How about I bring the girls by next week?"

"Anytime. My door is always open."

His words made her think of Will, and how often he used that same expression to let her know he would make time for whatever she needed. Like her dad.

Cherie grabbed her bag from the hook by the door. The comparison between these two men was disconcerting but comforting, she thought as she stepped out into the grey afternoon hoping Sunday wouldn't be a weather washout.

93

Chapter Nine

Will's choice for an afternoon with Cherie and the girls was a state park with an impressive multi-level play structure that looked like a fort with platforms, ladders, and rock walls to access the upper levels. A series of long blue slides, each with a different configuration gave a choice of ways to get down. Around the outside of the structure were a series of musical apparatus with chimes, drums, and a piano scale. One of the nurses he worked with had mentioned it. Will knew she had two boys of her own, so he'd done a quick recon mission yesterday to check it out then texted Cherie the address. She was meeting him here at noon after church. Will was early, but since this outing was his idea, he wanted to be here when they arrived. He chose a picnic table close to the playground and placed a small igloo cooler under the table.

He'd been looking forward to seeing Cherie since their phone call Thursday night. He knew this wasn't a date, but it felt like the start of something different. This outing was based on choice rather than a need for help, and though he would take either one, he found himself smiling at the thought that Cherie was choosing to spend time with him. Her time was as precious as his, little of it free and unscripted.

The morning's chill was giving way to a sunny afternoon, the sky cloudless, the crisp blue hue so intense it hurt his eyes to look at even as the vivid color drew his gaze skyward. A light breeze carried the delicate aroma of lilac from the blossoms behind the swing set.

He spotted Cherie's Jeep pulling into the parking lot and got to his feet, feeling a bit nervous but shrugging it off. By the time he crossed the parking lot, Cherie was already opening the door to the back seat. "Can I help?" he asked.

She turned to him with a smile. "I'll take all the help I can get. Could you grab the cooler from the back?"

Will lifted the tailgate and took hold of the rectangular cooler. He hoisted it from the cargo area. "Looks like you brought enough for dinner, too."

"You've never seen my kids eat after a workout on the playground."

"First table on the left," Will called over his shoulder as he carried the cooler across the parking lot. He set it on the tabletop and turned to watch Cherie and the girls coming toward him. The girls wore pants and sneakers with brightly colored T-shirts. Cherie was equally casual in jeans and a navy top.

"Girls, you remember Dr. Finnegan?"

"Can they call me Will?" he asked. "The doctor part sounds a little scary."

Carey wiggled to get down from Cherie's arms. "Doc Finn?"

Cherie chuckled. "How about we just go with that? She's going to call you that anyway."

"Works for me," Will said as Carey stood in front of him with a quizzical stare.

"No falling," she said, her expression serious.

Will squatted down. "I agree, no falling today and no boo boos." He tapped her forehead lightly.

She grinned as her sisters raced off to try the rock wall. Carey ran after them, not able to keep up but giving it her best effort.

Cherie glanced at Will as they fell into step together starting after the girls. "I hope you weren't planning on sitting down when you chose this place. We'll both be supervising so no one ends up in the ER." Cherie reached out and grabbed Carey who was trying to follow her sisters up the rock wall.

Watching the three of them going in different directions, Will marveled at Cherie's calm demeanor. Clearly, she had done this many times and knew the skill level of each one of the girls. And yet keeping an eye on all of them was a challenge, even with so few other kids on the playground. It was physically exhausting for the girls, their faces red and hairlines sweaty, but also mentally taxing for the adults on duty. Having never spent much time around children outside the ER, he was amazed at their prowess on the structure and their endurance.

An hour later, Cherie waved them all over to the table for lunch. Will watched the girls surround the cooler with eager faces.

"Sorry, not much time to talk," Cherie grinned as he stepped up to the table. "Welcome to my life."

"How do you do this by yourself?" Will asked as Cherie passed out moist wipes to clean hands before lunch.

"You get good at it after a while. I've had a lot of practice."

Will registered the flash of tension around her eyes before she met his gaze with a sad smile. "You do what you have to do to make it work."

"You make it look easy," he said, helping her unpack the cooler. "And I know it's not."

She handed him a thermos and three paper cups. "Not easy, but totally worth it. Girls, turkey and cheese or almond butter and jelly. Apples or grapes?"

The girls weighed in with their choices while Will poured the drinks.

He had thought lunch might be a time for a little conversation with Cherie, but he had underestimated the enthusiasm of three little girls who wanted to talk about everything from school to lacrosse, their favorite Disney princesses, and their Wednesday nights with their cousin.

When the sandwiches and fruit were finished, Will reached for the small cooler, glancing over at Cherie. "I brought dessert, if it's, okay?"

She nodded as the girls eagerly stood up on the benches to peer inside the cooler.

"I hope you like ice cream …" he said to squeals of pleasure. He handed each of them a chocolate-chip cookie ice cream sandwich. Molly and Sarah thanked him before they scurried off into one of the fort alcoves to eat their treats.

"This is going to be a sight," Cherie said, handing the treat to Carey. She settled the toddler on her lap and turned to face the fort to keep an eye on the girls. "We should take advantage, how about a little adult conversation. When I called you last Sunday, you mentioned lunch with your sister. Do you get to see her often?"

Will shook his head, leaning back against the table. "That was the first time I had seen her in years, over a decade. I'm one of five, all boys, except Maddie."

"That's a long time not to see your family," Cherie said, then frowned at the irony of her own words.

"We're not very close. My father's career as a judge spilled over into our house with high expectations and no leniency. We all followed Maddie's example and got out of there as soon as we could. We live all over the country now and rarely talk to each other."

"Sounds sad. I don't know what I would do without my sister, Amy."

"Well, Maddie seems determined to change that. Our lunch last Sunday was her idea."

"Did she have a reason?"

Will nodded. "She was diagnosed with lung cancer last year and had surgery to remove it. That seems to have prompted a few changes in her life."

"Understandable, hearing you have cancer can make you think about what's really important, like family," Cherie said, giving a wipe to Carey's chocolate-covered chin. "How is she doing?"

"Her most recent scan is cancer free, and she's got the best attitude I have ever seen in a cancer patient. She actually told me, God and cancer had given her back her life," Will said, his tone reflecting his skepticism.

"And you don't believe her?"

"I believe her life is different, that was clear just watching her with Scott. They didn't have a very good marriage, and now they're acting like two kids on their honeymoon."

"A scary diagnosis made them turn back to each other," Cherie said, getting to her feet and holding onto Carey as the older girls wandered over to the swings. "Time is a precious thing most of us don't appreciate until it's gone."

Walking beside her, Will could see the firm set to her jaw and knew she was thinking about Paul. "I'm glad Maddie has the support she's going to need, but I'm afraid she's not acknowledging the likelihood of metastasis."

"Spoken like a true doctor," Cherie said, settling on one of the swings adjacent to Molly and Sarah. She gently set the swing in motion as Carey continued to work on her ice cream.

"I'm just looking at the facts. I know how this usually goes," Will said, a touch of stubbornness creeping into his words as he took the swing beside her.

"I'm sure you do. Your life is all about how the body responds to different diseases," Cherie said, the gentle motion of the swing softening her tone. "But in that equation is also a future that for Maddie includes being a wife and mother. She's holding on tight to that."

Will wondered how this beautiful woman with all she had been through could listen to Maddie's story and choose optimism as a response. Cherie was cautious, yes, but she didn't default to the negative which he had to admit was sometimes his position, especially in his professional life.

"I think your sister and I may have something in common," Cherie said.

Curious, Will asked, "What's that?"

"Like Maddie, I chose out of necessity and desperation to put an impossible situation in hands bigger than my own."

"You mean God's hands?" Will met her gaze over Carey's head.

"You sound skeptical?"

"I am," Will admitted. "Maddie and I were raised in the Christian faith, but a loving father wasn't what I was seeing here on earth, and none of it ever made much sense to me. Turns out I'm a man of science, not faith."

"They aren't mutually exclusive," Cherie said with a smile. "I'm with Maddie on this one. She's choosing faith and hope, and so am I. I admire Maddie already and I haven't even met her."

"Interesting you should mention that. She wants to meet you, too."

"You told her about me?"

"I did when I called to accept her invitation for July 4th. And she invited you and the girls to join us. She's got a beautiful home on a lake in New Hampshire."

"I don't think we're ready to take this show on the road," Cherie said, holding out a hand to Will as Carey began to squirm.

Will took her hand, pulling her to her feet. "That's what I told Maddie, but she said it's an open invitation." He reluctantly let go of her hand as Molly appeared at his side.

"Thank you for the ice cream," she said seriously. "Do you know how to play the piano?"

"I do, a little bit," Will said. "Lead the way."

Sarah grabbed his hand and pulled, steering him toward the musical instruments encircling the playground.

"Lessons?" Cherie asked as he glanced back over his shoulder at her.

"I played keyboard in a band in high school," he replied.

"Of course, you did," Cherie said with what he thought was a hint of sarcasm. "Is there anything you can't do, Will?"

"Just one. I'll never be a triathlete. I can't swim," he admitted, before she was out of earshot.

The startled look on Cherie's face was worth the admission.

* * *

Cherie packed up the remnants of the snack the girls had just devoured after a final hour on the playground. She set the lid on the cooler before Will appeared at her side with Carey on his shoulders and Sarah and Molly right behind. It seemed he'd made a few friends this afternoon.

"Time to go, girls," Cherie said, noting their sweaty faces and the groan of dismay at her words.

Will lifted Carey up and handed her to Cherie. "All good things …" he said, reaching for the cooler to carry to the car.

"… must come to an end," Molly finished.

Will stopped and turned. "That's right. My grandmother used to say that. Who taught you that one?"

Molly smiled, looking up at him, her hair falling away from her face as she did. "My Pop. He's got a bunch of them."

"My dad calls them truisms," Cherie said. "Things that are true no matter how old you are."

"My kind of guy." Will lifted the tailgate and slid the cooler in. The girls scrambled into the car and fastened their seat belts as Cherie secured Carey in her car seat. Emerging from the back seat, she straightened with a smile. "This was fun."

"For me, too."

"Really?" Cherie asked.

"Yes, your kids are fun to be with. Is that surprising?"

"Not to me, but I wasn't sure how you would feel about it. Girls, can you say goodbye to Dr. Finn?"

Will leaned into the car amid a chorus of good-byes then straightened closing the door.

"Can I call you later?" Cherie asked. "There was something my dad mentioned the other day about Jake that I wanted to ask you about." She waved a hand at the playground. "And this setting wasn't exactly conducive to a serious discussion. Something called Disequilibrium Syndrome."

She noted the slight narrowing of his eyes. "After or during his dialysis?"

"During apparently. I'll call you tonight?"

"You can call me anytime," Will said, looking her in the eye. "You know that by now."

"I'm starting to count on it," Cherie said softly and was rewarded for her honesty by the look of sheer pleasure on Will's face as he opened the driver's door for her.

"That's not a bad thing, you know?" Will said, as she ducked inside and started the engine. "I'll talk to you later."

On the drive home the girls talked over each other about the merits of this new playground as Cherie considered her decision not to bring up the change in Jake's condition until the end of their outing. She knew she could have peppered Will with questions, and he would have answered, but she hadn't wanted to mar this spring afternoon with another medical discussion.

An image of Will with Carey on his shoulders made Cherie smile before a sudden sadness settled over her thoughts. After three years she recognized the feeling, a mixture of grief and regret, the pain less intense, but no less real. Thoughts of Will in recent days triggered reminders of Paul, which though natural were nonetheless disconcerting. In the years since the helicopter crash, memories of Paul had no competition in her thoughts, and now she felt a deep sadness that Paul's children would have few if any memories of him. He had been a great dad, involved in every aspect of their lives from diaper changes to bath time. But he had also missed so much. Months at a time when his deployments had taken him far from his family. Time they would never get back.

"Isn't that Grandy's car?" Molly asked from the back seat as Cherie made the turn onto their street.

Pulled from her revelries, Cherie tensed as the door of the Honda Accord opened. Clearly, her mother had been waiting for them.

Judith stepped from the car as Cherie pulled into the driveway. The girls scrambled from the back seat to say hello as Cherie unbuckled Carey from her seat.

"Have you been waiting long?" she asked, meeting her mother on the walkway.

"No, just a few minutes. Sounds like the picnic was a success. You discovered a new playground, I hear."

Cherie wondered how much the girls had managed to disclose in the last minute. "Yes, not too far from here."

"Dr. Finn found it," Sarah insisted.

"And he brought ice cream," Molly added.

Cherie inwardly winced. No skirting around what they'd been doing this afternoon.

"You girls must be tired after all that playing. How about a little quiet time with a movie?" Judith suggested.

Molly and Sarah raced for the door, taking the opportunity for a little screen time very seriously.

"I thought we could talk, if that's okay?" Judith asked, turning toward the apartment and matching Cherie's steps.

Cherie had no illusions about the topic of this discussion, so she simply nodded, standing behind Carey as she climbed up the steps. "Sure, just let me get them settled."

Having decided on a Disney movie, Molly and Sarah settled on the couch with Carey between them and Cherie joined her mother at the table, noting the tea Judith had made for them.

"So, I heard from Dad you went to see Jake on Friday," Cherie said, deciding to dispense with the small talk. "How is he?"

"Better, thank God. He made it through the dialysis yesterday with no seizures or complications," Judith replied, lifting her mug of black tea, and taking a sip.

Cherie noted the green tea in her own mug. Judith never forgot the things her children preferred. Cherie had always liked the lightness of green tea far more than the deep concentrations of its black cousin. "Could it happen again? The seizures?"

"That's what the hemodialysis team is trying to prevent. They slowed down the infusion rate, so it took quite a bit longer, but it worked."

"Did they let you sit with him?"

"I don't think they wanted to, in case something happened, but Jake insisted he wanted me there after making the drive." Judith looked up at her daughter. "He's got a lot more going on with his health than he has been telling us."

"That's not surprising. Jake has been hiding things from us since he was a teenager." Cherie sipped her tea, knowing where this was heading, but determined to stay calm and not let things get out of hand like last weekend. "He was coming home wasted when he was barely in high school."

"That's true. And all that drinking and then the drugs have left their mark on his liver as well as his kidneys. He's contracted Hepatitis B several times over the years, and that's damaged his liver."

"Jake's been using for close to a decade, Mom. His kidneys and his liver have been working overtime to get rid of that stuff."

Judith's eyes were fixed on the tea swirling in her mug. "I think in the beginning, your dad and I didn't see what was going on with Jake. I was back to work full time after years at home with all of you. We had college tuition to pay, and my working was the only way we could do it. And then your dad's accident and his recovery took all my time and attention. And Jake got lost, I think, lost in the drinking that dulled the pain and the friends who made him not feel so lonely. We knew he was drinking, and we should have been more alarmed. Of all the things he could have been doing, alcohol didn't seem so bad. I know how naïve that sounds now, but I was barely holding on, and I know I missed so much."

Curious at this sudden insight into her mom as an over-worked spouse and parent, Cherie asked, "So when did you know it was different with Jake?"

"When things started going missing in the house."

"I remember telling you my tablet was missing when I came home for Christmas, and you told me I probably left it at my apartment."

Judith winced. "We were just starting to put the pieces together then, and I still wanted to believe no child of mine could be stealing from his own family."

Cherie glanced over at the couch where Molly's dark hair was all she could see of her children over the back of the sofa. Yes, her life was hectic now, her days often chaotic just keeping everyone fed and healthy, but Judith's admission gave her a glimpse of the potential threats in the years ahead. Right now, her problems were directly proportional to the size of her children. Financial worries aside, because she would always have those, her days were consumed with dance classes, doctors' appointments, food shopping and laundry. But the idea of parenting these precious girls through their teenage years, and doing it alone, was terrifying. What if she missed something? Some Internet conversation with a new friend who was really a predator. A sleepover at a friend's house that turned out to be a lie. An abusive relationship with a boyfriend. Drugs. Alcohol. Bulimia. How did you parent three children through all the years ahead, help them navigate the treacherous waters and finally emerge as self-sustaining adults? It seemed overwhelming, and with that thought came the realization Judith and Joe had done just that. Not perfectly, of course, because no parent could. What did you do with a guilt you could never outrun? A guilt that you had missed signs you should have seen and with no way to go back and change it, much as you might want to.

"It isn't your fault, you know," Cherie said softly. The words came unbidden, one mother to another.

"Feels like it is sometimes." Judith looked up, her eyes wide and shiny. "The choices were Jake's, I know that, but I should have paid more attention. Maybe I would have seen how lonely he was, how what happened to your dad affected him, too."

"You did the best you could …" Cherie began.

"Did I? I don't know …" Her voice trailed off. "All I know is Jake finally managed to drag himself out of that pit, and now he won't have the time to start building a new life."

"Why are you here, Mom?" Cherie asked, her tone shaded with sympathy, never having seen her mother as a vulnerable parent.

"To ask you to think about moving ahead with the testing, just to think about it, in case something happens to Jake again during his dialysis. I'd like you to ask yourself one question: What would you do if it were Amy?"

"You've been talking to Dad, I see," Cherie said, recalling her conversation with Joe. "No secrets between you two."

"Not in 35 years. All I'm asking is you consider doing for Jake what I know you would do for Amy."

Cherie paused before answering. "I'll think about it."

"Thank you." Judith reached out a hand and brushed the hair back from Cherie's forehead, a maternal gesture that hadn't changed since Cherie was in grade school. "Now, tell me about Dr. Finn."

* * *

"So, what did you tell her?" Will asked, turning off the movie he'd been streaming when the phone rang. Conversations with Cherie at the end of the day were something he could get used to; he thought settling back into the couch.

"I wasn't planning on telling her anything until Molly and Sarah got to her first and started telling her all about the park and the ice cream. Big hit."

"I aim to please," he replied, tilting his head back with a smile. "So, how did you explain our relationship when we're just getting a handle on it ourselves."

"True, so I told her we're friends. Disappointed?"

Will knew the right answer. "No, because it's the truth. Good friends are highly underrated; we could all use a few more. Now, tell me why your mom was waiting for you in the first place?"

"And that plays into what I mentioned as we were leaving the park."

He could hear the shift in her tone, the lightness gone, reminding him of their conversation at the diner. "The Disequilibrium Syndrome?"

"Yes, what is it exactly?"

"It's a rare complication of hemodialysis that causes brain swelling. What kind of symptoms did he have?"

"The first time apparently the symptoms were mild, headache and blurred vision, but this past Thursday he had a seizure," Cherie explained.

Will sat up, shifting to a more professional mindset, knowing how imperative it was for the dialysis team to make a differential diagnosis for the seizure. "They must have kept him overnight and worked him up to rule out other causes."

"They did, and this disequilibrium syndrome is where they landed. What causes the seizures?"

"It's caused by a high blood urea level. When the urea is removed by dialysis it can cause a gradient shift that draws fluid into the brain producing increased intracranial pressure and the kind of symptoms Jake experienced. It usually happens to patients new to dialysis or those who don't come in for their dialysis regularly."

"So, what's the treatment?"

Will chose his words carefully. "Disequilibrium Syndrome is rare and not well understood. Management of the condition is aimed at prevention rather than treatment."

"They don't have a treatment?"

"More like a protocol to prevent any further seizures. When it's identified as a risk factor in patients like Jake, they do the dialysis differently, they slow down the infusion rate and alter the solution concentrations. Sometimes they give drugs like Mannitol to prevent brain swelling. Does Jake have a history of seizures?"

"He did as a kid. Does that matter?" Cherie asked.

"It puts him at higher risk for the syndrome."

"What happens if he has another seizure?"

Will paused, wishing they were having this discussion in person. It was hard to gauge her response to all this information with just her voice as a barometer. "There's a chance he could suffer neurological damage with repeated seizures, that's why the aim is to prevent them from happening."

"And what else? I can hear it in your voice."

"Repeated seizures can lead to coma and cardiac arrest."

"Does this move him up on the transplant list then?" Cherie asked.

He kept his words measured, trying to keep his feelings for Cherie out of the equation and found that wasn't possible anymore. "Many factors influence where a patient ranks on the transplant list. If Jake is getting regular dialysis and is no longer using …"

"The ranking isn't a factor with a living donation, right?"

"Yes, but I thought you had ruled out being his donor."

"I never actually had to think that through to its conclusion," Cherie said, her words pensive. "When Jake told me he didn't want me as his donor, I never went down that road to deciding if I would do it."

"And that's changed now?"

"My mom asked me to think about going ahead with the rest of the testing."

"And you're considering it?"

"I am. What do you think, Will? You are always so careful to just give me the facts, but what I need now is what you really think."

Will sat in stunned silence. How could he tell her that for all his professionalism, all his knowledge about the need for transplants that when he thought about Cherie having surgery, he was just another guy scared to death of losing her when they were just getting started.

"Okay, your silence is scaring me," Cherie said, and Will could hear the concern in her voice.

"Just gathering my thoughts," Will said, leaning forward with the phone in his hands. "To be honest I'm having a hard time separating my professional assessment from my personal feelings right now. Living donor transplant surgery is a safe and effective way to change the course of a patient's life. There are risks to laparoscopic surgery but in the hands of a team that does these surgeries multiple times a week, the chances of a bad outcome are minimal. In my head I know all that, but in my heart …" He broke off trying to find the right words.

"… you're worried about me," Cherie said, completing his thought.

"Yes, because now I know you and care about you and the girls, and I know your history with Jake," Will said, feeling the intense truth of that statement like a hollow hunger in his gut. "You and Jake have unresolved issues, and I don't think you trust him. In that respect nothing has changed except your awareness of Jake's condition."

"I keep coming back to what I told my dad the other day; if it were Amy I wouldn't hesitate."

"I get that. You're trying to be fair, but the bottom line is: can you forgive Jake? For the fire? For Molly's injuries?"

"I don't know," Cherie said softly. "It always comes back to that, and I never have the answer."

"Maybe it's time you figured it out," Will said. "Hold on a minute." He took the phone off speaker and pulled up the Facetime icon, connecting the call. It rang once before Cherie appeared on the screen; her smile immediate as the cameras connected them in real time. "Much better. I needed to see you for this part."

"Okay, now I'm intrigued."

Sitting there staring at her beautiful face, no makeup, hair pulled back in a messy bun, her eyes tired but smile warm, Will knew he was lost. He was falling in love with this woman who had taken up residence in his heart in the span of a few weeks. "If you decide to move forward with the testing, I'd like to go with you."

He watched her smile brighten and then slowly fade, concern furrowing her brow. "You don't have to do that."

"I know I don't have to, but I want to be there for you."

"You know I can do it …"

"… yes, I know you are perfectly capable of doing this on your own," Will cut in. "But wouldn't it be easier to have someone there to talk to."

"I admit that does sound better, but the hospital is on Long Island, and it takes forever to get there on the LIE. And what about work?"

"I can rearrange things, take a few vacation days unless, you don't want my company …"

"I never said that."

"So, you DO want my company?" Will asked, the question light, meant to bring the smile back to her face but it did just the opposite. Her features stilled, her gaze meeting his.

"More than I even realized." She shook her head. "How's that for an admission?"

At her words, Will smiled broadly. "Just what I wanted to hear."

Cherie paused, her tone quiet and reflective when she spoke. "To tell you the truth, it scares me. We've known each other for such a short time, and I've come to count on you in a way I haven't done in a long time."

"Since Paul died."

"Yes, and losing him almost destroyed me. I don't think I can do that again."

"I'm not going anywhere, Cherie. I'll be a part of your life for as long as you want me to be," Will said, the words, spoken in truth, were also a promise.

"And then you say things like that, and I'm caught between wanting to explore whatever this is we're becoming and knowing you deserve more than the remnants of someone else's life. It's not fair to you, Will."

"Don't I get to decide how I live my life and who I choose to care about?" Will asked, leaning forward, and wishing they were having this conversation in person. This was too important.

"Of course, you do."

"Then I choose you, Cherie Hollister. And all that comes with you."

"Why?"

The single word lingered in the air. Will knew he couldn't tell her he was falling in love with her without scaring her. And yet anything less than the truth did not belong in this moment.

"Cherie, look at me," he said and waited for her to lift her eyes to meet his. "Since the first time I met you in the ER with Carey, I felt a connection to you. Attraction, yes, but it was something more. But I figured it wasn't likely I was going to see you again, so I let it go, or tried to, until life or fate or destiny just kept bringing you back into my life. Meeting you in the registration center at the hospital and then again at the 10 K didn't feel like a coincidence somehow. I can't explain it and I know it sounds strange, but from that first run together the feeling just kept growing stronger. You needed me, needed the kind of help I could give, and I felt like I was in the place I was supposed to be. I still feel it now, like a tether that connects us. I don't know where this relationship is going but I need you to understand … I choose you, Cherie."

She smiled and even the inadequate screen could not diminish the gleam in her eyes. "That wasn't life or fate or some random coincidence, Will. That was God."

Will didn't know if that was true, didn't know if he believed that was even possible, but she did believe and so he replied, "Then I know who to thank."

"Me too," she said softly. "Call me when you get a chance this week."

"I will," he answered before her face vanished from the screen.

Chapter Ten

Cherie grabbed the bags of clothes from her car and started toward the church. She'd stayed late at school correcting papers which left her just enough time for this one errand before picking the girls up at after-care.

Cherie pulled open the door to the meeting area in the church basement to find a small crew of people organizing the donations. Their church had partnered with a large relief organization to bring much needed supplies of food, water, and clothing to victims of an earthquake in Central America. As always, Pastor Michaels was right in the mix sorting through bags of dry goods before placing them in the designated boxes for pick up tomorrow. Cherie waved and headed her way.

"Where do you want the clothing?" she asked, coming alongside the pastor. She stared at the table covered with bags and cans. "This is amazing!"

Gabby Michaels' smile was as wide as her enthusiasm. "I mentioned it yesterday and was hoping for a few donations, but the generosity of our community just makes me proud."

"Sorry, I can't do more." Cherie said, lifting the bags of baby clothes with a shrug.

"All donations gratefully accepted. We do what we can," Gabby said. "I've been meaning to call you. Do you have a minute?"

"Sure." She followed Gabby over to a table covered in clothing and surrendered the bags to an older man folding T-shirts.

Gabby grabbed two water bottles from a table by the kitchen and handed one to Cherie before settling on a stool by the counter. "When I saw you slip out the back of church yesterday, I was reminded of our phone call last week."

"You don't miss a thing, do you?" Cherie laughed. "We were on our way to meet a friend for lunch at the park."

"Play date?"

Cherie felt the blush start in her neck. "Something like that, yes."

"Interesting," Gabby said, the single word long and drawn out. "We'll talk about that some other time, but I was wondering if you'd talked to Jake this week?"

Cherie nodded. She filled the pastor in on the video call, her impressions of Jake and his new life as a groundskeeper for a church. She followed up with a recap of her conversation with her dad and the revelation of the precarious state of Jake's health. Through it all, Gabby listened without commenting, waiting until Cherie finished to ask a question.

"He doesn't want your help then?" she asked.

"That's what he said, but it looks like he needs it."

"Sounds like you're considering it."

"Thinking about it, yes," Cherie nodded.

"Any progress on the forgiveness we talked about?"

"Honestly no, I'm just stuck."

Gabby studied her for a moment. "Been praying about that, have you?"

"Not as much as I should," Cherie answered, realizing that she had spent more time talking about it than praying about it.

"Might be a good place to start, don't you think?" Gabby said, her tone quiet with a hint of concern. "I've been praying about your situation this week. God just keeps bringing you and Jake into my mind, and I have the distinct impression God has a plan for your brother."

"And does that plan include me?"

"I wish I could help you with that," Gabby answered with a wry smile. "But it's an impression, not a movie on wide screen in my head, more like a quiet whisper in my mind."

"At least He's talking to you," Cherie said, wishing for a little divine inspiration.

"That's because I'm listening," Gabby said. "Can I make a suggestion?"

Cherie nodded. "Always."

"Go for a walk sometime this week. Turn off the phone. Just walk outside, surrounded by all the beauty God has created, and talk to Him like He's there by your side, because He is," Gabby said. "You are trying to make one of the biggest decisions of your life, and I truly believe that if you ask for guidance, He's going to answer."

Cherie loved the surety of this woman who wore her faith like a warm sweater on a winter morning, it's touch soft and comforting. "I'm going to give that a try."

"And one more thing before you go," Gabby smiled, getting to her feet. "Your situation has got me thinking. Remember last year when Jessica Fielding needed a bone marrow transplant."

"I do. Twelve years old and she had leukemia. You asked the whole congregation to pray for a donor for her."

"And someone sitting out there listening told their sister about it, and she decided to get tested and brought along a few people from her office. And one of those co-workers was the match Jessica needed."

"An altruistic donor sounds like the answer to prayer," Cherie said. "And you were surprised?"

"I was. Sometimes the way God answers is so perfectly timed, it just takes your breath away. So many people today don't believe in the power of prayer. They use it as a last resort, like some celestial Hail Mary, waiting until things get so bad, He's the only one who can help. But why wait to involve the Almighty when He could be helping right from the start," Gabby said. "It got me thinking about all the other Jessicas out there."

"I'm sensing a plan here."

"You know me well." Her voice was animated, her smile broad like when she'd finished a great sermon. "I want to hold a donor drive here at Lakeview. Advertise it to all the other churches, mosques, and synagogues in the area and see if we can put a few more donors in the database and maybe save a few lives."

"I think it's a great idea. What can I do to help?" Cherie asked.

"You, my friend, have your hands full right now, but I will be in touch if I can get this plan off the ground."

"I might know someone at the hospital who could point us in the right direction. I could give him a call."

Gabby's smile grew even wider. "Interesting, and I think I'll take you up on that. Call away."

* * *

Mondays were usually the busiest day in the ER, and considering the large volume of patients they handled every weekend, that made it that much harder. The staff referred to them as Medical Mondays, a steady stream of patients coming through the door, and today was no exception. Will's shift had started with a cardiac arrest, a middle-aged man with no cardiac history. They'd done CPR and defibrillation for nearly an hour, and then finally had to pronounce him, his wife and teenage son waiting outside. Moments later a healthy thirty-year-old woman came through the door in respiratory distress that turned out to be a pulmonary embolism. She was now in ICU. And that was just the start of a long day.

Leaning against the desk at the central station, Will overheard the charge nurse taking report from an incoming rig, the anxiety in the ambulance driver's transmission clear from several feet away. Looked like a bad day was about to get worse.

Ginger Grant looked up at Will and put the call on speaker. "En route with an eighteen-year-old female with multiple stab wounds to the neck, chest, and abdomen. BP 88/50. Pulse 120 and thready. Respirations 26 and shallow. No time for paramedics. Happened right in front of us. Outside the coffee shop on Third. ETA three minutes. Two more victims on scene. Coming your way as well."

Will's pulse kicked up a notch. He nodded at Ginger. "I'll take the first one."

"Take Ben with you. Trauma Two."

Ben Reynolds had been a nurse in the ER for more than a decade. When Will had started his residency and knew almost nothing about ER medicine, Ben had often pointed him to the right diagnosis. Over the past four years they had become friends as well as colleagues. His experience was a welcome addition to any trauma team. Tall and burly, his bald head shone in the overhead lighting as they both grabbed gloves and headed for the ambulance bay. Behind him he could hear Ginger activating the mass casualty protocol while the unit secretary notified the trauma surgeon on call and the Operating Room.

The ambulance pulled up moments later, the young driver having the good sense to silence the sirens as he pulled up the ramp. He jumped from the vehicle as Will and Ben reached for the rear doors. His partner, a woman in her sixties, took one look at the help and gave a quick hand-off report as they unloaded the stretcher and headed inside.

"Crystal Jenkins, 18, multiple stab wounds. Last BP 78/50. Pulse 132, respirations 30. No breath sounds on the right. Unresponsive all the way in."

Pneumothorax. One of those wounds had collapsed her lung, Will thought, assessing her color, and noting the ashen undertone to her coffee-colored skin. Blood smeared her face, neck and arms with multiple dressings applied to her wounds by the ambulance crew. Hemodynamically unstable, Will knew they needed to act quickly. She needed surgery, and their job in the ER was to assess, stabilize, and get her to the OR as quickly as possible.

"I placed a vented dressing over the back wound on the right to allow air to leave the chest cavity," the first responder added. "And gentlemen, she's pregnant."

The ultrasound they were about to do to assess for blood in the abdomen would tell them the state of her pregnancy as well. One more thing to factor in as the team, a PA, RN, and an ER tech surrounded the stretcher in Trauma Two, placing monitors, cutting off the patient's clothes and starting two large bore IV's.

"Ben, grab the ultrasound," Will said. "We'll confirm the pneumo…" He didn't have to finish the thought before the ultrasound probe was in his hand and Ben turned to set up for a chest tube.

"Confirmed pneumo, let's place a chest tube and then intubate." He quickly moved the probe lower and scanned the belly, confirming what he had suspected. "Blood in the abdomen, she needs an OR. And tell the trauma team she's pregnant. Looks like twenty weeks."

Behind him the RN documenting the care they were giving, relayed this to the front desk.

"Sats are dropping," Ben said as he finished prepping the right flank with betadine.

Will reached for the scalpel and palpated the ribs finding the intercostal space between the fourth and fifth ribs. Making a vertical incision, he held out a hand and Ben placed the Kelly clamp with the chest tube attached into

115

his hand. He advanced the instrument into the incision and then followed the clamp's path with his finger before pushing the tube into the pleural space with a pop. He quickly sutured the tube in place as Ben connected the other end to a closed drainage system. "Let's get x-ray in here."

Will stepped to the head of the stretcher and opened the airway. Using the glide scope, he looked for the vocal cords, the pathway he needed to slip the tube into the trachea so they could breathe for the patient, but all he could see was blood. He suctioned the airway only to watch it fill up with blood again before he even had the endotracheal tube in the mouth.

"Ben, can you suction while I intubate."

The suction did its job but with it and the tube he was trying to place both in the airway, it was almost impossible to see the cords. And the patient's anatomy was making it harder, her airway so anterior he had to remove the tube and change the angle and still he couldn't get it in.

"Need help, Will?"

Dr. Anika Patel, the ER director, was at his side. "Try it one more time. Ben, switch out the suction catheter for a Frazier tip."

The slimmer suction allowed for a clearer line of sight but when Will tried to advance the tube it still wouldn't go through the vocal cords.

"I've got it," Anika directed. With a wave of remorse and relief, Will stepped aside and watched as this experienced ER doctor examined the airway. She then bent the endotracheal tube until it looked like the letter J and passed it through the vocal cords in one smooth motion. "I need two units on the rapid infuser," Anika directed. "Trauma team?"

"On their way," Will answered.

"Stick with me here, Will, that was a tough airway. No time to beat yourself up."

Will nodded. The feelings he would deal with later, what mattered now was their patient. An x-ray tech took a shot of the abdomen and chest as the RN's hung the blood using the rapid infuser to deliver the packed red blood cells quickly to the patient.

Later Will would recall the image on the x-ray screen as the moment he knew this young woman and her baby were slipping away from them. The image showed her abdomen was dense with blood. They tried to save her, infusing unit after unit of red blood cells as well as plasma and platelets. The trauma surgeon had arrived with his team and opened the patient's abdomen right there in the trauma bay because she wasn't stable enough to transport to the OR. With two other trauma victims in adjacent bays, the decision not to deplete the blood bank for one patient, who would most likely not survive, was a call finally made by Dr. Patel.

As Will changed into clean scrubs before going off shift, the bloodied face of Crystal Jenkins haunted him. He knew it wasn't his fault she had died, though his personal failure at not being able to intubate her lingered like a blaring song on repeat in his mind. They had done all they could, and in the end the blame for this tragedy lay with the young man whose rage had randomly fallen on unsuspecting people just out getting a coffee. As Will had sat with her parents trying to offer what little comfort he could, he'd been overwhelmed with guilt and grief held barely in check behind a professional façade.

He grabbed his keys and backpack from his locker. He could think of only one thing that would salvage this day from its many losses. He glanced at his watch. 9:15. Too late to call, though in the moment he almost did it anyway. Cherie had to work tomorrow, and he didn't want to keep her awake tonight with the images pulsing through his brain. With that option reluctantly set aside, all he wanted was sleep and a chance to put this shift out of his mind. But he feared, as in the past, staying asleep would not be so easy.

* * *

Cherie picked up her cellphone debating whether to call Will tonight or just wait to speak with him later this week. She wanted to run Pastor Michaels' idea about hosting a donor drive by him. She frowned as she realized she was calling to ask for his help again and wondered when she was going to admit to herself that she enjoyed talking to Will at the end of a long day. She hadn't felt that way in a long time, but the truth rang with the clarity of a bird's call on a summer morning, the sound clear and unexpected. With a soft smile, she pulled up her recent calls and hit the number.

"Cherie, how are you?"

She heard the lift in his tone as he said her name, but his voice sounded weary and beat down. "Better question, how are you? You sound exhausted."

"On my way home. It was a long day."

"Want to talk about it?"

"Don't think I can yet, still processing. Today was one of the sad ones."

She heard a quiet despair in the tenor of his words. "Did you lose a patient?"

He paused before answering. Beyond his silence she heard the acceleration of a car engine as it picked up speed. "More than one actually."

"Oh, Will, I'm so sorry. How can I help?"

"Just hearing your voice helps."

Cherie knew what he needed in that moment, what so many had given her in the face of loss. "Then stop here on your way home."

"I don't know … I'm not very good company right now."

"I'm not looking for company and you don't have to talk, but I'm here and I owe you one, remember?"

He inhaled deeply, the sound ragged and raw. "Making the turn. Be there in five."

Cherie stared at the screen as it went dark, glad she could offer Will what her parents and Amy had given her in the days and weeks after Paul's death, a quiet place to lay the burden down. She knew what that had meant to her, those people who stood by and listened, sharing her pain. They had given her a safe place to rest. And now she wanted to be that safe place for Will.

Cherie heard the low rumble of the car engine as it pulled up to the curb. She crossed the room and opened the front door. A week ago, she had stood in this exact spot and watched Will step from his car. She had needed his help then, and now he needed hers.

In the darkness, his green scrubs were a splash of color in the headlights as he rounded the front bumper and walked up the path. His shoulders were rounded, his eyes downcast, a sharp contrast to the man who had covered this distance a week ago with a confident step. Pushing open the screen door, she stood in the gap as he mounted the steps. He raised his gaze to meet hers, taking the final step to stand in front of her, his eyes dull with pain and regret. She didn't speak, simply lifted her arms and he stepped into her embrace. Heaving a great shuddering sigh, his arms closed around her, his breath warm against the side of her face.

And in that moment, it didn't matter this was the first time she had held a man in her arms in three years. Since Paul died. She felt no hesitancy or guilt. Will needed her help.

Under her hands his well-worn scrubs felt insubstantial, heat radiating through the thin fabric. A faint musky mix of sweat and the remnants of whatever shampoo he had used that morning mixed with an underlying scent both medicinal and strong. He held her gently, his hands trembling against her back.

They stood there a long time, simply holding each other before Cherie drew back, took his hand, and led him inside. The screen door closed behind them with its usual squeak.

"Thanks for the call," he said. "Very timely."

They crossed to the couch where Will sank onto the cushions, his head falling backward with a soft sigh. "First time I've sat down all day."

Cherie settled in beside him. "Do you want to talk?"

"In a minute, just enjoying the silence and the company," Will said quietly as he reached for her hand.

Cherie closed her eyes, enjoying the feel of this man at her side and wondering how Will had managed to navigate around all the barriers she usually put up to any new relationship. She knew she could be a bit prickly and stubborn. Perhaps even a little selfish in wanting to protect herself and her children, but Will had found a way around all that, creating a pathway where none existed, to forge a friendship she had not expected but was so thankful to have. She opened her hand, intertwining her fingers with his and gave a gentle squeeze.

His words started slowly as he told her the story of a father taken from his wife and young son by a massive heart attack. Of the St. Christopher metal around his neck. Of the ragged wallet that had fallen from his pocket as they cut off his clothes in their haste to try and save him. Of the holes in his socks and the tears of his boy.

His voice grew quieter and more strident as he spoke of the young woman covered in blood being taken from the ambulance. Of the chest tube he had placed and the unsuccessful attempt at intubation. Of the gentle swell of her pregnant abdomen and the blood that oozed from her nose.

His tone defeated, his words faded away as he released her hand and lifted his arm to encircle her shoulder, pulling her in closer. Cherie rested her head on his chest wishing she could quiet his guilt and sadness, but knowing she could offer nothing more than what she was giving, a listening ear and a solid presence at his side.

She lifted her head to look at him. Will's eyes were open, shiny and vacant as if the telling of the story had left nothing behind but guilt. She touched one finger to his chin, gently drawing his attention to her words. "You did everything you could for them, Will."

"But it wasn't enough." He captured her hand in his, resting them against his chest. "Her parents were devastated. I've seen a lot of grief in the last four years, but nothing compares to the loss of a child."

"I've known the terror of almost … almost losing a child," Cherie said, her words soft and her eyes stinging with the memory. "But I can't even imagine the rest."

Will nodded, gently squeezing her shoulder. "I don't know how you go home to a house that yesterday was full of conversation and petty little annoyances, and now it's all gone. Her parents told me they had decided as a family to welcome this new life as a blessing. They were eager to help their daughter and to meet their first grandchild."

"Oh Will, I'm so sorry," Cherie said, feeling the soft rise and fall of his breathing. "Those words sound so inadequate."

"That's what I thought too, even as I was saying them to her parents. It just seems so senseless. Makes you wonder why, doesn't it?"

Cherie had had that same thought many times in the days after Paul's death, and she had no better explanation now then she did then. But while she didn't know the why, she did know the God who had walked with her through those long, awful months. "They aren't alone, you know. Her parents, I mean."

Will met her gaze. "Funny, that's what they said, too. There I was trying to comfort them, and they were the strong ones. I watched them cry and cling to each other, the pain ripping them apart and yet drawing them closer together. I didn't know what to say, just sat there because somehow, I couldn't leave. And then her dad reached out a hand and asked me to pray with them."

"And you did?"

"Yes, because it was what they needed me to do. I bowed my head to give them a few moments to process before they went home to an empty house."

Cherie heard the subtle shift in his tone, a mixture of disbelief and wonder.

"And then this grieving father, this man who had lost his only child, started thanking God for giving them eighteen years with their daughter, for taking her home to be with Him and asking for help in the days ahead as they learned to live without her here on earth." Will's head fell back against the cushions, his eyes narrowing. "He was so sure, his words so beautiful and all

I could think was I hope he's right. I hope if there is a god, that he's listening with their daughter right beside him."

"That's a beautiful image," Cherie said softly.

"Yes, it is, but I don't think it's true."

"Do you believe in God, Will?"

"I don't think I do, not with all the suffering I see every day." His words were tinged with quiet anger.

Cherie rested her hand on his chest and pushed herself up to face him, her words soft and reflective. "Some people come to faith with such ease; I've always wished I was one of those. But for most of us, stubborn as we are, it takes a problem that drives us to our knees. And in that moment when you are out of options when you know you can't possibly handle the situation on your own, right there in that empty void, God steps in and lifts the load and you believe because you've seen Him do it. 'Blessed are they who have not seen but still believe', the gospel says. Well, I wasn't one of those, but I do believe."

"Because of Paul?"

"Yes, I was lost in the darkness after the crash. I'd always hung around on the fringes of faith, knew all about it in my head but never let it change my heart until I had nowhere to turn but to Him. I hope it doesn't take that for you, Will. I hope you can embrace the belief without having to find it on your knees."

"It's important to you, that I believe?"

"It is," Cherie answered, "because I care about you. It's a dark world out there, and you see some of the worst of it."

"The worst, yes …" He lifted his hand to touch her cheek. "… but also, the best. Thank you for listening. Now I might even be able to sleep tonight." He pushed himself to his feet, glancing at the clock on the wall by the table. "It's late and we both have to work tomorrow."

She walked him to the door. Will turned to face her with just a hint of a smile lifting the corners of his mouth. "So, are we even now?"

Cherie laughed. "Not even close. I still owe you at least one more. All you need to know is I'm here for you, Will."

He reached out, his arms encircling her in a hug, his words warm in her ear. "I'm counting on that."

He held her for a moment longer, and Cherie savored the embrace of this man she was coming to trust more and more with each day they spent together. "Call me tomorrow and let me know how you're doing, okay?" she said, looking up at him, glad to see the color back in his face and a slight gleam in his eyes.

"I will. And Cherie … thank you for this, tonight, for knowing exactly what I needed to get me though." He released her slowly and pulled open the door.

Cherie watched through the screen as he navigated the dark walkway, his shoulders square, and his stride easier than an hour ago. She smiled, wrapping her arms around herself as the warmth of his embrace began to fade.

She was glad she had been able to help him though a subtle disquiet tinged her contentment. She remembered teasing him yesterday at the park and asking him if there was anything he couldn't do, because clearly even the hard things he had attempted in his life, law school, medical school, had crumbled under the sheer force of his hard work. He'd persevered in making a career change most people would not even have attempted. His guilt and grief tonight highlighted how hard he pushed himself and how sky high he set the bar on his own performance. And despite his upbringing in what sounded like a dysfunctional family, he was strong and generous, kind and self-assured. Perhaps because he had never come up against a problem, he couldn't solve by just working harder to fix it. She recognized a touch of arrogance in his surety, perhaps because she had once had a good bit of it herself in the days before her perfect life was shattered by the flying shrapnel of a helicopter crash. It was disconcerting that this generous man seemed to want nothing to do with the God who had pulled her out of the wreckage of her broken life. Everyone was vulnerable, she knew, but few recognized it. Cherie shuddered, fearing what it would take to bring Will to that realization for himself.

Chapter Eleven

Cherie lifted the tail gate of the Jeep and reached for her sneakers. Leaning her back against the car, she exchanged the black flats she had worn to work for the more comfortable running shoes. She had an hour before she needed to pick the girls up, and she'd decided to take Pastor Michaels' suggestion and go for a walk. She tucked her cell phone into her back pocket. No music or podcasts today. Just walking and talking.

A brisk wind lifted her hair, and she grabbed a sweatshirt before closing the tailgate. When she had taken her class out for recess earlier, the day had been chilly but sunny. In the intervening hours, a cloud front had blown in, the sun now peeking out in flashes of brilliance before being obscured by gathering clouds. Pulling the sweatshirt over her head she was glad of the warmth as she set out for the trailhead.

The county park had a wide gravel pathway weaving in and out of the trees surrounding a man-made lake. The loop around was a little more than a mile and she figured she could get in at least two before heading over to get the girls.

She walked for several minutes, the fine gravel crunching beneath her feet, the breeze chilly on her cheeks. It felt strange at first not to be listening to one of her favorite playlists, but after a few moments she started to notice the sounds she would ordinarily have missed. The squawk of white geese in the lake's shallows. The whisper of new leaves as the breeze gusted. The gentle lapping of water against the shoreline as the wind created a light chop on the lake's surface.

Today, she didn't have an agenda. Instead, she was just walking, and if God wanted to have a word with her, she was open to listening though she wasn't sure how to get that started. Gabby Michaels had made it sound so easy, like it was the most natural thing in the world to go for a walk with the Almighty at your side. Unconsciously, Cherie glanced to her left then chided herself with a chuckle as the day grew blustery.

Through the trees she caught glimpses of the lake, the water a steely gray and capped with white crests. After one loop, the sun appeared around the edge of a cloud, the warm light returning gradually, brightening the day as it crossed the water from one side to the other. The lake glistened for a moment in the brilliant light somehow stronger in contrast to moments earlier.

Cherie felt her mind quiet, her thoughts not racing as they so often did when she focused on what was next on her to-do list. Instead, as the path turned away from the water and into the trees, a hint of pine scenting the air, she chose to focus on the blessings in her life. Her precious girls. Her good health. A secure job with meaningful work to do. Her parents. Her sister. And Will. A warmth settled in her chest, but she purposefully set aside that distracting tangent.

She backtracked a bit. Her sister was certainly a blessing in her life. But what about Jake? Could Jake be considered a blessing? Cherie instinctively grimaced. At one time that had been true. With eight years between them, she had been like a second mother when Jake was a toddler. She had helped him learn to walk and climb stairs, scooping him up before he could get into trouble. As a teenager, she had often been his babysitter, a job she remembered being less enthusiastic about, which had little to do with Jake and more to do with wanting to spend time with her friends. And when she left for college, he was rarely in her thoughts. So much of what happened with his addiction had become a burden her parents shouldered quietly. It wasn't that she didn't care what was happening to Jake but more the time intensity of her own life and her sheer inability to do anything to help him. Until the day her mother asked if Jake could stay with her because he was interviewing for a job.

So where did that leave her now? After the fire. After Molly's injuries. After willfully shutting her brother out of her life for nearly five years. The thought lingered as the clouds took purchase of the sky again.

In the dark days after the fire, when Molly had lived in the burn center, sedated and yet still restless with pain, Cherie had hated her brother. And Paul's rage had stoked her hatred making it hard for Cherie to let it go. Until the day Judith told her Jake had overdosed. Only the timely arrival of the police and the Narcan they carried in their first-aid kit had saved Jake from becoming a statistic in the opioid crisis. Fearing that the next time he would not be so lucky and knowing Jake's death would break her parents in a way only losing a child could, Cherie had driven to the hospital where they had Jake on a three-day psych hold.

The image of Jake huddled in a chair by the window of the locked unit came unbidden to Cherie's mind. She hadn't thought about that day in years.

Standing just inside the locked door, she had studied the brother she hadn't seen since the night of the fire nine months earlier. He looked old and, at the same time, impossibly young, his face pale and drawn, his arms wrapped around his drawn-up knees, his sandy hair dank and wild. Like a small boy huddled in a corner inhabiting the body of an old man.

Crossing the room, she knew what she had to do. And steeling herself for the task, she stepped up next to him.

"Jake?"

He turned, shoving his hair from his face with a shaky hand. His eyes, vacant a moment earlier, were filled with dread. "What are doing here?"

"How are you?" Cherie asked, ignoring his question.

"I'm here. On a locked psych unit. How good could I be?"

"But you're alive."

"If you call this living. They won't let me leave. They think I tried to kill myself," he replied, his tone angry and desperate all at the same time.

"Did you?"

"Does it matter?"

"It does. A lot of people are worried about you," Cherie responded.

"Mom and Dad told you to come, didn't they?"

"That would be just like Mom, but no, I came on my own, to tell you something."

Jake cringed, retreating from an expected onslaught. "Tell me what?"

"I came to tell you about Molly."

He visibly shuddered. His bloodshot eyes gleamed as he turned his head to stare out the window. His voice when he spoke was quiet and filled with regret. "How is she?"

"She's recovering, thank God. The burns to her face and neck are healed. She needed a skin graft which the burn surgeon took from her thigh. The reconstruction of her ear will take a few more surgeries though."

"Can she hear?"

"Very little on that side."

His back heaved, his breathing coming in short gasps as he began to cry. "I'm sorry, Cherie. I'm so sorry."

She heard the sincerity in his tone, and still the words caught in her throat, strangled by all the things she wanted to shout at him about abandoning her child. She purposefully cleared her throat before opening her mouth. "I forgive you, Jake."

He turned back to her, wiping his runny nose on his sleeve, his eyes wide in surprise. "Why would you do that?"

"Because it's the only way I know to let go of the anger and to move on with my life," she replied, which was half the truth. "And I want to put this in the past, for my family."

"Is that even possible when looking at Molly reminds you every day what I did?"

"I'm doing it for Molly, so I can be the best mother I can possibly be for her. I need to forgive you so I can do that." She knew the words were true even as she said them.

"Thank you. I don't deserve it, but thank you," Jake said, the tears making his cheeks shiny.

She considered reaching out to touch him, but she couldn't do it. All she wanted now was to get out of here. "I have to go." She turned but then stopped. "Jake, you have a chance right now to change your life. I hope you take it."

Then she fled and never looked back. As she climbed into her car for the drive home, she knew Paul would never understand what she had done. His anger was so deep and visceral he was incapable of changing, even for her. And she knew that for the first time in her marriage, she would lie to Paul about what she'd done that day.

The wind's chill cut through her sweatshirt making her tremble, or was it the memory, so long buried, that had her feeling cold. She picked up the pace breaking into a jog.

But the memory had shaken loose the truth. She had known it then, had recognized the need to let go of the anger to be a good parent. And yet, as evidenced by the years of silence that followed with no contact with her brother, she had retained an ember of anger, a smoldering coal of resentment, buried deep in her soul. She had said the words, had thought at the time she meant them, but she had never believed them. She had done it for her mom and dad, to salvage the family they loved from being torn in two by the tragedy.

So, what now, God? She felt the question rise in her consciousness, the words whispered from her mouth and snatched away by the wind. She remembered Gabby's words. Forgiveness doesn't mean you forget. Forgiveness is a choice you make, to offer a gift of grace to the undeserving, because we are all undeserving, and to move beyond what you can never change.

She stopped suddenly, her sneakers punching deep divots into the gravel, transfixed by the sudden truth.

Forgiveness was a choice. She would never forget, couldn't possibly ever forget, but she could make a choice.

She drew in a deep breath and exhaled the words into the wind.

"I forgive you, Jake."

And with that simple admission the way forward seemed as obvious as the God who had guided her to this moment. All she needed to do was take the next step as she had for so many years.

The sun broke through the clouds as she jogged to the car.

Cherie was looking forward to pizza night as she did every week, and the girls were eager to see their cousin. She had spent her lunch hour on the phone, making appointments, and now what remained was telling her family. As in the past, she chose to start with Amy.

"When will they be here?" Molly asked, pencil in hand, as she looked up from her math homework.

"Any minute now," Cherie answered. "Just about done?"

"I'm all done," Sarah said proudly, waving a single worksheet in the air.

Molly frowned. "How come Sarah gets one page and I get all this?" She waved a hand over the work in front of her before a knock sounded on the door, and she bolted from her seat. Throwing open the door, she looked upward. "Grandy?"

Startled, Cherie turned to see her mother standing awkwardly in the doorway. "Mom, come in. You're just in time, Amy should be here ..."

"Right now," Amy said, appearing on the steps, pizza boxes in hand while Mark scrambled around her legs to find his cousins. The bottleneck in the doorway eased as Molly reached for his hand and pulled him clear, the kids disappearing into the girls' bedroom. "Mom? Joining us for pizza night?"

Judith's smile didn't make it to her eyes. "If you have enough?"

"More than enough," Cherie answered, her voice welcoming even as she wondered why Judith had stopped by unannounced.

Amy placed the pizza on the counter, the spicy aroma of sausage and peppers filling the apartment. "Everything okay with Dad?"

This wasn't about Dad, Cherie thought, clearing away the homework on the table and placing it on the bench by the door. This was about Jake.

"Dad is fine. He's playing a pick-up game of wheelchair basketball with a few guys from the rehab center right now." She paused, glancing from one daughter to the other. "It's Jake. They've moved him up the transplant list. He's had another seizure."

Amy stepped up next to Judith. "Is he okay?"

"Now, yes, but they had a hard time stabilizing him this time. It lasted much longer than last time."

Cherie joined Amy and Judith, mother and daughters forming a tight circle, dinner forgotten.

"Where does that leave Jake now?" Amy asked.

"He needs a transplant," Cherie said, softly.

Judith nodded. "Yes, he does." She turned to Cherie, reaching for her hand. "You said you would consider taking the next step ..."

"Already done, Mom. I have an appointment for the testing on Friday," Cherie answered.

"You do?" Judith's eyes filled with tears as she squeezed Cherie's hand.

"I was going to call you tonight and tell you." Cherie extended a hand in Amy's direction. "I'm going to need some help with the girls though."

"Whatever you need," Amy responded instantly, as Cherie had known she would. "I could pick them up, do dinner, even keep the girls overnight for a cousin sleepover if you need me to."

"Thank you, I might take you up on that. And Mom …"

"Whatever I can do …" Judith said, her eyes shiny.

"Mom," Cherie interrupted, needing to make sure Judith understood. "I'm taking this one step at a time. The tests may show I'm a good candidate to be a donor and they may not. Whatever way it goes you need to be okay with it."

Judith nodded. "Of course. I only want the best for all of you. Can I go with you on Friday?"

"I have that covered, thank you."

Amy and Judith exchanged a knowing glance that in any other circumstance would have made Cherie laugh at their obvious assumption she wasn't going alone. Which was true, or at least she hoped it was true. She still needed to talk to Will. And then she had one more call to make before heading to Long Island on Friday.

The bedroom door flew open amid a gaggle of shouts about pizza and starvation. The noise filled the somber space with the joy of children's laughter.

Hours later, after a stress-free dinner where Judith had actually eaten two pieces of pizza, Cherie closed the bedroom door behind her. She smiled, hearing Molly and Sarah's whispered giggles filtering out into the hall.

Feeling the telltale vibration in her back pocket, Cherie reached for the phone. Glancing at the number, her smile grew broader as she stepped into the living room and settled on the couch.

"I was just about to call you," Cherie said.

"Great minds really do think alike," Will responded.

"I don't know how great our minds are, but we do seem to be in sync lately."

"Just trying to make myself indispensable," Will quipped.

"Well, it's working," Cherie said, trying to keep her tone light and failing.

"Tell me what you need, Cherie," Will asked, his tone serious.

"I've made a decision to move forward with the donor testing for the transplant and you said that you wanted …"

"Yes, I'll go with you."

"I haven't even told you when it is."

"Doesn't matter, I'll make it work."

Cherie smiled with relief as Will responded exactly as she had been hoping he would. She was coming to rely on him, a thought that last week would have scared her and now felt as comfortable as the couch she was sitting on. "It's Friday at 11:00."

"I'll pick you up at 8:00 then," Will said without hesitation. "The LIE on a Friday moves like a snail. Have you told your mother about this?"

"Yes, a few hours ago."

"She must have been relieved?"

"She was, and yet, as she was leaving, I got the feeling she was afraid, like she just realized she might have two children having surgery at the same time."

"She's a mom, worry comes with the territory, so they tell me. Judith has spent a good part of her life looking out for you," Will said.

Intrigued by a tone she couldn't quite identify, something akin to wistful but with a harder edge, Cherie said, "You know so much about my family, especially my mother, and I know almost nothing about yours. Can you tell me a story about your mom, Will?"

The silence that followed, though not more than the length of a full breath, spoke louder than his response. "She's complicated, Cherie. Not a bit like your mother, always out there advocating for her children. My mother was a ghost."

Chilled by his somber words, Cherie waited to see if he would explain this part of his past he rarely mentioned.

"I don't have any stories, Cherie. My mother was beautiful, fragile, and clinically depressed. She was in and out of hospitals most of my childhood, and even when she was home, she spent more time behind a closed bedroom door than she did with us. Five kids in nine years. We were just too much for her, all of us. And she was never able to stand up for us when it came to my dad. My grandmother was the only one who could do that."

"How is your mom now?" Cherie asked.

"Better. Her doctors finally found the right combination of drugs to help her, but she missed so much, and she knows it."

"Do you see her often?"

"No, we speak on the phone, but I rarely go there. And she never travels outside the town they live in. Maddie seems to be the only one who has made a real effort to keep in touch with her. Maybe because she's the only one of us who has children." Will paused, his tone reflective. "I know Judith isn't easy to deal with sometimes, but she's there in the mix with you, helping with the kids and loving you through all of it. You're lucky to have her."

Cherie knew that was true. For all the problems and petty annoyances, Judith's love for her family was unwavering. She didn't always get it right, and sometimes it might have appeared she loved one of them more than the others, but that had never been true. Cherie knew that instinctively, had always known Judith's time and attention was measured by their need. Where the need was greatest that was where she invested her time, and there was no question she loved with her whole heart.

"I think you're right about that," Cherie agreed, understanding now why Will had always tried to be so even-handed when it came to Judith. "I was thinking of making a stop on the way home on Friday. Any chance you have time for dinner for three? Could get us back late."

"Whose joining us for dinner?" Will asked.

"My brother, Jake. I want you to meet him."

Will paused, clearly surprised. "Of course, I'd like to meet him."

Sitting in the darkened living room, the light from the hall casting the room in shadows, Cherie wondered what this steady, dependable man would think of Jake. "You've heard so many things about my brother, most of it awful, do you think it's possible for you to see him objectively?" Cherie asked, putting her thoughts into words.

"If I've learned anything working in the ER it's not to judge people by their history or what others have to say about them. I'll do my best," Will responded. "Have you made a decision about the transplant?"

"Just taking it one step at a time for now."

"What changed your mind?"

Her decision was still new and though it felt right, she was still getting used to it herself. "Mind if we talk about it on Friday?"

"Of course, we'll have the whole day to talk about it."

"Will, thank you," Cherie said, her tone filled with gratitude and relief. "I don't think I even realized how much I was counting on you going with me until you said you would."

"Glad I could help. See you Friday."

Chapter Twelve

Cherie closed her eyes, feeling the smooth powerful acceleration of the Porsche as it merged onto the highway. Amy had picked the girls up for drop-off at school and day care, and she had taken their suitcases for an overnight stay. Molly and Sarah had been so excited at the prospect of a sleepover with their cousin they barely asked Cherie where she was going or when she would be back. She wouldn't have to worry about the girls today which left a host of other thoughts vying for her attention. A day of tests at the hospital. A conversation with a psychologist about being a possible donor. A dinner with Jake. It was going to be a long day.

Glancing over at Will navigating the dense traffic, Cherie was so thankful she wasn't doing this alone. "How did you manage to get the day off?" she asked.

"I switched shifts with another resident. He was only too happy to take my shift today when I offered to take his weekend duty."

"Sounds like you got the short end of that deal."

Will shrugged. "Depends on how you look at it. Personally, I think I got the better part. You won't be seeing me this weekend though."

"But you're here now and I appreciate it. Thank you."

"Can't think of anyone I'd rather spend the day with," Will replied. "How did your call with Jake go?"

"He was surprised and a little relieved to hear I was moving forward with the testing. And he wasn't expecting the dinner invitation."

"What made you change your mind?' Will asked, his tone curious but his eyes on the road, the commuter traffic increasing with each mile as they drove east.

"I realized in many ways my mother was right when she said I never really forgave Jake," Cherie said, her tone reflective. "A lot of my anger in the months after the fire was fueled by Paul's rage with Jake. It wasn't that I didn't feel the same way every time I looked at Molly, but Jake is an addict which isn't a reason to forgive him as much as it's just a fact."

"But your husband didn't see it that way?"

Cherie paused, searching for the words to explain, and yet not betray, the man she had loved with every ounce of her being. "Paul saw Jake's behavior as willful, something he chose to do, like a lot of people think about addiction. He hated Jake until the day he died, and I think a lot of that spilled over on to me. A few days ago, I remembered something I hadn't thought about in years, Jake's remorse, and his tears at what he had done. I told him I forgave him then and never meant a word of it. But now I do."

"Do you think Paul would ever have forgiven him?" Will asked, switching lanes to take the exit for the Goethals Bridge to Staten Island, the GPS on the console showing it the fastest route to Long Island.

"I don't think so. He was a wonderful man, a great husband and father, but he had a stubborn streak. Changing his mind was hard to do." Cherie turned toward Will. "I didn't think you'd want to talk about Paul."

"Actually, just the opposite. Paul is part of who you are. He's the father of your beautiful children. He's still here with you in many ways."

Cherie studied his profile, hearing the calm certainty of his words. "How does that make you feel?"

Clearly, she had caught him off guard with the question, making her more curious to hear the answer. His gaze fixed on the cars around them exiting the highway, he replied, "Feel? I would say privileged to be the man you have allowed into your life. In another universe, we might not have had this chance, and I for one am glad to be here with you today."

"Me, too," she said quietly, wondering just how this remarkable man was still single. He must have been a hermit during medical school after that breakup with Jen. Cherie was amazed some would-be-doctor hadn't snatched him up by now.

They fell into a comfortable silence, the traffic heavy but moving as they drove across Staten Island.

"You're pretty quiet this morning," Will said as they neared the Verrazano Bridge.

Cherie turned toward him. "Just wondering how long this is going to take."

"Hopewell Atlantic is a major transplant center. They were just acquired by our parent company, Atlantic Regional Health. They do more transplants than we do at Mercy; I would think they have a pretty streamlined testing process. Probably going to take a few hours though," Will said, glancing at the GPS on the console. "The coordinator explained about the tests they need, right?"

"Blood work, chest x-ray, CAT scan, something called an intravenous pyelogram …"

"To check the structure and vessels in the kidney."

"The mammogram is making me nervous," Cherie admitted. "Why do I need that to be a donor?"

Will put on the blinker to change lanes as they crossed the bridge. "They need to rule out the possibility of any cancer."

Cherie flinched. "Okay, I was worried about the pain I hear all the women at work talk about after they get their mammograms. Now, I'm going to worry about what they're going to find."

Will reached over and squeezed her hand. "It's going to be fine, Cherie."

"From your mouth to God's ears," Cherie said, turning her hand upward to rest in his for a moment before releasing it.

"You really do believe there's someone up there listening, don't you?"

"I do. You don't though, do you?"

"Honestly, no, that just hasn't been my experience." His jawline tensed. "I gave the praying thing a shot as a kid, but it never made a difference."

"What were you praying for?" Cherie asked softly as they drove across the expansive arc of the bridge, the water below shining and dotted with boat traffic.

"For my grandmother. She took a fall down the front steps of our house and hit her head on the stone walkway. The impact created a massive brain bleed because of the medication she was taking for her A-fib. She was in a coma for a week before she died, and no amount of prayer changed that."

"How old were you, Will?"

"Nine," Will said, taking the exit for the Belt Parkway. "She was the only person my father ever respected enough to listen to and after we lost her, all his worst instincts took over. He was a hard man to live with." Will checked the rearview mirror, his tone reflective. "Nothing was ever the same after Nan died, and I remember thinking if there was a god that he died right along with her or maybe he was never there at all."

Cherie heard in his tone a remnant of the little boy who had lost the one love in his young life. Recalling what he had told her on the phone about his mother's illness, Cherie ached for him. As dysfunctional as she sometimes thought her own family was, there had never been any doubt about the love in their family. It had sometimes felt overbearing, but Cherie had never doubted she was deeply loved.

Her phone vibrated with a text message. She glanced down at the phone in her lap.

> **Drop off done. Sarah thought she forgot her homework but Molly found it in her backpack. There's a good reason I don't have four kids! Just kidding, I got this, Cher. No need to worry. Tell Jake I said Hi when you see him.**

An hour later, Cherie spotted the sign for Hopewell Atlantic. The hospital, just over the line dividing Nassau from Suffolk County, was a massive complex with wings fanning off the central building as if the medical campus had recently undergone a major expansion project.

Leaving the confines of Will's comfortable car, Cherie found her anxiety coiled like a spring at the top of her spine, making her shoulders stiff as a shiver ran down her back despite the warmth of the day. Instinctively, she stepped closer to Will, and he reached for her hand as if sensing her mood. Making this appointment had been the easy part, keeping it was a whole other level of putting forgiveness into practice.

The day took on a rhythm of its own as they stepped through the main entrance and were directed to the registration area. A pretty, older woman wearing navy scrubs and a white lab coat approached them. "Cherie Hollister? My name is Brook Sheraton. I am one of the transplant coordinators here at Hopewell, and I will be helping you through the testing process. I know you came a long way this morning. How was the drive?"

136

"Remarkably easy for a Friday morning," Cherie said recalling the voice from her initial news about the tissue match.

"I'm glad to hear it. We have a series of appointments laid out for you today to minimize your wait time. I'll be checking in with you throughout the day to answer any questions you may have along the way."

"Thank you. This is my friend, Will Finnegan. He came along for moral support."

"Of course, we have many candidates for donation who choose to have a family member, or a friend come with them." Brook led them over to a small seating area. "Before we get started, I will need you to fill out some basic registration forms. HIPPA disclosure, emergency contact information, all the usual hospital paperwork." She handed Cherie a clipboard. "Let me know when you're ready."

Cherie and Will sat down on a sleek vinyl sofa. She flipped through the first few pages, repeating her name and address on the top of several. The emergency contact form gave her pause. For years Paul's name had automatically filled that spot, written without even thinking about it. In the years since the crash, she had put her parents' names, but today feeling the weight of the donation process, she wrote Amy's name on the designated line. She repeated the same on the HIPPA disclosure which specified who the doctors could talk to about her medical condition.

She paused, glancing over at Will. "Is it okay if I put you down here?" She tapped the page with her pen.

Will leaned over, reading the top of the sheet. "Of course, but are you sure you want to do that?"

Cherie nodded. "I'm going to tell you about it anyway so on the off chance something happens …" Her words fell away as she copied Will's number from the contacts on her phone.

"I'm honored you would trust me that much," Will said, his shoulder brushing hers.

Cherie lifted her gaze to meet his. "I do. I find that remarkable myself, but it's true."

Will's eyes grew wide and then narrowed, the crow's feet at the corners deepening as a smile touched his lips. She saw in his eyes what she had known she would, his devotion radiating outward with an intensity that made her eyes sting as she glanced away. A few short weeks ago she had been answering Will's questions about Carey in monosyllables, trying to get away from him and the hospital as quickly as possible, and now she was rapidly coming to a place where she couldn't imagine her life without him.

Brook Sheraton appeared in front of them. "Ready to get started?"

* * *

Cherie had never been a fan of hospitals, and ever since Molly's stay on the burn unit her aversion had grown. She knew lifesaving work happened in hospitals, having been on the receiving end of many talented clinicians' efforts to save Molly. Still a nagging unease, sometimes approaching panic, assailed her the moment she stepped through the hospital doors. She felt like she couldn't draw a full breath until she put the building behind her and filled her lungs with fresh air in the parking lot. Today, that anxiety was a subtle undertone rather than an escalating panic as they began the testing with a blood draw in the lab. Her stomach was growling, but her breathing calm as the phlebotomist took several tubes of blood.

Cherie kept waiting for the anxiety to bubble to the surface as she began the tests in the radiology department. But it never did, perhaps held at bay by the cheerful competence of every technician she met, from the radiology tech taking the chest x-ray to the RN explaining the CAT scan and pyelogram. Her description of the body's usual reaction to the contrast dye, given through the IV, had been spot on, Cherie thought as she lay on the scanning bed and felt a warm flush pulse like a wave through her body.

"How was it?" Will asked, getting to his feet as she joined him in the waiting area.

"Fine, just a weird sensation with the contrast, something between a hot flash and sinking into a warm bath. Not painful, but strange."

Brook Sheraton joined them, pocketing her phone. Cherie wondered with all the donors she must deal with how she had the time to spend with just one possible candidate. Cherie appreciated the guidance, but knew it came at the cost of a good portion of the coordinator's day.

"We built in a little time for a break before we go over to the Women's Center. Are you hungry?' Brook asked.

"Starving," Cherie answered.

"We'll stop by the cafeteria then. We understand asking our would-be donors not to eat before the testing is tough, especially when the appointment is later in the day like yours."

Brook led them down a long modern hallway with floor to ceiling windows flooding the space with sunshine. They stopped outside the cafeteria entrance and Brook handed them two meal vouchers. "These are good for whatever you like. I'll be back in thirty minutes."

"That's a nice touch. Free lunch," Will said. "They seem to have thought of everything."

"If you're impressed, I'll take that as a good sign," Cherie said.

The cafeteria was well organized with separate stations for soup, sandwiches, and a hot meal option. Alongside the usual grill fare, there were healthy choices from salads to vegetable platers with hummus and guacamole. They found a table in the crowded room where scrubs, surgical caps, and white lab coats dominated the attire.

"What were you doing while I was getting scanned?" Cherie asked, digging into her Cobb Salad and wishing she'd chosen the cheeseburger and sweet potato fries Will was enjoying with all the enthusiasm of a ten-year-old at McDonald's.

"Reading articles from the annual conference on emergency medicine. I downloaded the presentation on difficult airways, but I had a hard time concentrating," Will responded, glancing up at her, cheeseburger in hand. "I send my patients for these tests every day and never give it a second thought, but I'm finding there's a big difference between being the ordering physician and the friend waiting for the test to be over."

"You were worried about me?" Cherie sipped her iced tea.

"Not worried exactly, this is pretty routine stuff. Uneasy is a better word. It's giving me insight into what the families of my patients are going though. It's hard being the one waiting for answers rather than giving them."

Cherie remembered so clearly the waiting and the powerlessness. "It seemed like hours before the doctor came out to talk to me about Molly the night of the fire. It was just me and Sarah, alone in the middle of the night. My mom hadn't gotten there yet, and Paul was still a day away." Cherie set her fork down, a slight tremor in her hand at the memory. "When the burn surgeon came through the door, I could barely breathe, the fear was suffocating. All I could think was, 'please God, just let her be alive'. I have never been so terrified in my life."

"Those memories are exactly what you need to be talking about with the psychologist this afternoon."

"Then this is a good run through. I'd much rather do it with you first," Cherie said, as her thoughts lingered on that terrible night. "I don't think about the fire often anymore though there were years when I thought about it every day, every hour in the beginning when I was beating myself up about leaving Molly in the house with Jake. That surgeon, that kind woman, saved my sanity. Her caring and her detailed explanation of what would happen in the coming days, grounded me in the reality Molly was going to live, that we had a hard road ahead, but there would be a day when it would all be a memory. What you do matters, Will. It matters to the people you help and send home, and it matters to the families of the patients you lose like the parents on Monday night. You are in this job for a reason, and you're good at what you do, never doubt that."

"Not as good as I will be with a few more years of experience," Will said, then paused pushing aside his plate. "I want to thank you again for Monday night. I would have replayed that shift over and over in my mind, if you hadn't been there for me."

"All I did was listen," Cherie said, returning her attention to her half-eaten salad.

"That's not a small thing. You knew I needed a place to tell the truth about my own failings and a hand to hold while I did. I was able to sleep that night because of you." He extended his hand across the table, palm open.

Cherie looked up and without hesitation placed her hand in his.

"I feel like something changed that night," Will continued, "like we stepped over some invisible line from what we've been to what we can be. Am I alone in that?"

Having had the same thought, Cherie shook her head. "No, you're not alone, but what we could be ... "

"... is still a long way off and a road with many hurdles," Will injected as if reading her thoughts. "But where I want to be at the end of the journey is crystal clear to me. I want to be the family member in the waiting room who gets to hear the answers."

Startled, Cherie saw the calm intensity in his eyes even as she processed his words, hearing his sincere vision for a future together. "You want us to be a family?"

Will's gaze never wavered. "I do, if you want it, too."

Before she could even consider a response, Brook Sheraton appeared at the table, surprising them both. "The Women's Center is running a bit ahead of schedule, which almost never happens, so I hope I gave you enough time to eat something."

*   *   *

Was that a proposal? Cherie thought, distracted from the poking and positioning of the mammogram by Will's surprising declaration. On autopilot, she held her breath as instructed by the technician administering the test, her thoughts still with the man whose hand she had reluctantly surrendered before resuming the reason they were here today. Her thoughts were a jumble of images from the last few weeks.

Sitting across from Will at the diner, his hair still damp with sweat from the 10K. The standoff with her mother in her apartment Will had calmly defused. Her words of caution about their friendship spoken into the darkness as Will stood on the walkway looking up at her. She had known then she had the potential to hurt him. He wore his emotions on his face for anyone with eyes to see and the tenor of his words spoke clearly of the feelings behind them. It was rare in this world, but Will was a man with no guile. What she had vastly underestimated was how safe that made her feel. She didn't have to worry about ulterior motives or pushy advances or someone trying to score points with her by pretending to be nice to her children. Will was exactly what he appeared to be, a strong confident man who had chosen to help her, and then amazingly had stuck around and become a part of her life. She knew he was falling in love with her, had seen it coming and had thought of saving them both from the hurt of unrealized expectations with her words of caution. And then instead had been drawn word by word, day by day, to this place of comfort and ease where she found herself able to tell Will anything.

The mammogram done, but with no results given to the patient, Cherie exited the Women's Center to find Brook Sheraton talking with Will.

"All set?" Brook said as Cherie approached. "We're just going to cross over to the west wing for your final appointment."

Cherie noted the studied expression on Will's face and wondered what they had been talking about as they walked up a wide flight of stairs and passed through a glass causeway connecting the main hospital to the ancillary building.

Brook checked with the receptionist and then turned to them with a smile. "Sylvia Cummings is the psychologist you are going to speak with today, and she's ready for you. Feel free to share with her any concerns you may have about the transplant process. That's what she is here for. Not to convince you but to listen."

Cherie nodded. "Thank you for making this day so easy. You have a remarkable facility here."

"We think so, too. I am going to say my goodbyes now, but I want to thank you for considering being part of our transplant team. We are all in this together, the patient, the donor, and the staff, all part of the same team." She extended her hand first to Cherie and then to Will. "You'll be hearing from me after the transplant committee meets to review your testing. I enjoyed meeting you both. Have a safe trip home."

Cherie watched her disappear back through the glass causeway. "I like her."

"I do, too," Will said. "She's genuine. This is more than just a job to her. Hopewell is lucky to have her."

"What were you two talking about when I came out of the exam room?" Cherie asked.

A shadow of surprise played across Will's features. "I was asking her about the numbers, how many transplants they do every year, how many living donors as versus deceased donations, that kind of thing."

"Ms. Hollister? Dr. Cummings is ready for you now."

Cherie looked up to find the young receptionist holding open the door from the waiting area to the offices beyond. Feeling unsettled, Cherie glanced at Will, wondering where this sudden trepidation was coming from.

Will rested a hand on her shoulder and leaned toward her, his lips close to her ear. "You got this. Just tell her what you told me."

Cherie nodded, her stomach feeling like she'd stepped onto an ocean liner, a bit nauseous, the ground beneath her feet not quite steady as she followed the young woman. The feeling began to ebb as Cherie stepped through the office door and Sylvia Cummings rose to greet her.

She was in her early sixties, her short hair a generous mixture of dark brown and gray. Casually dressed in navy pants and a turtleneck sweater, with an antique pocket watch hanging on a gold chain around her neck, she had a commanding presence despite her short stature. Her smile was warm as she came around the desk, making Cherie briefly recall her grandmother.

"Cherie, I'm Sylvia. It's very nice to meet you. Shall we sit?" She waved a hand towards two comfortable wing-back chairs facing each other, a small coffee table between them.

"Long day?" Sylvia asked as they both settled into the leather chairs.

"A bit, yes, but remarkably smooth overall," Cherie answered, wondering just how this conversation got started.

"Tell me about your relationship with your brother, Jake," Sylvia said, leaning back in her chair and cutting right to the reason they were here.

"Our relationship is ... complicated," Cherie began.

"How so?" Sylvia asked, her manner attentive.

Cherie paused, wondering where to begin. "Because the baby brother I loved became the man I hated."

After that the words came of their own volition, almost as if they had been waiting years to be heard. Words of love for the baby who learned to walk on his tip toes and the toddler who loved Batman action figures. For the boy who could sink a basket from the line before he finished kindergarten, followed by expressions of anger for the teenager who had stolen his parent's car and crashed it into the Holland Tunnel on a joy ride to NYC. Jake had put her parents through hell as he ran from the family who loved him to the drugs he craved. Cherie described the hope at each commitment to rehab and the crushing disappointment at each relapse. And then finally, she spoke of the fire. Molly's burns. Paul's death.

"You were right, complicated is a good word," Sylvia said when Cherie finished. "So, how is it with all that history you are here thinking about being your brother's living donor?"

"To be honest, thinking is the operative word here," Cherie responded, meeting her gaze.

"You just put yourself through a morning of procedures and discomfort to what end?"

"I need to know if I'm a possible donor. If there is something in those tests that disqualifies me then I can walk away knowing I did everything possible to help my brother."

"And if you are a medically sound donor? Then what?" Sylvia's words were soft, her question probing.

"If we were sitting here talking about my sister, Amy, my donation would be a given, so how can I not do the same for Jake? I can't just sit back and watch him die knowing I could have saved him," Cherie answered, feeling the weight of her words.

"Not quite an answer which makes me think you're still working that part out," Sylvia said and then continued, "How long was it after the fire before you and Jake reconciled?"

Cherie considered the word. Reconciled.

Picking up on the pause, Sylvia went on. "Perhaps a better question is, when is the last time you saw your brother."

Cherie looked up and saw no judgement in Sylvia's eyes but noted the concern in her voice. "I'm meeting him for dinner tonight, but I haven't seen my brother in four years."

"And the last time was?"

"Nine months after the fire when he was in the hospital on a psych hold because my parents and the police thought he tried to kill himself."

Sylvia leaned forward in her chair. "And did he? Try to kill himself?"

Cherie shook her head. "I don't know. He was filled with guilt after what he'd done to Molly. My parents were barely speaking to him. It certainly was possible. I don't think anyone knows except Jake."

"Have you talked with him regularly since then?"

"No, we spoke for the first time three weeks ago when I learned from my mother he needed a transplant."

"And are you experiencing any pressure from your family to help your brother?" Sylvia asked.

"Some from my mother, yes, though that's not why I'm here. My mother aside, this is about me and Jake."

"And you are meeting with him tonight?"

"Yes, my friend, Will, and I are taking Jake to dinner."

"I think I have a better picture of your situation now," Sylvia said, concern apparent in her tone. "Is it possible for you and I to speak again, perhaps early next week? I would like to follow up with you after your dinner with your brother."

"Yes, any time after 3:00. I work until then."

Sylvia got to her feet. "I'll have my scheduler call you. How are you feeling about seeing your brother tonight?"

Cherie stood, reaching for her purse by the side of the chair. "I'm a little nervous. When we spoke a few weeks ago, I was startled by how together he is. He seems like a different guy, but I guess I'll find out if that's true. I am glad not to be doing it alone."

"So, you're dating again?"

Cherie looked up. "Dating? I don't know what we're doing to tell you the truth. Why do you ask?"

"Just something I sensed in your tone when you said his name. Sounds like he's important to you and you trust him, so I'm glad he'll be there with you tonight." Sylvia walked her to the door. "I look forward to speaking with you next week. Have a good evening."

* * *

Will closed his eyes, trying to get comfortable in the swivel chair in the waiting area. His phone back in his pocket, he had given up on getting anything productive done and simply decided to enjoy this quiet time while Cherie completed her final appointment.

His thoughts diverged in two different directions, his conversation with Brook Sheraton in the Women's Center and the interrupted conversation with Cherie in the cafeteria, the two events inextricably linked. Admittedly, he could have chosen a better venue than a crowded cafeteria to give voice to the vision that had been with him all morning. He had been surprised at Cherie's request to include his name on the HIPPA form. That she trusted him to receive information about her medical condition reflected a level of confidence and intimacy both staggering and welcome.

Monday night had changed them. He had felt it then and knew it now. When he had stepped out of his car, his thoughts consumed with self-blame, Cherie had known instinctively what he needed. Stepping into her arms, all Will could do was hold on, guilt and regret making his eyes sting. And as he stood in her embrace, he felt the pain ebb, receding slowly like the first light of dawn pushing against the night sky, at first so little you can barely see it and then slowly increasing in degree until the day displaced the darkness. When she took his hand and led him inside the tenor of their relationship shifted, the change increasingly clear.

With Cherie, he seemed to have little filter, saying the things he probably should have held back, though it was no less true for the telling. He wanted a future with her and the girls. He'd known it the day of the picnic but had buried it deep, not wanting to scare her after knowing each other for such a short time.

Which turned his thoughts to the discussion with Brook Sheraton. He'd told Cherie the truth about his questions, the lack of time eclipsing the rest of the conversation. Hopewell Atlantic was a major transplant center, one of the top ten in kidney transplants performed each year. The living donor surgeries represented a smaller percentage of the whole, about a third. Will remembered scrubbing in for the laparoscopic donor nephrectomy on two occasions during his intern year. The surgery was performed through four small incisions in the abdomen that allowed a camera as well as dissecting instruments to be inserted into the inflated abdomen making the entire procedure visible on a video screen opposite the surgeon. The kidney, renal artery, and vein were identified and freed from the surrounding tissue as was the ureter leading from the kidney to the bladder. The kidney was removed by enlarging the incision in the right lower abdomen and then retrieved by the transplant surgeon and placed on ice. A second surgeon stationed at a separate sterile table would then evaluate the kidney, flushing the vessels with an irrigating solution before carrying it into an adjacent operating room where the recipient's abdomen had already been opened to receive it.

The procedure was performed at transplant centers all over the country every day, the major complication to the donor the possibility of excessive bleeding, a scenario he had seen play out in the second surgery he had scrubbed in on.

"Will?"

His eyes flew open to find Cherie standing in front of him, a quizzical smile lifting her lips. "You weren't sleeping, were you?"

"Just resting my eyes," he said. "How did it go?"

"Pretty painless," Cherie replied. "I just had to tell the truth."

"Which is?"

"Easier to talk about than it was a few weeks ago."

"You've come a long way in a few weeks."

"I guess we're about to see just how far I've come," Cherie said, looking a bit flustered. "I just texted Jake. We're meeting him in an hour."

146

Chapter Thirteen

The restaurant Jake had chosen was twenty minutes west of the hospital, which would cut time off their drive home, Will thought, wondering if Jake had selected it for that reason as they pulled into the parking lot. Or more likely, he'd picked it for the water view of Long Island Sound, glimpses of the late afternoon sun reflecting off the water visible through the trees on either side of the rustic building.

Cherie had been quiet on the drive from the hospital, and Will had chosen to give her the space to work through whatever nervous anticipation she might be feeling.

He shut the engine off. "We're a little early. Want to take a walk down by the water. I think I spotted a dock."

Cherie nodded. She reached for the door handle but then turned back to him. "Thanks for today, for coming with me and waiting through all those tests, but right now for not filling this space with conversation when all I can think about is the next hour. You knew that didn't you?"

Will nodded. "Suspected. I knew if you wanted to talk, you'd let me know."

"Getting to know me pretty well, aren't you?"

"Starting to, yes. I've got a long way to go though."

"And we're going to talk about that later."

"Whenever you want, just not in the car. Face to face and in a quiet location with no interruptions would be my choice."

"Mine, too."

They exited the car, heels sounding on the black-topped parking lot. "So, how are you feeling about this evening?" Will asked, pointing toward a brick pathway that skirted the rustic restaurant, its shingles weathered with age.

"Surprisingly, the best word to describe it would be, curious." Cherie stepped onto the path with Will beside her. "I wonder if Jake is really the man I saw on that call a few weeks ago."

"And what did you see?"

"I saw a man finally comfortable in his own skin with a stillness … like this." Cherie stopped in her tracks at the view of open water spread out before them.

Through an open doorway, they could hear the clanking and bustling of a kitchen preparing for the dinner crowd, but in front of them the expanse of water was breathtaking, the surface surprisingly smooth for late afternoon. On a long, weathered dock, its planking grey, a lone fisherman reeled in an empty line.

Will stepped up behind her, placing his hands on her shoulders. "Tell me what you're hoping for tonight."

Staring out over the water, her words came softly. "I'm hoping its real, that finally after all these years, he's moved beyond the cravings and manipulation to be the man I knew he could be."

She leaned back against him, her hair tickling his chin as she turned her head to look at him. "Maybe I really am my mother's daughter, which should scare you a little."

"I don't scare that easily and I rather like your mother," Will chuckled, wanting to wrap his arms around her but knowing this was not the time.

Cherie stepped forward, watching the fisherman packing up his gear on the dock. The baseball cap he wore fell from his head as he secured the tackle box. "That's Jake."

Will studied the lone fisherman wearing jeans, sneakers, and an oversized windbreaker. His sandy colored hair was cut short, almost military in style but a bit longer. Broad shouldered with an even gait, he started up the dock carrying his fishing pole and tackle box, which he stowed in a small shack by the shoreline. He took the steps to the patio two at a time. Reaching the top he spotted his sister, his look of surprise followed instantly by a smile.

"Cherie, you're early," Jake said, covering the distance between them with an easy stride.

"And apparently, you're still not catching anything." Cherie waved a hand at the water. "I thought Dad taught you better than that."

"He did, though these days it's more about the quiet than the catching. I'm finally starting to understand what Dad loved about fishing."

Will had been expecting a more awkward reunion but this pivot to a memory they both shared started the conversation off easily.

"Dad could spend hours out on the water, though he doesn't get a chance to do it that often anymore," Cherie said with a sad smile before taking up the introductions. "Jake, I'd like you to meet Will Finnegan."

Jake extended his hand to Will. "Thanks for coming out here with Cherie today, so she didn't have to make the trip alone."

Will noted his firm grasp and calloused palm as the two men shook hands. "My pleasure."

Jake turned toward the restaurant. "I checked on the table when I got here, so why don't we go in." He led the way up an exterior stairway to the second-floor seating area overlooking the water. Pulling open the French doors, Jake waved at a group of waiters talking with the hostess before he led then to a window table set for three.

The restaurant looked like a hunting lodge with its wood finishings and autumn colors of yellow, red, and green in the carpet. Solid varnished tables with straight backed chairs in matching cherry furnished the dining area. A bit dated in its interior design, it felt like a place for locals though the water view must draw a few new customers, Will thought. It reminded him of the place his grandmother used to take them for brunch after church on Sunday. Pulling out the chair facing the window for Cherie, he and Jake took seats on either side of her.

"You seem pretty comfortable here," Cherie said, as a waiter stepped up to the table and handed them menus.

"I worked here as a bus boy when I first came out of rehab." Jake shrugged off his oversized jacket, revealing a plaid dress shirt, the collar open. "The owner likes to help people get a fresh start."

"Cherie tells me you're working as a groundskeeper at a church now," Will said, opening the menu and noting the reasonable prices.

Jake nodded. "I left the job here after a few months. I was glad of the work but the access to alcohol, at least in the beginning, was too tempting. Neil, he's the owner, gave me a good reference and helped me find the job at the church. He's my NA sponsor."

Narcotics Anonymous. Will was glad to hear Jake wasn't trying to manage his addiction on his own.

The waiter, an older man with a distinguished beard, returned to take their drink order. Club soda with a splash of cranberry for Cherie. Will ordered the same, watching Jake shake his head.

"Just water for me," Jake said. "Thanks, Gabe."

Eyeing the glass of water in front of him, Will suspected it would be the only drink Jake had during dinner. Cherie had told him Jake had a Tuesday, Thursday, Saturday dialysis regime which meant he was due to go in tomorrow. While some dialysis patients still produced a small amount of urine, for most the kidneys were too impaired to produce any significant amount. Anything he drank became part of his circulating blood volume and increased his blood pressure. And drinking any liquids in excess could tax the heart's ability to pump all that volume.

"When did you take up fishing again?" Cherie closed her menu and set it aside.

Will studied the dinner options, listening to the exchange between brother and sister.

"Shortly after I got here. Neil has an old motorboat he lets me use. I take it out a few times a month to go trolling early in the morning. I enjoy the quiet, just the purr of the engine and the silent pull of the line through the water."

"Sounds relaxing."

Jake nodded. "I love the peace of the sunrise breaking the horizon. All the creator's beauty on full display. 'The heavens declare the glory of God', isn't that the verse?"

Will glanced up, seeing Cherie's eyes widen. Clearly taken by surprise, she smiled. "Yes, it's in the psalms."

"The 12-step program is based on a power greater than ourselves. I see that so clearly in nature." Jake reached for the water glass and took a small sip. "When I first started attending NA meetings the idea of turning my life over to God was an abstraction, something I heard people talk about and never really understood. But I had failed at getting clean so many times, and I finally realized I couldn't do it on my own."

All the right words, Will thought, wondering why hearing them wasn't reassuring. Exactly the opposite, in fact. Cherie had asked him to keep an open mind about Jake, and he had assured her that he could, but clearly that might be more difficult than he'd anticipated.

The waiter returned with their drinks and took their dinner order. Without much of an appetite Will chose quickly, noting Jake's order of chicken and steamed vegetables.

An older man in his sixties, tall and fit with weathered hands and a face to match stepped up to the table, placing a hand on Jake's shoulder. "I hope I'm not interrupting, but I wanted to meet your sister."

Jake smiled introducing the restaurant's owner, Neil Russell, to Cherie and Will.

"You have a beautiful place here." Will stood and the two men shook hands.

"We're a nice local haunt, a bit too far from the LIE to draw the trendy crowd, which suits me just fine," Neil replied. "This place has been in my family for a lot of years. My wife says, too many. She's trying to talk me into retiring to one of the Carolinas. I'm holding out for the time being."

"Do you have children in the area?" Cherie asked.

Will noted the brief flash of sadness in Neil's eyes.

"No, we lost our son to a drug overdose a few years ago."

"I am so sorry," Cherie said, her sympathy matched only by her obvious regret at having asked the question.

"Eric was a bit too much like his dad. And yet, I could never reach him and pull him back," Neil said. "That's a parental hell I never want anyone else to know. So, I'm using this place to save the ones I can." He squeezed Jake's shoulder. "It was nice meeting you both. Enjoy your dinner. I spoke to the chef, Jake. No worries about the sodium."

Jake nodded his thanks, watching his sponsor cross the nearly empty dining room. "Neil's a great guy. Over the last two years he's fielded a lot of phone calls from me. He's a gift in my life, one I don't deserve but am happy to have."

Will glanced at Cherie, watching the tension in her jaw fade slowly, her lips lifting in a soft smile.

A shiver of fear crept up Will's spine until it settled at the base of his skull, making his shoulders twitch. He'd only experienced that sensation twice in his life. The day their family dog had bolted across the street after a deer and been hit by a car. And the day his grandmother had fallen, hitting her head on the pavement, and dying a few days later. He struggled to shake off the ominous sensation, refocusing on the conversation continuing in front of him.

"Have you made a few friends out here?" Cherie asked.

"A few, yes, not easy to do though when I'm not going to bars or using dating apps. Not ready for that yet."

"So, no one special then?"

Jake eyed his sister. "Not really, why?"

"Because you keep looking over at the hostess station and the pretty red-head I noticed on the way in. Friend of yours?"

"I see your sibling radar is still in working order," Jake laughed. "Like the time you picked me up from that sixth-grade pool party and managed to zero in on the one girl I had a crush on. Is that an inborn thing?"

"More like good powers of observation. I just watch where your eyes go. What's her name?"

"Jamie. She's worked here since she was a teenager. And now it's her second job. She's a graphic designer, web sites mostly. And we're just friends."

"I think I've heard that before," Cherie said, glancing over at Will.

He focused on Cherie's smile and the teasing look in her eyes. It was the very look of easy comradery he'd wanted to see in the early days of their relationship, and the ease with which she offered it to him now stole his breath away.

Their dinners arrived, three waiters setting them down with a flourish before smiling at Jake. Clearly, he was well liked by his former colleagues, which should have blunted Will's growing trepidation but didn't. He needed to get out of his own head about this and give Jake a fair hearing, not one colored by his own prejudices and fear.

Around them the restaurant started to come alive, a sizable early bird crowd filling the tables. After cutting into his steak and sampling the scalloped potatoes and garlic spinach, Will could understand their patronage. The food was well prepared and hearty, priced reasonably and with an ample portion to take some home for another meal. Cherie seemed to be enjoying the sole almondine though Jake had less of an appetite for the bland fare on his plate. The conversation over dinner shifted easily from Cherie's job to Jake's new skill set as a groundskeeper at the church.

Setting his half-eaten plate aside, Jake asked, "So, Will, what do you do?"

Will looked up, a bit surprised Cherie hadn't mentioned his profession. "I work in the emergency room at Mercy Medical Center."

"You're a doctor?"

"Still a resident. I graduate from the program in a few weeks."

"Will has been helping me understand the transplant process," Cherie added.

"Have you seen the actual surgery?" Jake asked.

"I have scrubbed in on a few in my residency," Will responded, sitting back in his chair. "The precision involved in suturing arteries to arteries and veins to veins in the hands of a transplant surgeon who does it every day is amazing to watch. All I did was hold a few retractors so they could see what they were doing."

"Does it always go well?"

"As with any surgery there are risks involved," Will said, not wanting to overstate the outcomes or underplay the risks. "But the transplant process has been around for decades and getting better each year. In the hands of an experienced team, the surgery is life changing." Will had asked the post-residency doctor who was doing a transplant fellowship at Mercy to fill in a few gaps for him about the Hopewell program. He had been relieved to hear that their complication rate for both donors and recipients was among the lowest in the country.

Their waiter stepped up to the table offering a dessert menu.

Will thought about ordering coffee but then dismissed the impulse. It felt rude to enjoy a drink after dinner when Jake couldn't join them. Tuning back into the conversation, he caught Jake's follow up question.

"And the donors? What exactly are the complications?"

Will glanced over at Jake. "Complications for the donor include bleeding during the surgery and postoperative infection."

"And the recipient?"

"The list for the recipient is longer with the biggest complication being possible organ rejection resulting in a non-functioning kidney."

"So, it's possible the donor gives their kidney, and the transplant is unsuccessful?" Jake asked.

"It happens, not often, but yes, that's a possible outcome," Will said.

"I know all this already," Cherie said to her brother. "Why are you making Will tell you things I suspect you already know?"

Jake turned toward her, his expression earnest. "I can't tell you how glad I am to be sitting here with you after what I did to your family, to Molly," he said, dodging her question with words that cut straight through all their dinner pleasantries to the real reason they were all here tonight. "I never thought it would happen. I wanted it, prayed for it, but never dreamed in those first few months of my sobriety that this moment would come about as result of a life-threatening illness I brought on myself. My end-stage renal disease is a direct result of all the bad choices I made for so many years, and the fact that you are here even considering helping me is a gift of forgiveness and grace I don't deserve. Narcotics Anonymous tells me I need to make reparations for the hurt I caused, but there are no amends for what I did, no way to make whole Molly's beautiful face and hearing." He ran a shaky hand over his face. His eyes closed briefly before he looked up with a clear penetrating gaze at his sister. "I believe God has a plan for me in all this, Cherie. Kind of ironic, I know, coming from a guy who wasted a good portion of his life seeking instant gratification, but I'm willing to wait on God's plan."

Will remained quiet, watching the conversation play out, amazed at this sudden declaration of faith.

"And you don't think that plan includes me?" Cherie asked, her eyes widening.

Jake shook his head. "I know you seem like the obvious answer …"

"Maybe the only answer at this point," Cherie offered.

"It looks that way right now, but maybe us getting here, to this moment, is what it's all about. We wouldn't be here today except for my illness, wouldn't you agree?"

Cherie nodded, conceding the point.

Jake leaned forward. "And if that's what it took to get us talking again then I'm glad of it. Truly, I am. There's a verse from scripture I kept coming across when I started my job at the church. It's in the book of Jeremiah, chapter 29:11. 'For I know the plans I have for you, says the Lord. Plans to prosper you, not to harm you, to give you hope and a future.' Right up until now it feels like we've been walking in that plan, but where we go from here, I'm not sure. I'm willing to wait until God shows me the next step."

"That's a whole lot of faith," Cherie said.

"Just a mustard seed actually," Jake responded.

Clearly Cherie understood the reference. She smiled. "I do believe that's all it takes to move a mountain."

"I think we're about to find out," Jake said, lifting the glass in front of him and finishing the last of it. "And now, Will, I think it's about time you take my sister home to her beautiful little girls."

More than ready to do just that, Will turned to try and find a waiter to get them the check.

"The bill has already been taken care of." Jake got to his feet and placed his napkin on the table. "Neil's generosity knows no bounds."

"You'll thank him for us," Cherie said.

"Already have but will again." Jake led them out the way they had come, down the exterior stairway to the patio overlooking the water.

Will blinked, his eyes adjusting from the restaurant's dark interior to the sunlight of a spring evening. It felt like hours since they had first stood here taking in this beautiful view of Long Island Sound, but glancing at his watch he realized it had been just ninety minutes.

Jake extended his hand. "Nice to meet you, Will. Take care of yourself and my sister."

"I will." And despite his best efforts, Will couldn't quite keep the two words from sounding more aggressive than congenial. He noted the assessing glance Jake directed his way before he turned to his sister.

Cherie held out both hands to him, bringing the two siblings face to face.

"Thank you," Jake said, with a soft smile. "For coming all the way out here today, and for the forgiveness implicit in being willing to be tested as my donor. I didn't understand how you could ever forgive me until I met the God who forgives us all."

"We can't change the past Jake, but we can move forward. This feels like the first step." She squeezed his hands and released them. Stepping back, her hand reached for Will's. "Take care, Jake. I'll call you when the test results come back."

He nodded. "Have a safe trip home."

Hand in hand, they crossed the parking lot in silence each with their own thoughts, Will trying with each step to shake the feeling of disquiet that had settled over him. He knew Cherie was going to ask him what he had thought about meeting Jake, and he needed time to think about it himself. It wasn't a straightforward answer.

155

Will pulled open the passenger door for Cherie, surprised when she spun back to him in the confines of the doorway looking up into his face.

"I know I could have done that without you, but I'm so glad you were there, thank you. Would you mind if I just take some time to process before we talk about it?"

Relieved at the question, Will nodded. "Sure. We've got a long ride. A quiet start sounds like an excellent idea."

He found a slow jazz station on the radio and programmed the GPS for the fastest time home. Pulling onto the LIE, he settled in for the drive, knowing at this time of day on a Friday, it would be hours before they made it back to Jersey. He glanced over at Cherie, her head resting back against the seat, her eyes closed. He didn't think she was sleeping but could well understand if she was. It had been a long day.

The GPS took them home the way they had come via Staten Island. That had not been Will's initial thought, but he trusted the navigation system would make more timely choices than he would. The irony was not lost on him; he found it easier to trust a computer and a satellite than he did the man who had spoken with such certainty about God's plan.

Jake had seemed so sincere, wearing his faith on his sleeve with such ease, no longer a man consumed by addiction. So why did it feel like a con, Will thought, finally identifying the root of his concern. It had been lingering in the periphery of his mind all evening, unnamed until now. Could he trust what he had seen with his own eyes? Because if not, then the man they had just had dinner with was a master manipulator, willing to use anything, even God, to get a new kidney. Will shifted in his seat, the thought unsettling. And at the same time, he knew the reason for his doubt had more to do with his inability to grant the basic premise that faith in God could change anyone that much.

"Do you think he's for real?" Cherie asked suddenly.

Caught off guard by the very question he had been considering, Will realized he had underestimated the savvy of this strong woman beside him. Here he'd been thinking she needed his protection when she was more than capable of protecting herself and her family. She'd done so on her own for the last three years. She didn't need his help, but she wanted it, Will mused, feeling the sensation of disquiet that had been riding him for the past few hours begin to dissipate. "I was just wondering the same thing."

* * *

Cherie sat up straight, pushing her hair out of her eyes. "I know having a serious illness can change someone, and I believe in God's ability to change the hardest of hearts, but it seems like a timely about face."

Will glanced sideways at her, his expression a mixture of surprise and relief. "What does your gut tell you?"

Cherie turned to him. "Okay. Here's the thing, sitting there talking to Jake, it felt sincere, but thinking about it with a little bit of distance, it just feels off and I was hoping you could help me figure it out. Your impression of Jake doesn't come with all the baggage I've accumulated over the years. So, what did you think?"

Will hit the blinker changing lanes, clearly weighing his words. "I think he was trying to make a good impression. The dress shirt, the new haircut, the introduction to his sponsor. But something put you off," Will continued. "What was it?"

"Honestly, and here's the strange part, it was all the talk about God that threw me."

"The NA program is based on a belief in a higher power. It's a faith-based program," Will responded.

A bit frustrated with his measured answers, Cherie studied his face in the gathering darkness. "I think you have an opinion you're not sharing, and I need an honest answer. What did you think of Jake?"

Will paused, his hands at ten and two on the steering wheel, his attention focused on the road. "Okay, I think he came across as thoughtful, likable even. I tried to stay out of the conversation and just listen, which wasn't easy because I realized about halfway through that my objectivity is totally shot, and I will always and forever be on your side."

Cherie smiled, his word choice touching her heart as she waited for him to continue.

"But for what it's worth, I thought Jake had all the right words, he said them in the right tone, and somehow it all felt scripted to me, like he knew what he was going to say before we even sat down. That may be the cynic in me or the fact that I find the whole faith element hard to buy into as you know." He paused, glancing over at her. "I will tell you the part that felt genuine was his remorse about Molly."

"I agree, so why tell me I'm not meant to be his donor?" Cherie said, posing aloud the question she had been asking herself. "And why say it before

157

the tests are even back? Because if Jake's right about God's plan, then this whole discussion is a moot point. The tests will come back, and I won't be an eligible donor and this will all be over for me anyway. So why say it?"

"To gain your trust," Will suggested, a steady stream of headlights revealing his frown. "To make it look like he doesn't want something from you he desperately needs."

"A little reverse psychology? So, when I am eligible, I default to being his donor as if it's a part of God's plan?" Cherie wondered aloud, not liking the sound of that.

"Could be, but that implies a degree of manipulation I'm not comfortable with," Will said, his jaw clenched.

"And one I'm all too familiar with when it comes to Jake. It wouldn't be the first time he talked a good game to get what he wants."

"But you agreed to be tested, clearly you weren't thinking this way when you made the appointment."

Cherie could hear the growing concern in Will's tone, though in the dark car it was harder to see the nuances in his expression. "I told Dr. Cummings I agreed to the tests because I couldn't let Jake die, knowing I could have saved him."

"And that might still be true."

"I know," Cherie said, leaning back against the seat. "Feels like we're talking in circles."

Will's hand tightened on the steering wheel. "I think you need to be clear in your own mind about what you are willing to do, before the tests come back, before the added pressure of eligibility slips into your decision making."

"That's a good idea. I'm supposed to have a call with Dr. Cummings this week. She wanted to talk about the meeting with Jake."

"Then you need to tell her everything we just talked about. And since your reservations have to do with Jake's faith, how about talking with Pastor Michaels. I know you trust her, and I am not well equipped to help you wade through the waters of faith."

"Think you might be able to learn to navigate those waters someday?" Cherie asked.

"Maybe, for you," he said with a smile.

"You can't do it for me, Will," Cherie said, a hint of sadness coloring her tone. "Faith is a decision we each need to make for ourselves."

She found it disconcerting, though she and Will were in sync about many things, when it came to God, they were very different. She hoped that would change, believed it could, but knew he might have to walk through a wall of pain before it did. And knowing that, she wanted to save him from the struggle, to help him find the answers without crawling through the darkness.

Will pulled off the exit, navigating the quiet roadways to Cherie's house. "Do you want to pick the girls up?"

Glancing at the dashboard clock, she shook her head. "Too late. And the girls are counting on breakfast with their cousin. Amy's pancakes and Taylor ham are legendary."

And then they were back where they'd started more than twelve hours ago. Will parked at the curb in front of Cherie's apartment and killed the engine.

"Do you want to come in?" Cherie asked, turning to face him in the dark car.

"I do," he answered quietly.

A shiver of anticipation, the sensation foreign and yet somehow familiar, made her breath catch in her throat as they exited the car. Starting up the walkway, Will reached for her hand and Cherie grasped his, a bit unsure if what she was feeling was desire or fear or both. She and Will had never truly been alone together. Even on Monday night as they sat on the couch the awareness of the girls sleeping in the next room and the tenor of their conversation had kept them well within the bounds of friendship. But their interrupted discussion over lunch had blown away that pretense. They had moved beyond friendship now. The next few minutes would give them both a clearer picture of where they were going.

Cherie reached into her bag as Will pulled open the screen door. Finding her keys with a shaky hand, she glanced back at Will, a man who had in a few short weeks taken up residence in her mind and heart. She had come to trust Will implicitly, and her biggest fear up until this moment had been her potential to hurt him. And while that was still a concern, she was beginning to understand hurt could be a two-way street.

Will took the keys from her hand and opened the door.

* * *

In all the time he had known her, Will had seen many of Cherie's moods and emotions. Her strength. Her caution. Her gratitude. Her love for her children. But he had never seen her nervous. And he didn't like it.

She had offered him a glass of wine which he had politely declined. He didn't drink often, and when he did a good IPA was more his style. In any case, any alcohol tonight seemed unwise. It would only muddy the waters of a discussion he wanted to be crystal clear. He watched Cherie silently pour two glasses of seltzer, her concentration far exceeding the task's simplicity.

He stepped up next to her in the tiny kitchen, taking her hands in his. Meeting her gaze, he noted her surprise in the quizzical lift of her brow. "It's going to be okay; you know. Whatever we decide tonight we're going to do it together, and then I'm going to kiss you good night and leave you to get a good night's sleep after a long day. Sound like a plan?"

Cherie's eyes widened and she started to laugh. "Do I look that nervous?"

"Yes." Will smiled. "And the good night kiss is optional by the way."

"Good to know. I'll think it over." She smiled up at him and Will could see the tension leave her shoulders.

"You really are getting to know how I think," she said, leading him over to the couch where she collapsed with a chuckle.

Sitting down next to her but keeping some distance between them, Will said, "So where do you want to start?"

Cherie's expression softened; the laughter gone. Shifting to face him, she rested her arm on the back of the couch. "How about with always and forever."

Will nodded, realizing his words in the car, not chosen deliberately but flowing from his heart, were a good place to begin. Not wanting to miss one nuance of her reaction, he turned toward her, so they sat face to face. "First off, I want to say I could have chosen a better place for putting our future out there on the table. A hospital cafeteria was not the best place to do it. Did I scare you?"

Her eyes were warm. "No, just took my breath away. I spent the afternoon trying to figure out if that was a proposal."

"More like an expression of intent. I know I'm probably out in front of you on this, but I hope I'm not completely off track." Will waited, relieved to see the relaxed set of her shoulders and the slight smile that tweaked the edges of her mouth upward.

"You're just moving a bit faster than I am," Cherie said, extending her hand to him, her palm up.

"Good to know." He covered her hand with his, amazed and encouraged by her words. "I know this is early in our relationship to be talking about this but sitting there with you today in the hospital just sped up the normal timeline. I know you trust me as a doctor and look to me as a friend, but I want to be the man whose face you see when you wake up from surgery if you decide to do it, and I want to be the man you wake up to every morning if you don't."

Her eyes widened at his words. "And you know this after less than a month?"

"I do. The bottom line is, I can't imagine my life without you, without you and your beautiful girls."

Will watched the subtle sigh that softened her expression at the mention of her children. "And I'm not talking about next week or next month, but sometime in the near future, I want to marry you and start a life together as a family, our family, always and forever."

Having put it all out there he waited, knowing this beautiful woman had the power to shatter his heart but somehow knowing she would not. He saw it in the shine of her eyes, suddenly moist with tears. In the flash of white teeth that stilled her quivering lip. Her hand reached up, one finger tracing the line of his jaw from ear to chin igniting a wave of heat from his face to his heart. He hadn't known if they would ever get to this moment, when she would reach out to him, not out of need but out of wanting. Then she closed the distance between them, her lips touching his in a kiss he had never experienced the likes of in his life, a mixture of longing and wonder, expectation and tender desire.

His arms closed around her, holding her with care, purposefully checking the impulse to pull her into him. There would be time for passion later, much later he thought, glad she had the good sense to do what at least in this moment he could not. Her lips lingered on his then backed off just an inch. She rested her forehead against his, her breathing as rapid as his own.

"You can't marry someone you've never even kissed," she said softly, her breath warm on his lips.

"Glad you took care of that for us," he whispered. "Now we're one step closer to starting that life together."

"I think we are," Cherie said, her tone filled with wonder and surprise.

At her words, Will's chest tightened in a strange sensation of awe and deep joy that felt like his heart would burst, a pleasure so deep it was almost painful. And with her breath warm on his skin, the intensity of his gratitude for this display of trust and desire made his eyes sting. He lifted one hand, cupping her cheek in his palm, his thumb gently moving across her lower lip. He felt the shiver that made her shoulders tremble. His hand slipped to the base of her neck as he drew her to him.

How was it possible one simple kiss could be so perfect, the rational thought fleeting, soon eclipsed by his mounting passion and her matched response. With the last remnants of anything resembling a coherent thought, Will backed off, his lips settling on her forehead, his breathing ragged. He wasn't willing to sacrifice this moment to a wave of passion that would leave them both questioning their relationship tomorrow, not when they were finally headed in the same direction.

"I think I'd better go,' Will said, his words whispered against her skin.

She leaned back against the couch, her face flushed. "Just stay for one minute. I just need to process while you're still here."

Will smiled, settling into the couch next to her and taking her hand. "Are you okay?"

"I'm waiting for the guilt to kick in." She turned her head to look at him. "I haven't kissed a man in three years."

"Regrets?" He studied her face, open and glowing, relieved to see no signs of remorse.

"No, this feels … right."

"I was thinking the same thing."

"I'm glad one of us managed a little self-control though," Cherie added. "My body remembers the way, but my mind knows I'm not ready to go there."

"I agree, a little anticipation is a good thing." He stood holding out a hand to her. "Something we're going to get a lot of in the next few days when all I get to do is work and sleep."

"After spending the whole day together, I'm going to miss you," Cherie said walking him to the door. She stopped at the entryway and turned to him amid the coats and scattered shoes.

Will drew her to him, his hands linked at the base of her spine. "You are making it very hard to leave." Now he was on his feet and a step from the door, Will bent to meet her upturned face for one last kiss. He savored the feel of her lips on his, the pressure sweet with growing hunger, noting her quick intake of breath as he lifted his head and looked into her eyes. "And just to be clear, when I do propose to you, there won't be any doubt about what I'm doing. You will know beyond a shadow of a doubt I am asking you to marry me."

"Good to know. I'll look forward to it." The look in her eyes was piercing though her tone was light, and Will knew he needed to leave now.

"I'll call you tomorrow when I get off shift," he said, pulling open the door and wanting to linger but knowing he was already pushing his limits.

"Right now, I'm having a hard time thinking about anything but tonight," Cherie said with a slow smile.

"I'm leaving now," Will asserted, stepping beyond the screen.

"That's a very good idea," Cherie said softly. "Good night, Will."

Chapter Fourteen

"Mommy, we missed you," the girls screamed, jumping down from their seats at the long trestle table in Amy's kitchen and rushing to engulf Cherie in a hug. She took the full weight of their enthusiasm with open arms. She hugged them to her, taking in the sweet smell of maple syrup, clean clothes, and a soap that smelled like bubblegum. Clearly yesterday's activities had required a bath. "Did you have fun?"

"We went to the petting zoo after school, and Mark almost fell into the pen 'cuz he was climbing on the fence," Sarah said, pointing at her cousin, who looked up smiling and then dug back into his pile of pancakes.

"Then we had to talk about setting a good example for our cousins," Amy said, joining the conversation. "I've got coffee."

The girls scrambled back to the table to enjoy the rest of their breakfast. Amy filled a mug and handed it to Cherie. "Long day yesterday?"

"For both of us, I think." Cherie lifted her head, nodding at the table where a gaggle of voices made the actual words a blur. "How did you manage four kids at the zoo?"

"I had some help. John took the afternoon off and went with me." Amy flipped the last of the pancakes onto the serving plate. "You look incredibly well rested. One night away and you're practically glowing. Next time I'm leaving Mark with you."

"Anytime." Behind her uplifted cup, Cherie felt the blush warm her face.

"If I took you up on that you would need some help to manage all four of them. They're a handful. Maybe you could ask Will to help you," Amy suggested, with a wry smile.

Cherie shot her a sidelong glance, knowing what was coming.

"You didn't think you could walk in here and not tell me, did you?" Amy added the hot pancakes to the stack in the middle of the table as Mark plucked one from the pile. "I've been watching you since we were their age."

Amy knew her so well. Cherie had woken up this morning and wanted nothing more than to share the amazement of last night with the one person who had always been on her side. "He wants to marry me."

"Will proposed last night?" The glee on Amy's face was contagious. "Mom is going to go crazy. You should hear what she's telling everyone about the handsome doctor in your life."

"Wait," Cherie laughed. "It wasn't exactly a proposal, more like a discussion of our future."

Amy sobered a bit. "And you're good with that?"

Cherie nodded, still a bit surprised herself as she leaned back against the counter and wrapped her hands around her mug. "Talk about something I never saw coming. A month ago, I never would have considered getting married again. And then I met Will." She sipped her coffee, staring at the table where her kids were devouring the last of their breakfast. "After all the heartache, it feels like a gift," Cherie said softly. "There is one problem, though."

"Just one?" Amy chuckled, elbowing Cherie in the side. "Okey, what is it?"

"He's too perfect. I keep waiting for his Achilles heel to show up, and it hasn't yet. He's intuitive and thoughtful, never has a bad word to say about anyone, even defends Mom when I get too hard on her. He's protective, in a good way. And harder on himself than he is on anyone else."

"Will's just been on his best behavior trying to impress you, but he's not perfect, none of us are." Amy looked up as the kids cleared their plates, intent on sneaking off to play while their moms were still talking. "How did he handle meeting Jake?"

166

Distracted by all that had happened with Will she hadn't given much thought to the dinner with Jake. But it needed more consideration. She gave Amy an overview of the evening as the kids scampered off to the family room, concluding with Jake's surprising declaration about wanting to wait on God's plan.

"Will hung back and listened mostly. He was a good sounding board for me on the way home, but nobody knows Jake as well as you and I do. Did you know he's a Christian now?"

Amy nodded, starting to stack the breakfast dishes in the dishwasher. "Sure."

Her tone implied she'd known for a while. "How often do you talk to him?"

"Since he got sober, about once a month."

Startled Cherie finished clearing the glasses and napkins from the table carrying them over to the counter by the sink. "You never told me that."

"I wasn't trying to hide anything, but I knew you didn't want to talk about Jake."

Cherie stiffened. Amy was right, of course. After the fire, Cherie never voluntarily mentioned Jake's name. So why did this feel like a secret Amy had been keeping from her?

"How about before he got sober, were you talking to him then, too?" Cherie said, the question she had never thought to ask spilling from her mouth.

Amy grew still, then closed the dishwasher door, looking up at Cherie and meeting her gaze. "Yes, not often, but I did."

Her sister's words felt like the sudden sting of a wasp on a summer day, the pain searing and unexpected. "Why would you do that?"

"Because he had no one else," Amy said, her tone soft and measured, but with no hint of apology. "After the fire everyone abandoned him, even Mom and Dad. He needed someone to care about what happened to him. So, I stood in the gap between where he was and where he could be, if he could finally manage to accept help."

"I can't believe you never told me," Cherie said. "After all he'd done, to Molly and me?"

"You had every right to be angry, but that didn't mean we all had to make the same choice," Amy replied. "You thought he was worthless. I can remember you saying those exact words to me after the fire. You were so furious, and deservedly so, but no one is worthless, and no one is beyond redemption. I thought when you went to see him on the psych unit that you might see it." Amy stepped closer, reaching out a hand, her gel nails glittering in the reflection of the kitchen's recessed lighting.

Cherie recoiled from her touch. It wasn't rational after all Amy had done for her, but still the ember of betrayal burned, smoldering beneath the surface of this sin of omission.

Cherie backed off a step. "Thank you for taking care of the girls last night. I need to get Molly to practice."

"Cherie, I never meant to hurt you."

"And the rational part of my brain knows that, but I'm just having a hard time finding it right now. You have done so much for me; I just need a little space. I'm going to go corral the girls."

Separating the girls from their cousin took a fair amount of patience and Cherie's was in short supply. After an awkward sibling goodbye, the girls safely buckled in, Cherie backed the car out of Amy's driveway. The ride to the lacrosse field was just long enough for some form of rational thought to reassert itself.

She was being unfair to Amy. Yes, she should have mentioned being in touch with Jake, but considering Cherie's fury with their brother it was understandable Amy hadn't wanted to talk about Jake. Logically, Cherie knew that. Still, she wondered how she hadn't put the pieces together; any sister as generous as Amy wouldn't just choose one sibling over another. She must have been blind not to see that. And if she could be that obtuse about Amy what did that mean for the other relationships in her life. Was she missing things there as well? In her relationship with Judith? And with Will.

* * *

Will was still riding the adrenalin high of having Cherie agree they had a future together. Even the 6:00 a.m. start of his Saturday shift hadn't diminished the joy of last night. It took until mid-morning for the grin on his face to fade when they received the victims of a car T-boned by a delivery van that blew through a red light. The family of four never saw it coming. All the injuries were relatively minor except for the front passenger, a 45-year-old mother of two. Unconscious and intubated in the field, she was in bad shape.

Will scanned her abdomen for blood, the ultrasound probe sliding across the patient's pale skin. The team in the trauma bay had already started two IV's, sent labs, and placed a foley catheter, which was draining pink tinged urine, indicating a possible kidney injury.

"Abdomen is full of blood, looks like a ruptured spleen," Will said, glancing up at the EKG tracing and blood pressure with a strange feeling of déjà vu.

"Broken right femur," the PA added, the image up on the portable x-ray screen.

"Alert the OR and the blood bank and initiate a massive transfusion protocol," Will ordered, knowing her best chance at survival was getting the packed red blood cells, plasma, and platelet units infusing prior to the start of surgery.

The trauma surgeon arrived with his team just as they were hanging the units. Will reported out the care they had given and then helped them pack the patient up for transport to the operating room as he eyed the clock: 29 minutes since she had come through the door. To surgery in just under an hour from the time of injury. They'd given Virginia Holloway her best chance to survive. Now, for Will, came the hard part.

Dr. Patel met him as he stepped out of the trauma bay. "Her family is in Bay 10. Father insisted on staying with the kids. Nice job in there, Will. I'm glad you're staying on with us. You're good at what we do."

Jim Holloway was a big man, built like a linebacker, his head bowed and resting in his hands as he sat in the tiny room's only chair. His children, ten-year-old Moira and eight-year-old Luke, were sitting side by side on the stretcher.

"Mr. Holloway, I'm Dr. Finnegan. I was leading the team caring for your wife."

Jim Holloway surged to his feet. "How's Ginny?"

Will chose his words carefully knowing these two kids were about to hear every word. "The surgical team has just taken her to the operating room. She has a broken femur and a ruptured spleen which has caused bleeding into her abdomen as I'm sure the surgeon told you when he had you sign the consent for surgery," Will said, glancing over at Jim's children, Moira's arm wrapped around her brother's shoulder. "We were able to start giving her blood products to replace some of what she had lost from her injuries …"

"She's going to be okay, right?" Jim interrupted; his tone desperate for reassurance.

Will knew Jim was hearing what he wanted to hear in this discussion. "We've given her the best possible chance at a full recovery."

"And how long will that take?"

"It's likely to be several months. Does your wife work outside your home?"

"She's a teacher," Luke spoke up, his tone high-pitched and his eyes scared.

"Then she'll have the whole summer to start feeling better," Will replied, making eye contact with the little boy before turning back to Jim, who was barely holding it together for his children. Anxiety bordering on panic shone in his reddened eyes, his forehead creased with worry.

Out in the hallway after spending time answering Jim's other questions, Will knew he had left them with a more optimistic picture than perhaps was warranted. And perhaps that wasn't a bad thing. Jim was left with hope, and he would need it in the days ahead.

Still the image of Jim and his children lingered in Will's mind as he went about the rest of his shift. Some families he connected with on the job left a lasting impression. Why one family and not another was sometimes hard to figure out but, in this case, he knew exactly what it was. Ginny was a teacher. With pale skin and dark hair. With children and a man who loved her.

Like Cherie.

Will felt Jim Holloway's anxiety on a visceral level, knowing if Cherie was the one on the operating room table this morning he would be as crazed as Jim. And that could happen. Not here at Mercy, of course. But at Hopewell Atlantic, if Cherie's testing from yesterday came back and the transplant board accepted her as Jake's donor.

Will had watched it begin to play out last night. Cherie's words of skepticism in the car had been a welcome parallel to his own musings, but knowing her as he did, her kindness, her desire to be fair, he doubted her qualms would last in the face of another dialysis complication. She would do what she always did, give generously. She did it daily for her girls, and she would do it for Jake. That thought just kept resurfacing throughout the day forcing Will to finally acknowledge the bottom line.

He didn't want her to do it. He didn't want Cherie to undergo a voluntary surgery to save a man who might well be using her to get what he wanted.

He and Cherie were finally on the same page, and he wasn't about to jeopardize that now. He knew it sounded selfish, even a bit controlling. He cringed at the thought he might have more of his father in him than he realized, but then dismissed the idea. He was fighting for Cherie and her family, the family he hoped to be a part of someday. And the more he thought about it, the more he began to see his conclusion, not as selfish, but as necessary to protect Cherie and the girls. Admittedly all the talk of God in the decision-making was coloring his thinking. He had never given much credence to the idea of a higher power, and certainly not one who took the time to be involved in the calamities of one individual life. And the idea of a divine, loving father was so far from his own experience of fatherhood; even the concept was a cross between laughable and cruel.

But Jake's relationship with God had been on full display last night. If Jake really was a believer, and if the God he believed in was so powerful, they didn't need Cherie to solve his health issues, Will thought. God could certainly work it out some other way.

Some other way that didn't include the woman who would one day be his wife.

✳ ✳ ✳

Cherie took a chance after lacrosse practice and pulled into the church parking lot. The weekend yoga class held in the church's all-purpose room was just letting out. Cherie held the door open for several of the older women as they exited with a smile. A volunteer from a local yoga studio had started a low-key class for older adults. Trying to set an example for the yoga squeamish, Gabby had been the first one to sign up. After a few months the instructor had bowed out of what had become a successful program, and not wanting to lose the momentum, Gabby had stepped in as an interim instructor. The ladies loved her blend of simple movement, music, and a closing meditation based on scripture.

Cherie shepherded the girls into the ground floor room where multiple French doors allowed for sunlight to fill the space. Dressed in bright swirling yoga pants and a tunic top, Gabby spotted her and waved her over.

"You're a little late," she said. "And about three decades too young for this class though we do take all comers."

"I'll keep that in mind when my Saturday mornings aren't filled with lacrosse practice and birthday parties," Cherie answered. "I just stopped by to ask if you might have some time later to talk? I had dinner with Jake last night and I wanted to run it by you."

"How about now? I don't have anything for the rest of the morning." Gabby straightened to her full height after rolling up the final mat. "Girls, we're going outside to the playground to get some fresh air." She led the way to the small fenced in play area used by the pre-school, the girls scampering behind her. Covered in wood chips, the playground was a toddler's delight with half a dozen Little Tikes play structures, all donations from parishioners well past their childbearing years.

"Miss Molly, can you watch your sisters so your mom and I can talk?"

Molly nodded, dashing off after Carey.

Gabby sat on the bench by the fence. "Dinner with your brother. How is he?"

"Sober, gainfully employed, and he seems to have found the Lord," Cherie said, taking a seat beside Gabby and watching Sarah push open the windows to the cottage, playing hide and seek with her sister.

"Well, that's a nice surprise."

"Surprise would be a good word for it, yes."

"I'm sensing a little skepticism here," Gabby said. "But before we go into that, tell me what you saw with your eyes."

Startled by the request, Cherie stopped to think. Gabby seemed to always have a way of looking at things from a different angle. "Okay, so I saw a clean-cut young man, who was happy to see me. His job as a groundskeeper means a lot of outside work so he's in good shape. I saw a man with friends and a generous NA sponsor. A man who blushed when I mentioned the young hostess he couldn't stop staring at. A man who carefully followed the dietary restrictions imposed on him by his illness."

"Good observations. Now tell me what you heard?" Gabby said, pulling on one ear lobe to illustrate the point.

Cherie watched Molly helping Carey navigate the slide. "I heard a man with a sense of humor who shares many of the same memories I do about my dad. I heard admiration and gratitude for Neil, his sponsor and friend. He sounded in awe of the dawn God created and could quote the scripture that points it out. His remorse about the fire and Molly's injuries rang true."

"Okay, now we're getting somewhere," Gabby said, leaning forward and bracing her elbows on her knees as she turned to meet Cherie's gaze. "What else?"

"And he said, he wants to wait on God's plan for his life, and he doesn't think that plan includes me."

"Interesting. It would appear the 12-step program has helped your brother find his sobriety and the Lord. That would be a good thing. So where is your skepticism coming from?"

"How do you know it's real?" Cherie said, giving voice to the question she couldn't seem to answer. "His faith in God, his new life, all of it."

"Good question, how do you know?"

"I guess it all comes down to a matter of trust. Can I trust Jake …"

"Let's turn that around for a minute," Gabby injected. "Who is it you need to trust?"

Cherie knew the answer. "God, not Jake."

"That's right. Is the God you believe in, the God you found in the darkness after Paul's death and clung to in the weeks and months after, is that God big enough to do the same for Jake?"

"Of course, he is." Cherie insisted.

"So can you trust Him enough to offer the one thing you've been struggling with since your beautiful little girl was hurt?" Gabby said quietly, as she inclined her head toward the trio of sisters scrambling up and over the Little Tikes cube.

"You're talking about forgiveness."

"Yes, and that doubt I hear in your voice has its roots in the very thing that has held you bound since the fire."

"I thought I had forgiven him," Cherie said, feeling a bit defeated.

"People think forgiveness is an event, something you say and then move on. But forgiveness is a choice we make every day. Only God's forgiveness is a one-time deal, literally one and done. For the rest of us, it takes a bit longer."

"So, this was never about Jake? It was about me?"

"Both of you, actually. Each a part of a greater whole. True remorse and true forgiveness," Gabby said. "It doesn't always happen that way. Some people have to choose to forgive when there is no remorse from the person who hurt them, but ideally as with God, a truly repentant heart is met with an outpouring of forgiveness." Gabby turned on the bench to face Cherie. "Now tell me what you felt in your heart when you talked to Jake. What was your gut telling you right in that moment?"

Cherie paused, a mental picture forming in her mind of standing by the water, hand in hand with her brother. "I felt peace and awe that we were face to face for the first time in years."

"And when did the doubts start?"

"On the ride home with Will when I started dissecting the evening in my mind."

"And is Will the 'play date' you had with the girls last weekend?"

"Don't miss a thing, do you?" Cherie chuckled.

"It's my job to put the pieces together," Gabby said with a wink. "Besides the blush makes it easy."

"Will is a doctor in the ER at Mercy." Cherie glanced over at the girls making piles of the wood chips. "He's been helping me understand the transplant process."

"What did Will think of your brother?"

"He was careful with his words, but I could sense his suspicion. I think Jake's quoting scripture threw him off, threw us both. Will's still figuring out where God fits in his life."

"You're helping him with that, are you?" Gabby asked.

Cherie nodded. "He also has a sister who seems to be a strong believer after a struggle with cancer."

"Do you feel like Will is trying to influence you one way or the other about the transplant for your brother?"

"No, he's been very neutral, providing a lot of good information. He was the one who suggested I come and talk with you today. Feels like he just wants to be there for me whatever I choose to do," Cherie mused.

"I'm sensing you might be getting serious about Will."

Cherie nodded slowly. "I think we are, yes."

A frown flickered across Gabby's features; the expression gone so quickly Cherie would have missed it had she not been paying attention.

"Just one last question, and this one is more like homework. The doubts you are having are they about Jake being worthy or about the transplant itself?"

Taken aback by the stark question, Cherie didn't know what to say.

"You don't have to answer now, and I could be wrong," Gabby continued, "but I think there's still a part of you that believes Jake has to earn your forgiveness, that he has to be living some perfect sober life before he deserves your help."

Cherie felt the words drive home like the shake of someone waking you from a deep sleep.

"Like I said, I could be wrong," Gabby stated, meeting her gaze. "But before you move forward you need to finally put this to rest. Can I pray for you?"

"Yes, of course."

Gabby bowed her head. "Oh Lord, you are our great God and this daughter of yours is struggling. She needs your help to make a big decision. You have carried her through these last few difficult years, and I ask that you guide her again as you and she work through what we have talked about today. Give her your wisdom and your peace in the decision she will make, in Jesus' name we pray. Amen."

"Thank you." Cherie reached over and squeezed the pastor's hand before standing, grateful as always for her wisdom and guiding strength.

Gabby wrapped her in a warm embrace. "Let me know what you and the Lord decide."

Cherie nodded. "You know I will."

* * *

Cherie's hands encircled the warm mug of green tea as she settled on the stoop. Through the screen door behind her she could hear Molly and Sarah setting up a board game on the table. Chutes and Ladders. With Carey down for a nap, Cherie had a few quiet moments to herself. Didn't happen often and she needed to take advantage of it.

Gabby's final question haunted her. Cherie felt like she was back where she'd started. Did she still consider Jake unworthy of her forgiveness? Is that why she kept finding ways to second guess his motives? Amy's words from this morning floated to the surface of her musings. Had she really called her brother worthless? She couldn't remember saying the words, but she had no doubt Amy's recollection was accurate.

"Lord, I'm a bit of a mess here. I keep thinking I've already forgiven Jake, but it isn't as easy as that. How do you do it? How do you forgive and then set it aside and move on? Clearly, I don't know how to do that."

She was beginning to think that forgiveness was more like an onion with many layers that needed to be peeled back one at a time. Each one a bit slippery, some paper-thin, but all with the potential to bring tears if not handled carefully.

How did you move beyond the agony of knowing you could have prevented the pain your child had experienced but you didn't, Cherie thought, before a flash of insight made her breath catch and her chest tighten.

"Why?" The single word escaped her soul, whispered into the warm breeze of a spring day. "Why did you let that happen? You could have stopped it, but you didn't."

The images came to her mind in rapid succession. A brawny fireman holding Molly in his arms. Cherie's desperate prayers as she followed the ambulance to the hospital. The long agonizing wait for news about Molly. All alone. No Paul. No Judith. No one.

But me. The single phrase landed softly.

Cherie closed her eyes as tears blurred her vision. God had been there. He had heard every desperate plea. And He had saved Molly that night. Cherie knew it then, and she knew it now. She would never understand why, but she knew the One who had delivered her child back into her arms. A Father who knew the agony of watching his Son suffer in pain and who delivered Him three days later, delivered all of them.

Pastor Michaels had hit this one square on the head. On some level, not quite conscious, Cherie believed Jake needed to demonstrate his worth, that his abuse of his own body made him unworthy to receive the gift of life he had been willfully tossing aside since he was a teenager. For years she had believed he was incapable of breaking free, that he would never change. The thought came unbidden but crystal clear.

He didn't deserve her help.

Cherie cringed at the ugly truth, the subtle prejudice that had anchored her in an attitude that set her apart from her brother. Her heart beat faster. Some part of her had never wanted to admit that truth. She had buried it deep because it went against everything she believed about herself and exposed the ugly reality that she had been looking down her nose at her brother for years.

Tears stung her eyes. She had been trying to find forgiveness when what she needed was repentance. For her pride. Her judgment. Her lack of love.

"I'm sorry, Lord," she whispered.

Behind her she could hear Molly and Sara laughing, the sound like a flute, high pitched and beautiful.

There were things she would never understand this side of heaven. Why Paul had been taken from his family. But God had walked her through that tragedy, every minute, every step, every tear and every angry scream. She had learned to trust Him out of desperation, and what she had learned in the darkness she needed to display in the light.

Trust me now, as you did then.

The silent revelation settled like a fallen leaf on a still morning lake. Because she had known the truth all along. Had told her dad as much that afternoon in his kitchen. If it was Amy, she had said, she would put things in the hands of God and trust He would take care of her. Which left her feeling a bit like Dorothy trying to make her way home from Oz. The answer had been there all along. She just needed eyes to see it.

"Is that the answer, Lord? To the transplant, to all of this?"

A silent peace settled over her.

The test results would not be back for days, and they would tell the final tale. For now, all she needed to do was wait to see if God's plan for Jake included her.

Cherie felt her cell phone vibrate in the pocket of her sweatshirt. She pulled it out and glanced down at the screen. A text message. Three simple words that made her smile.

I miss you.

Cherie closed her eyes, savoring the feeling of joy and anticipation at that simple phrase. Holding the phone in both hands she quickly typed an equally simple reply.

Me too.

Do you realize we've never actually gone on a date?

Are you asking me out?

Dinner. Monday night. Pick you up at 7:00. Can you get a sitter?

I'll find one.

You might want to dress up.

Have you got a plan?

Oh, yes. Gotta go. See you then.

Chapter Fifteen

Three days of twelve hour shifts now behind him, Will stepped from his car. He shrugged into his blazer and adjusted his tie. He hadn't set eyes on Cherie since Friday, hadn't managed more than a few quick phone calls when his weekend shifts had morphed into fourteen plus hours of non-stop work. He was just glad he'd gotten out on time today; he'd been looking forward to this all weekend.

Molly opened the door to his knock, smiling up at him. "We knew it was you, so Mommy said it was okay to open the door."

"She's wearing make-up." Sarah appeared from behind her sister, her stage whisper seeming to indicate it was a secret.

"Doesn't she do that every day?" Will asked, following the girls inside.

Molly shook her head. "Not like this."

Will grinned, enjoying the candor of Cherie's girls and the eager expressions on both their faces. He looked up as the bedroom door opened and Cherie backed out of the room, closing the door softly. She turned, her vivid blue dress hugging her slim frame and literally driving the breath from his lungs.

The girls rushed forward, hugging their mom with upturned faces.

"You look so beautiful," Molly said.

"Like a princess," Sarah added.

"My thoughts exactly," Will said, finding his voice.

"Thank you all." Cherie hugged the girls. "Grandy's reading Carey a story if you want to listen."

Molly shook her head, pulling Sarah by the hand toward their bedroom. "No, we'll just play in here 'til she's done."

Cherie met Will's gaze in the sudden quiet space vacated by her children. "Dressy enough? I wasn't sure what you were planning."

"Perfect," he said, crossing the room to her.

She reached up to straighten the collar of his shirt, the gesture so simple and yet somehow so intimate, making Will glad they were going to a public place for dinner. Out in the close quarters of his car Will knew that had been a wise decision, the scent of rose and jasmine shampoo filling his senses.

"You called your mom in for tonight?"

"She was more than happy to do it."

"She approves of you dating me?"

"Gleeful, would be a good word to describe it."

Will studied her face, her expression open and inviting. "I just need to do one thing before we go."

"What's that?" Cherie asked, a slight smile lifting the corners of her mouth.

He leaned toward her, his eyes fixed on hers before he kissed her. His lips lingered on hers just long enough to make his pulse race. "I've been thinking about that since Friday night."

"Worth the wait?" Cherie said, pushing the hair back from his forehead.

"Absolutely," Will responded. He squeezed her hand and then started the car.

After two days apart, the conversation flowed easily as they headed eastward. Will steered clear of the solemn stories of work, choosing to share the peculiar rather than the tragic. He heard Cherie's quick intake of breath as they pulled into the parking lot twenty minutes later.

The restaurant shone like a palace, its two exterior staircases sweeping up to an entryway with a vaulted ceiling. The old-world architecture of rough-cut stone on the exterior and shiny marble on the interior was dwarfed only by the breathtaking view as they stepped through the doors. The expanse of New York City shone in the final hour of daylight, the setting sun glinting off the windows of a dozen skyscrapers. They were a few minutes early for their reservation and the hostess led them to the outside bar on a semicircular balcony facing the city.

Standing beside Cherie as the setting sun colored the skyscrapers with a deep orange glow, Will reached for her hand. "One of the residents I work with told me about this place. He proposed to his girlfriend here a few weeks ago."

Cherie turned her head, looking up at him. "But we're not doing that tonight, right?"

"On our first date?" Will said, feigning innocence. "And no, we're not here to do anything but have a good meal and enjoy the view."

Cherie leaned into his shoulder. "Are we crazy to be talking about a future together after knowing each other for such a short time? Feels like we're two high school kids so crazy about each other that caution is taking a back seat to emotions."

Will stepped up behind her, his words infused with deep pleasure and spoken close to her ear. "Did I just hear you say you are crazy about me?"

"I am," she answered, leaning back against him. "But we're two adults with jobs and responsibilities, not to mention my family."

Will wrapped his arms around her, gently pulling her back against him, and savoring this perfect moment. "It's not a straight line from here to there, but we agree we're headed in the same direction?"

She turned her face to study his, a look of wonder in her eyes. "Yes."

A single word. Spoken with surety. Will found his heart overflowing with gratitude for Cherie. "Let's just take it slow then, give your girls a chance to know me better and give you a chance to meet my sister."

"I do want to meet Maddie."

"Then how about we accept her offer to have us for July fourth. We'll take the girls to New Hampshire and they can swim in the lake and get to hang out with two great would-be cousins."

"Sounds wonderful, but I'm just concerned about the timing." Cherie paused, returning her gaze to the view as the hostess appeared announcing their table was ready.

Moments later they settled in at a candle-lit table for two by the window, the place settings positioned at a ninety-degree angle to maximize the view.

"I talked to Pastor Michaels this weekend." Cherie unfolded her linen napkin, placing it in her lap.

Will had never felt the need to consult a spiritual advisor, but he understood this relationship with Pastor Michaels was important to Cherie and had given her comfort in some very difficult days. "What did she think?"

"She rarely comes right out and tells me what she thinks, instead she asks a lot of questions to make me look at things from every angle."

"She guides rather than decides."

"Yes, and she always sends me home with something to think about." She paused, lifting her gaze to meet his. "In the car on the ride home from Long Island, you suggested I needed to make up my mind about being Jake's donor before the test results came back …"

"So, your eligibility wouldn't be the only factor in your decision, yes." Will had been hoping to have this discussion later this evening, having had the last two days to think about what he would say, but he never got the chance to finish that thought.

"I've decided to be Jake's donor," Cherie said, her voice quiet and resolute.

Having anticipated a conversation Will realized the decision had already been made. And he found his professional pride at her bravery at war with his personal fears for her safety. It wasn't his place to convince her one way or the other, but rather to support her in whatever decision she made. As a doctor he knew this, but as a man truly in love for the first time in his life, he was scared, scared to death of losing her. It didn't make sense from a medical point of view, but feelings rarely did. And his reservations about this surgery had more to do with Jake's motivations than with Cherie's generosity. All these thoughts passed through his mind in the time it took him to extend his hand to her, his eyes fixed on her face. "What changed your mind? Friday night you seemed to be questioning Jake's sincerity?"

Cherie placed her hand in his. "I realized this wasn't about Jake, not really. It was about me and whether I trusted in God's plan for my life."

Startled by the origin of her decision making, his disbelief was evident in his tone. "How can you know what God's plan is? How can anyone know that?"

Cherie squeezed his hand. "I know this may be hard for you to understand when you question whether God even exists, and I know He does. I have literally felt His presence holding me in the darkness when I couldn't see the path forward, couldn't envision a time when I would smile again, when the farthest thing from my mind was imagining a night like this."

She smiled softly, her eyes filled with both wonder and sadness. "That God, who drew me out of the darkness, has a plan for me. So, this wasn't ever about trusting Jake and his sobriety, it's about relinquishing my judgement of him, letting go of the ugly part of me that doesn't think he's worthy of a second chance after the way he's lived his life. And then I had to decide if I truly trusted in the God who had walked with me through the darkness."

"And you do?"

"Without question," Cherie said. "I know that's a lot to take in. Are you okay with this?"

Will paused before answering, trying to unite the warring factions in his head. How could he tell her after that heart-felt revelation that he didn't want her to do it, that he didn't trust her brother and his convenient use of the God Cherie trusted with her life.

Seeing the concern on her furrowed brow, Will forced a smile. "This was always your decision to make."

"But now it affects both of us. I never saw this coming, Will. I never thought my decisions would impact anyone but my children ever again."

The words he'd been planning since Saturday sprang to his mind, wanting to be heard, needing to be said, before this went any further. Words, not of fear for her safety, but rather words of doubt about the motivations of a man he didn't trust and a God he didn't believe in. A God who had stolen the only stability he had known in his young life in a household filled with his mother's depression and his father's ire. His grandmother had been his only constant during his mother's many hospitalizations. And when she fell, her skull shattered, Will's world splintered into episodes of silent pain. He couldn't take the chance a mercurial God and another man with selfish motivations could threaten the happiness he had found with Cherie.

Will opened his mouth, choosing his words carefully. The warmth of her hand resting in his drew his gaze downward, her slim fingers clasped around his. Staring down at this simple joining, the words he had been about to say stilled on his tongue.

Her hand was bare, devoid of the wedding ring that had rested there since he met her.

Will lifted his gaze to meet hers, pulled from the problems of his past to the promise of his future. And he knew in that moment she had been courageous enough to do what he had not.

His words when he spoke were unscripted, the emotions flowing from his heart.

"You have changed my life, Cherie Hollister. And it occurs to me we've been talking about our future together and only one of us has been brave enough to demonstrate why we need to make that a reality, because if you don't know already, and I suspect you do, I love you, Cherie."

He watched her eyes widen, the shimmer of candlelight reflected in their glistening depths. He lifted her hand, running his thumb across the pale silhouette on her ring finger. "When did you take it off?"

"This morning. I realized if we were talking about being a family then I couldn't do that wearing Paul's ring. It didn't seem fair to him or to us."

"That must have been hard to do," Will said.

Cherie nodded, her expression thoughtful but not sad. She studied him for a moment before she spoke. "I can't say it yet, Will, I hope you understand."

Will knew instantly what she meant. They were words he had held inside for weeks before breathing them into life. "You don't have to. I think you have demonstrated very clearly how you feel about me."

"What I do need to say is this." She met his gaze, her words strong and sure. "I have needed your help from the moment we met in the ER. The difference now is I want you by my side. With or without the transplant, whatever way it all plays out later this week with the test results. I know I can do it on my own; I have proved that to myself over the last three years, but I want you there beside me."

And with that, any thoughts he had been harboring about dissuading her from her generous instincts hung in the air unsaid. If she wanted him by her side, then he was going to be there and if that included a hospital room then so be it.

* * *

Maddie couldn't say why she kept thinking about Will. It had started Monday night and persisted at random moments throughout the last two days. She had spoken to him less than two weeks ago which, given their history, could be considered recent, and yet she couldn't shake the feeling he needed her. Which was silly, of course. Will was a grown man she had only spoken to a handful of times in the last decade. And yet the feeling persisted. After dinner she decided to stop ignoring the obvious and just call him.

Grabbing her phone from the counter, Maddie pulled up his number.

"Looks like you're about to stick us with the dinner dishes," Scott said, stepping up next to her as Kiley and Shaun cleared the table. He peered over her shoulder. "Will, huh? Let me know how it goes." He kissed her softly, then joined the clean-up crew in the kitchen.

Stepping out onto the deck, Maddie connected the call with a touch to the screen.

"Maddie?" Will said, sounding out of breath. "Now this is strange, I was about to call you."

"Calling to chat or did you have a reason?"

"I was hoping I could take you up on your offer for July 4th. Is the guest house still available?"

"It is, and I would love that," Maddie said with a smile as she settled into one of the Adirondack chairs facing the lake and put the phone on speaker. "And you're bringing Cherie and the girls?"

"We're a package deal."

"Really." The word hung on her lips. "I think I need a few details."

"I'm in love with her, Maddie."

The simple statement hung in the air between them. "I'm so happy for you, Will."

"No words of caution about jumping in too quickly?"

"You are a grown man who knows his own heart. I trust you know what you're doing. I can't wait to meet her."

"And that plays into the other thing I wanted to talk to you about."

Maddie heard a faucet running as Will filled what sounded like a very large glass. "Now I'm even more intrigued."

"Cherie might be donating a kidney to her brother in a few weeks which could alter the timing on our plans."

"That is an incredibly generous gift, and we can get together anytime you're available," Maddie said, sensing in Will's words an undertone of disquiet. "How are you feeling about that?"

Will paused, and whether he was rehydrating or choosing his words was an open question.

"You may be the only person in my life I can say this to, Maddie, but truthfully, there's a part of me that wants to talk her out of it. Is that as selfish as it sounds?" Will asked. "You don't have to answer that. I know it is. You would think being a physician would make it easier. I understand about the need for transplants, and I know all the statistics about donor safety and living a full life with one kidney, but she has three little girls who love her and need her …"

"And you're scared of losing her."

"Yes, but it's more than the surgery …" He broke off, clearly searching for the right words. "How do you know what God's will is for your life?"

Startled by the question, Maddie stared out over the water and offered a silent prayer that she in her new faith could help her brother find his. "God has a plan for each one of us. Whose life are we talking about? Yours or Cherie's?"

"Both. But for you to understand, I need to tell you a story. Do you have time?"

"Always for you little brother," Maddie said with a smile.

"I used to hate it when you called me that," Will responded.

"I knew that. When we were kids, I said it to remind you that I was the oldest, kind of a control thing, but now it's a term of endearment. Tell me a story, Will."

Maddie watched the setting sun turn the water into a myriad of oranges and reds, shifting in hue from the soft glow of the lake's center to the deepening shadows of the shoreline, as Will told her about the fire. About Cherie's oldest daughter who barely escaped losing her life and was left with the scars to prove it. About a drug addicted brother, his negligence and repentance.

Will finished the telling with a simple statement. "I don't understand how she can forgive him and do it so gracefully and generously."

"I'm sure that wasn't an easy choice for Cherie to make," Maddie said, the right words coming to mind in a flash of insight. "Forgiveness isn't a feeling, it's a choice, and when you have been on the receiving end of that gift of grace you stand in awe of the struggle it takes to make that decision and the love it takes to live it out."

"I can't imagine you ever doing anything that requires that kind of forgiveness," Will said.

Maddie knew in that moment she needed to share her story, all the ugliness, the bad decisions, the testimony of a love and a life almost lost, but for the hand of God. She fell silent, gathering her thoughts. She had never told anyone this story, didn't want to even now, but sensed the telling would serve a greater purpose. "I had an affair, Will."

Her heart racing, she drew in a deep breath. "Two years ago, I auditioned for a summer show on a whim and was cast in the leading role opposite a man who became very important to me. Scott and I had neglected our marriage for years and I thought it was shattered beyond repair. That's not an excuse. What I did was willful and wrong. I saw the attraction building between Adam and I, and I did nothing to stop it. I had wanted someone to love me for so long and I found it, in the wrong place and with the wrong man." Tears stung her eyes and blurred her view of the deepening twilight as she remembered how close she had come to losing everything.

"The only thing that kept me from throwing my marriage away was Kylie and Shaun. I knew I couldn't shatter their lives with my selfishness. Although I almost did it anyway when Scott confronted me and accused me of sleeping with Adam. I told him that wasn't true, but he was so angry and hurt, and we both said a lot of things we'd been holding back for years. Mean, angry accusations and thoughtless words. When I ran out of the house and got in my car, I fully intended on going to Adam and telling him my marriage was over. I was furious and driving way too fast when a deer stepped into the road, and I crashed into a tree."

"Oh, Maddie," Will said softly.

"They found the cancer that night and operated on me a few days later. My whole life was turned upside down in the space of a few days, and I was left having to rely on the one man I thought I hated who I thought hated me for what I'd done." Maddie wiped the tears from her eyes. "What I didn't know until months later was that Scott had given his life to the Lord that day of the crash, had prayed for help and healing, for me and for our marriage. And as I watched him care for me through the chemotherapy treatments and take care of Kylie and Shaun, I knew he was a different man. A man who loved his family with his whole heart. Finally on Christmas night, four months after the accident I told him I was sorry for what I had done. I was surprised and humbled when I realized he had already forgiven me, because he loved me and he had seen how God had brought out of our anger and heartache, a new commitment to each other and to Him. So, to answer your question, I think the level of forgiveness you are talking about only comes with God's help."

"Which would explain Cherie's decision to move forward with the transplant. She is a woman of strong faith."

"Where does that leave you on the faith question?" Maddie wondered aloud.

"With a lot of questions and no answers," Will said, his voice taking on a hard edge. "How do you reconcile it, Maddie? Where was God when we were growing up without a mother and left in the care of an overbearing father who cared more for his image in the community than he did his own kids?"

Maddie could hear the pain in this voice.

"He was an abusive father, Maddie. Not physically, but verbally and psychologically, what he did was abuse. As an adult I've come to see that."

"You're right, he was, and you and the boys caught more of that than I did."

Will's tone softened. "I've spent my whole life trying not to be like him, trying to give others the grace no one gave me. So, you can understand my reluctance to see God as a father. Not the best associations for me."

Maddie didn't have the answer but even as a new believer herself, she could see God's hand in the aftermath of that tumultuous upbringing. Out of those years had come a man brave enough to change his career path in his thirties and determined to find a way to help others. Having been given a glimpse at Will's inner struggles, Maddie found she admired him even more.

"There's a chance Kylie and I may be coming to New York for a college visit to Columbia in the next few weeks," Maddie said. "Can we meet for dinner if that happens?"

"Absolutely. Just let me know when. Thanks for calling, Maddie. It's like you knew I needed to get that off my chest with the only person who could understand where I was coming from."

"I'm here anytime, Will." Left staring at the dark screen after they said good night, Maddie sensed his presence before she felt Scott's hand on her shoulder. "Did you hear all that?"

"Most of it, yes. I wondered what was taking you so long and came out to check, and you telling our story just drew me in. I know how it ends but I'm still so grateful for the path that brought us back to each other." Scott pulled Maddie to her feet, wrapping her in his arms.

"He's bringing Cherie and the girls to meet us for the 4th."

"It will be good to have little kids around here again."

Maddie nodded, looking up into his eyes. "He seems to be very serious about her."

"Isn't that a good thing?"

"She's a believer …"

"And he's not." Scott finished, understanding her concern. "Does he even realize that's important?"

"I don't think so. And it seems his struggles with that go a lot deeper than I realized."

"Maybe this is the way God draws him closer."

"He's asking questions at least," Maddie said. "Who would have thought when we reached out to him that more than a sibling reunion was in the works. That's an awesome privilege and a big responsibility to try and answer his questions."

"Good thing you don't have to do it alone. I get the feeling we're a small part of a much bigger plan," Scott said, wrapping an arm around her shoulders and leading her inside.

Chapter Sixteen

Now there was nothing left but the waiting. Cherie tidied up her classroom before heading home for the weekend. She had spoken with Dr. Cummings earlier in the week and explained she wanted to be Jake's donor, a statement she had been unable to make last Friday, but now felt like the right one. The transplant board would review all the tests, as well as Dr. Cummings' recommendation, before making a decision. Knowing she had done all she could, the mental tension of the last few weeks lifted like wisps of fog fading in the light of dawn.

The only note of disquiet that still lingered had nothing to do with Jake and everything to do with Will. He had said all the right words, and Cherie could feel his support, but with an undertone of something she could only identify as apprehension.

Which didn't make sense, Will had been her biggest supporter through this whole process. But standing in front of him on Monday as they said good night, something felt different. Gone was the teasing glint she so often saw in his eyes, his features still as he studied her upturned face. Then instead of the kiss she had been expecting, he had gently drawn her to him until her head rested on his chest, his arms enfolding her in an embrace somehow more intimate than a kiss. In that moment, Cherie had wanted nothing more than to simply rest in Will's arms, his lips pressed against her forehead, his breath warm on her skin. She closed her eyes hearing the steady beat of his heart but sensed a tightness in the arms that held her so gently, a subtle juxtaposition of tension and tenderness. She turned her face upward, questioning what she was feeling and meeting Will's gaze she saw in his eyes his deep love for her and his fear.

The sound of ringing bells filled the room, making Cherie wish she'd turned down the volume after speaking with Judith at lunchtime. She reached for the phone on her desk, recognizing the number and feeling the stillness of the space around her.

"Cherie, it's Brook Sheraton from Hopewell Atlantic. The transplant board just finished their meeting."

"Have they made a decision?" Cherie asked, feeling strangely calm.

"They have," Brook replied. "You are an eligible donor for you brother, Jake."

Cherie waited for the panic to set in, the fear that had plagued her for the last few weeks. But surprisingly, all she felt was peace as if she had known this would be the outcome from the beginning, which in a way she had. And the first person she wanted to tell was Will.

Cherie quickly finished up the call with Ms. Sheraton who said she would be in touch about possible procedure dates. Cherie sent a quick text, hoping Will wasn't too busy to answer.

Time for a run tonight?
Yes, I get off at 6:00.
Meet you in the parking lot.

* * *

Will exited the ER to find Cherie sitting on the hood of his car, her bright pink sneakers matching her sleeveless T-shirt. He grinned relishing the unexpected pleasure of seeing her tonight, even as his steps slowed at the realization it was dinnertime. Surprised by the text, and eager to see her, he hadn't thought this through. If Cherie was here then someone else was feeding her kids dinner, which meant she had called upon her family for the second time in a week. Much as he wanted to believe she had done this to spend some time alone with him, he suspected there was a more urgent reason for this get-together.

Spotting him across the parking lot, she waved, her smile tugging at his heart as he recalled the day of the 10K race when all he'd wanted to do was make her smile exactly like she was right now.

"Nice surprise," he said, stopping in front of her. "I didn't think I was seeing you until tomorrow. Good thing I keep my running gear in my locker." He held out a hand to her as she slid off the hood. "Who is watching the girls?"

"Amy. She's doing pizza and a movie at her house." Cherie placed her hand in his.

"I'd love to think you missed me so much you planned this all week, but I suspect you have something to tell me," Will said. He pushed back a stray strand of hair that had escaped her ponytail.

She nodded. "I do, and just for the record I did miss you this week."

"Good to know. Okay, let's hear it."

"The transplant board approved me as a donor for Jake."

He had expected this after their dinner on Monday, and yet that didn't diminish the sudden ache in his gut. Cherie's full and uncoerced consent to donation had always been the stumbling block. With that removed, she was the obvious answer to Jake's end-stage renal disease and a lifetime of dialysis. A part of him had been hoping she might be ineligible from a medical point of view. But apparently, Cherie was as perfect on the inside as she was on the outside. "Have you told Jake yet?"

Cherie squeezed his hand, looking up into his eyes. "I haven't told anyone yet. Not my brother or my mom. Not even Amy. Only you."

The heavy weight in his core lifted just a bit at her words.

"I know you're afraid, Will. I can see it in your eyes."

"Not of the surgery, Cherie," he replied. "I know this donor procedure is done all over the country, every day with few complications. So, it's not the procedure." He struggled to find the words to explain the powerlessness in a situation beyond his control. "It's standing back and watching the woman I love give so generously and being unable to do anything but watch and wait."

Cherie stepped toward him, placing her hand over his heart. "Will, don't you understand how every word of support and encouragement you've spoken has given me the confidence to do this? I truly believe you are the man God placed in my life to show me I could love again. I don't know if that makes any sense to you …"

His finger on her cheek stilled her words. "That would explain why I couldn't stop thinking about you from the moment I first met you. All God's doing then?" He lifted her chin with his knuckle.

Cherie smiled, then nodded slowly. "All I know for sure is this: I was a widowed mother of three who firmly believed I would never fall in love again, until I met you."

Her words landed gently, settling into his heart, and calming his soul. If that was as close as Cherie ever came to saying the words, he was okay with that, and he knew he would do everything in his power to help her through these next few months so they would have the chance to build a life together. He drew her into his arms as Cherie lifted her hands and turned his gaze to meet hers. She paused for just a moment, her eyes studying his face with an expression of joy and wonder.

"Just in case that wasn't perfectly clear, I do love you, Will Finnegan."

Will felt his eyes sting as he bent his head to kiss her.

* * *

The Porsche pulled up to the curb in front of the yellow ranch, the yard as colorful as the dwelling with pink azaleas in full bloom, pansies and impatiens of every color planted in an orderly pattern in the window boxes and bordering beds.

When Cherie had called Judith on Friday night and asked if she would be willing to host a dinner, her mother had eagerly agreed and had done so without asking a lot of questions about the reason for it. She simply took the guest list and made her plans.

"Are you nervous?" Will asked, meeting Cherie's gaze over the roof as they exited the tight confines of the car.

"A little," Cherie answered. "Which is silly, right? They're all my family."

"Right, so there's nothing for you to be nervous about," Will said, reaching for her hand as he rounded the bumper. "I, however, have every reason to be worried since I'm about to meet your father for the first time."

"He's not that fierce, believe me. Protective, absolutely. But the only thing my dad has ever wanted was for me to be happy and meeting you has made that possible." Cherie squeezed his hand as they walked up the path to her parents' house. "I do love you, you know?"

"And I'm blown away by that every day. I love you, too," Will said as they stepped up onto the porch.

A wave of warm aromatic scents flooded the senses as they came through the door. Rich roasted meat, freshly baked biscuits, a tinge of rosemary and sizzling potatoes. Judith was in her element, preparing a feast for her family, her labors a pleasure not a chore. Joe was putting the finishing touches on a triple layer cake, brandishing a pastry bag with chocolate icing after auditing a baking class at the community college. Amy was setting the table outside on the deck with John's help while Jake lit the candles on the deck railing.

Cherie hadn't seen her parents this happy in a long time and this without any idea what she was about to tell them. This evening was all about a family sitting down to dinner together for the first time in years. A reunion of hearts after too long apart.

Judith spotted them as they came through the door, her smile broadening as she hurried over to them. Gone was the reserve that had held her bound, the caution that made her worry when the next disaster would strike. Gone as well was the worry that had furrowed deep lines in her brow for so many years.

Had she done this, Cherie wondered? By forgiving Jake had she freed her mother from the burden of worry and regret? Was it possible her decisions could have such a profound impact on her mother? Watching Judith now, her expression open and excited, Cherie knew it was true. How had she never realized, even as a mother herself, that the welfare of her children and their relationships with each other was everything to a parent, that the all-encompassing love she had for Molly, Sarah, and Carey was a mirror of the love Judith felt for her, for all her children.

A long-forgotten memory surfaced; its images as clear as if she was watching it on a wide screen. Judith as a young mother, enveloping her in a suffocating hug when she picked Cherie up from a two-week stay at summer camp. And the arms that embraced her now were just as filled with that fierce love. Judith held her tightly for a moment, then released Cherie and turned to Will, hesitating just the briefest of seconds before enveloping him in a similar hug. Cherie saw the look of surprise on Will's face melt into pleasure before Judith stepped back and studied them both.

"Now we can start this party," she said, turning back to the kitchen as Joe joined them.

"You must be Will," he said, one hand locking the brake on his wheelchair as he extended the other. "All the women in my life have been buzzing about you. It's nice to finally meet you."

"You as well, Sir," Will said, clasping the offered hand.

"I think we can dispense with the formalities. Just call me Joe."

Will nodded as Cherie bent to hug her dad. "Thanks for having us. I know I didn't give you much notice when I asked you to do this."

"No notice necessary, you are welcome here anytime, though perhaps I should be thanking you. I haven't seen your mother this excited about a dinner in a long time." He glanced over his shoulder with a soft smile and Cherie marveled at the depth of love it took to endure the trials of the last thirty-five years and emerge on the other side still smiling.

"When did Jake arrive?"

"About an hour ago and your mother put him right to work."

"Of course, she did," Cherie said, before being engulfed in Amy's arms.

"So, why are we here? Are you making some big announcement I know nothing about?" Amy whispered in her ear, pulling back, and looking up at Will.

"Not the one you're thinking." Cherie watched John introduce himself to Will, noting how Jake hung back as the men began to talk. "Excuse me a minute."

Stepping over to Jake, Cherie registered the look of longing in his eyes as if, even in his parents' house, he felt like an outsider. He was dressed casually in jeans and a white dress shirt with rolled up sleeves, his hair recently cut. "Can I talk to you outside for a minute?"

Jake nodded, following her as she led the way onto the deck festooned with white fairy lights just beginning to shine in the gathering darkness. A long rectangular table covered with a linen tablecloth was set for seven with Judith's best dishes and flatware, the candles in its center already gleaming.

Cherie sat down on the wide steps leading to the backyard, her back to the house for a bit of privacy as Jake settled beside her.

For a moment she stared out into the backyard, the darkness gathering first beneath the trees and then spreading over the lawn, finally held at bay by the lighted candles on the deck railing and the light pouring from the kitchen.

Cherie turned to her brother. "The transplant board reviewed my tests and approved me as your donor."

She heard his quick intake of breath, his surprise clear with none of the relief or joy she had half-expected. In the set of his shoulders rounded inward, she saw his remorse. In the downward turn of his gaze, she felt his shame. In the hand that reached up to massage his brow, she sensed his reluctance.

"Have you told anyone yet?"

"Only Will. I wanted to tell you in person, not over the phone."

"Cherie, you don't have to do this …" Jake insisted, his tone firm.

"I know you said you don't want me to be your donor," Cherie interrupted, "but I think that's your guilt talking. You said you wanted to wait on God's plan and His timing, and I think He's speaking loud and clear. I'm not just a match, Jake, I'm a perfect match for you."

The irony of her trying to convince Jake to agree was not lost on Cherie. For weeks she had been running full tilt away from the decision that now had been made with such ease. She realized in offering her forgiveness to Jake, she had found it as well. Forgiveness from God for all the anger she had been clinging to and the hatred that had kept her rooted in a time before the fire when she had been living the perfect life, married to the man she adored. The fire had incinerated that perfection, and in the aftermath, she had seen the darkness of her husband's soul and of her own. And year after year as she harbored that malice toward her brother and continued her unwillingness to forgive, she had shackled herself to the past.

"I don't deserve your forgiveness," Jake said quietly.

Cherie held out a hand to him." No one deserves forgiveness, Jake. It's a gift offered from one flawed human being to another." She took a breath as Jake took her hand. "Actually, I think I need your forgiveness."

Startled, Jake started to speak before Cherie cut him off. "Just let me say this, while I still have the courage to get the words out." She hadn't planned this, but the timing and the phrasing seemed to have a life of their own.

"I gave up on you, Jake. I didn't think you would ever change so I didn't fight for you like Mom did. And though you were my brother and I loved you, I couldn't watch you continue to fail at rehab after rehab. I was convinced the drugs would rule your life until the day you died. And as I sit here and look at you now, strong, and sober, a man who has given his life to God, I feel ashamed that I stopped hoping for you, stopped praying for you, and stopped believing that you were capable or worthy of another chance. That's an ugly truth, and I'm sorry."

Jake met her gaze. "I knew all that, Cherie, and I was as disgusted with myself as you were with me." He raised a hand. "No, don't deny it. Disgusted is the right word. But for me those temptations are still out there, still a real part of who I am. Some days, I still feel the pull of them, other days not quite so much, but it's why, whether I feel it or not, I still go to an NA meeting every day." Jake buried his face in his hands for a moment. "That's the thing that scares me about the transplant. I don't know if I can live up to the trust you are placing in me with a gift like this. It's the reason I don't want to accept it. What if I screw up again? It could happen. Every day I wake up and fight to stay clean, but it could still happen."

"I know that, Jake, and to be truthful that was part of my reservation about even being tested. But this isn't about the future, it's about making the right choice now, today, and then taking the rest as it comes. I'm not doing this for who you'll be next week or next year, I'm doing this for the man you are right now, who has worked so hard to get here. It's about trusting God to see us both through the surgery and the healing. I believe with His help we are both going to find our way to a healthy future and a healed family."

"How can you possibly be so generous to me?" His eyes were wide with the question, their brown depths shiny as he studied their joined hands.

"You already know the answer to that," Cherie said with a smile. "I didn't do it on my own."

He lifted his eyes to meet hers. "I can see that, but somehow I never expected to see Christ's love literally poured out for me in such a life changing way."

"So, you'll accept me as your donor?"

"With faith like that, how could I do anything but gratefully accept."

Jake got to his feet, taking her other hand and pulling her to a stand.

Cherie stepped into his arms, realizing she had never hugged her brother as a fully grown man. He was half a head taller than she, his torso strong and solid, no longer the gangly teenager who had let drugs take the place of nourishment.

"Thank you," Jake whispered, taking a step back, his hands resting on her shoulders. "I don't even have the words … I think you should be the one to tell them."

"If you insist," Cherie replied. "I do believe Will has already poured the toast."

"Mom is going to totally lose it," Jake said as they turned to the table. "Shouts of joy or a flood of tears?"

"Definitely tears," Cherie replied. "If it were one of mine, I'd be crying my eyes out."

They joined the others carrying covered dishes to the table. The plates, white with blue and gold rims, reflected the candlelight, the table shimmering.

As they took their seats, Cherie took in the festive scene seeing Judith's soft smile and shiny eyes, Amy's easy laughter, John and Will talking easily across the table, and Jake's attentive focus on whatever Joe was telling him. Over the years there have been many dinners, some joyful and celebratory but others rife with arguments, voices raised in pleading and tears of sorrow. All those moments had brought them to this one, Cherie realized, feeling blest to be here with Will beside her and to share this evening with her imperfect family.

"Can we start with grace," Joe said, holding out a hand to Jake and Cherie who did likewise creating a circle of joined hands as Joe bowed his head. "Bless us O Lord, and these thy gifts we are about to receive from your bounty." He paused after this traditional prayer and then added, "and thank you Lord for bringing us together tonight as we unite as one family to share this long-awaited reunion feast. Bless those who consume it and the hands that prepared it, in Jesus' name we pray." He looked up and winked at his wife before turning his attention to Cherie and Will. "Now who is making the toast? And what exactly are we celebrating?"

"That would be me," Cherie said, reaching for her glass and holding it aloft as the others did likewise. "To Jake's new kidney, a bit used but a perfect match from one sibling to another."

A shriek erupted from the end of the table. Judith covered her mouth with one hand and burst into tears.

Cherie met Jake's gaze across the table, mouthing the word. "Both."

Chapter Seventeen

The restaurant's rooftop dining area was perfect for the send-off party. They had taken a chance with the open-air seating area, having chosen it for its spectacular three-sided view of the vast meadow studded with colorful wildflowers undulating down to the distant river's shoreline. And though it had rained heavily last night, the day had dawned with the sun rising to drive away the last of the clouds. Normally, such a venue would have been well beyond Cherie's limited budget, but Will had insisted on paying, and when her dad found out and made a fuss, the two had agreed on splitting the tab. The men in her life wanted to create the perfect send-off for her and for Jake.

It had been three weeks since the phone call with Brook Sheraton and now, the scheduling all worked out, Cherie would travel on Tuesday to Long Island where in side-by-side operating rooms, she would donate her kidney to Jake.

For now, though, all she wanted was to enjoy this beautiful Sunday evening with all the people she loved. Judith and Joe. Amy and John. And Mark, of course, who was showing Molly the binoculars he'd gotten for his birthday as they stood next to the railing overlooking the meadow scanning for birds. Sarah was playing campout with her two favorite stuffed animals under the long table set in the middle of the rooftop. Jake had driven out from Long Island this morning and would be returning tomorrow for his last dialysis treatment before the surgery. He stood talking with Pastor Michaels, who was telling him about the donor drive being held at the church next week, her expression animated and her laughter easy. Cherie smiled, her gaze coming to rest on Will who stood listening to them holding Carey in his arms.

Over the last few weeks as the arrangements for the transplant had been finalized, Will had spent nearly all his time away from work with Cherie and the girls. He came over in the morning when he wasn't working and helped them get ready for school. He ate dinner with them many evenings, then read the girls' stories before bed. In doing so, he and Carey had formed a unique bond. Perhaps it was their encounter in the ER, but the trust she saw in Carey's eyes whenever she looked at Will was heartwarming.

Will had told her he wanted to be ready to help when she came home from the hospital and knowing the girl's routine would make that easier. Cherie didn't need a reason, she just wanted him with her every waking minute. As for the rest, she and Will had decided this was not the time to add another dimension to their relationship. She loved Will, of that she was sure, but the physical intimacy still seemed like a bridge she wasn't ready to cross, the final severing of her marriage to Paul. It didn't make sense in some ways, but what she had shared with Will was her concern not about the act but the after. There would be no going back, and she didn't want to wake up the next morning with any regrets. What had made Cherie love him even more, if that was possible, was his commitment to honor her feelings and to wait.

She watched Will's distracted expression as he listened to Jake and Gabby, knowing he was keeping a lookout for the two final guests. Cherie could tell the moment they arrived, the smile on Will's face going from polite attention to full wattage. Glancing to her left, she saw a pretty woman with blonde curly hair and a tall, statuesque teenager coming up the exterior stairway from the parking lot. Will excused himself and, still carrying Carey, hurried over to meet the new arrivals at the top of the stairway, unlatching the gate for them. Cherie started toward them as Will embraced his sister and niece.

"You must be Maddie," Cherie said, joining the group.

"Cherie, it's so nice to finally meet you. Thanks for inviting us to join you. I know this is a family party."

"I'm glad you could make it."

"And this is my daughter, Kylie." Maddie said, eyeing her brother who couldn't seem to stop smiling.

Cherie turned to the beautiful young woman. "How did you like Columbia?"

"I liked it, it's the first campus I've seen that's really a part of the city. Not sure I can get in though," Kylie said with a very teenage shrug.

"You do have a few other schools to see, perhaps something in Boston?" Maddie suggested.

"That's Mom's not so subtle way of saying she wants me closer to home," Kylie said with a good-natured smile as she held out her hand to the toddler in her uncle's arms.

"This is Carey. You can see Will's handiwork right there on her forehead. It's how we met." Cherie reached up and ran a finger over the pink scar on her daughter's brow.

"You do nice work, Uncle Will," Kylie replied, distracting the toddler with the bangle bracelets on her wrist. She cast a questioning glance at her uncle, who smiled and handed Carey over into her waiting arms.

"I could tell Will was smitten from the first time he mentioned you," Maddie said, returning her attention to Cherie.

"And when was that?" Cherie glanced over at Will, noting the color in his face. It could have been a touch of sunburn from their outing in the park but certainly looked like a blush creeping up his neck.

"Okay, you two," Will said with a laugh, wrapping his arm around Cherie and pulling her close. "I'm going to save myself the embarrassment and just own up to the fact that I was crazy about you from the moment I set eyes on you in the ER."

"Wise move, Uncle Will," Kylie whispered. "It's written all over your face anyway." She set Carey on her feet as the toddler held tightly to her hand and dragged her away to meet Sarah.

"I certainly hope I do a better job hiding my feelings from my patients than I do in my personal life," Will said. "My transparency is evident to all the women in my life, even those I haven't seen since they were five."

Cherie smiled at him. "That's not a bad thing, you know. You are a man without guile."

Maddie smiled at her words. "He is, isn't he?"

He glanced back and forth between the two smiling women. "That's some biblical reference you're going to have to explain to me later, isn't it?"

Maddie nodded. "Yes, but it's a good thing, don't worry."

"Let me introduce you to Cherie's parents," Will said, wrapping his other arm around Maddie and turning toward the larger group.

A raw, angry crack of splintering wood rent the evening air. Immediately sensing the danger, Cherie spun to see Molly leaning over the railing reaching for the binoculars tumbling to the ground. Cherie bolted to the railing and grabbed Molly around the waist before the railing gave way completely. Turning, she pushed Molly into Will's arms. Too late, she realized her mistake, the momentum of the push propelling her backward. Her arms flailed, reaching for the severed railing but finding no purchase. She met Will's terrified gaze, his hand reaching for hers as she plunged to the ground.

* * *

Will watched in horror as Cherie disappeared. He didn't need to look over the deck's edge to know a fall from the second story would produce multiple traumatic injuries. His heart pounding, he acted instinctively, his mind barely able to grasp what he had just witnessed. He quickly set Molly on her feet and raced to the exterior stairway, vaulting down the stairs with Amy's husband, John, right behind him.

Cherie had landed on her back, her arms splayed, the left one resting at an unnatural angle. Will covered the distance between them at a run, feeling his shoes sink into the sodden grass. Though his mind raced with terror at her stillness, his training kicked in automatically as he sank to his knees beside her. He saw John do likewise, placing one hand on either side of Cherie's head to stabilize her spine. Will was going to need every one of the first aid skills John had learned in his police academy training.

"911?" Will said aloud.

"Done," John replied. "Amy called it in. My guys will make it first. Paramedics will take longer."

"Cherie, talk to me!" Will said loudly, tapping her uninjured shoulder firmly with his hand to try and solicit a response. None. He pressed two fingers against the supraorbital notch, the bone just below the eyebrow, to check for a pain reaction. A semi-conscious patient would groan or even recoil at this painful stimulus. Nothing. A shiver of pure fear raced up his spine. Airway, Breathing, Circulation, Disability, Exposure, he reminded himself, going back to basics as he bent close to Cherie's face, keeping his eyes on her chest for movement as his fingers palpated a carotid pulse.

In the distance, Will heard the sirens, their piercing yelp growing louder. "Breathing shallow and rapid. I've got a carotid, fast and thready."

He needed to give the paramedics as much information as possible when they arrived. He began a head-to-toe assessment, gently palpating the back of Cherie's neck and looking for any fluid draining from her ears which would indicate a skull fracture. He palpated her shoulders and clavicle feeling for any obvious fractures, but without a pain response from the patient, it was a gross exam at best. He ran both hands down her rib cage hoping a broken rib had not punctured her lung. Her abdomen was soft for now. Will checked each hip for any obvious fracture points. Without the x-ray and ultrasound, he was used to having in the ER, he was flying blind out here unable to determine what was happening internally.

Will felt the panic rise in his chest. They had one hour. One golden hour from injury to operating room to give Cherie her best chance at survival. His eyes stung with unshed tears as he forcibly pushed the fear away and turned his concentration to examining Cherie's left arm checking for a radial pulse.

Around the corner of the building two police officers raced to join them with the medical supplies they carried on their cruiser. John greeted his colleagues by name. "Sanchez, how far out are the paramedics and the rig?"

"Less than a minute for the medics," Sanchez replied as his partner opened the jump bag of basic medical supplies. "They were just wrapping up a call not far from here when we got the dispatch. Ambulance is still five minutes out."

"This is Dr. Finnegan from Mercy's ER," John explained. "He's calling the shots 'til the paramedics get here."

Will reached for the BP cuff, wrapping it around Cherie's uninjured arm. "Let's get the pulse oximeter on her and some O2, non-rebreather mask at 15 liters/minute."

He took a quick BP reading, 84/58. Not good. And her breathing was changing. More rapid and shallow. He felt for the carotid again, noting it was faster and still thready. Glancing at the portable monitor, the pulse ox flashed its first reading revealing the level of oxygen in Cherie's blood: 90 and falling. Will could feel his panic fighting to break free.

He heard the slamming of doors and felt a wave of relief as two paramedics, a burly older man and a petite young woman, appeared on the lawn carrying their gear. In those bags were the advanced airway management equipment, drugs and IV supplies they needed to stabilize Cherie for transport.

John recognized them and Will noted his look of relief. "Lisa, Ralph, Dr. Finnegan will fill you in. He works in the ER, and he was at the party when she fell."

Will noted John's careful introduction, leaving out his relationship to the victim. They would never let him help if they knew he and Cherie were dating.

Will launched into his professional assessment. "Cherie Hollister. Thirty-two. Fell from the second floor." He gave a quick rundown of his findings keeping his tone even though it was taking everything in him to stay calm. "She needs to be intubated and two large bore IVs started."

He shot another glance at the pulse oximeter. In the eighties now.

"I've got the airway," Ralph said. "Lisa, get the lines."

John moved out of the way and Ralph laid down on his belly on the grass, his head positioned just above Cherie's as he inserted the laryngoscope into her mouth to visualize the airway. "Doc, can you give me a jaw thrust to open the airway? I don't want to create a spinal cord injury if she doesn't already have one."

Will placed his thumbs underneath Cherie's jawbone just below her ears and pushed the mandible upward without moving the neck. He heard a child's wail and glanced upward, his fingers remaining firmly in place. He took in the scene above, the image lasered into his retina when he returned his gaze to Cherie's ashen face. Judith with her arms wrapped around Molly. Amy holding a crying Sarah in her arms. Kylie standing next to Maddie and holding Carey's face turned away from the scene below. And Gabby Michaels standing protectively in the empty space left by the splintered railing, her eyes lifted to the sky in prayer.

Ralph attempted to pass the tube but couldn't see the vocal cords well enough to thread the tube through the narrow opening to the lungs. He suctioned the airway with the rigid tipped catheter John handed him and then tried again. "I can't get it in."

Will spoke calmly. "Ralph, let me try. I do these every day in the ER, and sometimes a new set of eyes is what we need to help the patient."

Ralph looked up and nodded. "John, take over on the jaw thrust while I suction, and Doc has got the tube."

With no time to second guess himself, Will mimicked Ralph's body position, feeling the wet ground soak through his shirt. He moved his head directly over Cherie's mouth. He couldn't look at her. In this moment, he needed her to be just another patient because if he couldn't intubate her now, she was going to go into cardiac arrest. John opened the airway, and Will saw the problem immediately, his stomach clenching in fear. Feigning calm, he pulled the tube out without attempting placement and changed the angle on the tube by bending it with his fingers until it resembled the letter J, just as he had seen Dr. Patel do that night weeks ago in the ER.

"It'll never go in that way," he heard Lisa whisper as Ralph suctioned the airway.

Will inserted the tube to the back of Cherie's throat, saw the cords but couldn't pass the tip through. Withdrawing it, he changed the angle, ever so slightly and offered up a silent prayer to the God Cherie spoke of with such confidence.

Please, help me.

He inserted the tube and moved it to the back of the airway, trying to visualize the cords.

"Give me some cricoid pressure," he said aloud and watched as the external pressure Ralph applied to the front of the neck created a perfect view of the cords. He advanced the tube and slipped it easily through the small gap between the vocal cords and into the trachea. Will blinked, tears of gratitude blurring his vision. "Let's bag her."

Behind him, he heard the ambulance's motorized stretcher being lowered to the ground. With the endotracheal tube taped in place and the airway secured, John joined the paramedics and EMTs as they log rolled Cherie onto a backboard while Will monitored the airway and squeezed the bag valve mask. They quickly secured the straps and head blocks and lifted the board onto the stretcher, covering the distance to the ambulance in a minute despite the sodden ground.

"Can I ride in with you?" Will asked Lisa as she climbed into the back of the rig.

"Sure Doc, take the jump seat."

John squeezed his shoulder. "We'll meet you there." He closed the doors and pounded on the rear panel, signaling to the driver all was secured.

The ambulance, sirens wailing, pulled out of the restaurant's parking lot headed for Mercy. Will checked his smart watch. 18 minutes on scene.

He glanced up at the cardiac monitor as he continued to squeeze the bag valve mask delivering oxygen to Cherie's lungs and brain. He watched Lisa lift Cherie's eyelids to check for a pupil response with a pen light, feeling his gut clench until the paramedic looked up at him and said, "Equal and reactive."

Behind him, he heard the driver calling into the ER. This was the part he never saw, Will realized in a flash of insight. All the people who worked as a team to bring patients into the ER as quickly and as safely as possible.

Hearing the driver winding up his report, Will turned and asked to speak to the ER. The driver passed the cell phone back over his shoulder and Lisa took over operating the bag valve mask for him.

"Ginger? It's Will."

"You're the doctor on scene who witnessed the fall?" Ginger responded, surprise clear in her tone.

"Yes, can you find Dr. Patel for me? And Ben too, if he's there."

"Will do. The patient's a friend of yours?"

"Yes," he said softly, his mind racing, his world turned upside down in less than an hour.

Taking hold of the bag valve mask once again, he felt the difference immediately. The bag beneath his hands was growing tighter as they covered the last few miles to the hospital. Will fought the panic rising from his gut to his chest as they pulled up the ramp to the ER.

The rear doors swung open as soon as they stopped moving, and Will blew out a sigh of relief as Ben and Anika reached for the stretcher.

"She's getting hard to bag," Will said as they released the stretcher and rolled into the ER. In the background, he could hear Lisa giving her hand-off report to the team as he studied Cherie's beautiful face, the side of her mouth distorted by the endotracheal tube keeping her alive as he continued to breath for her.

At the entrance to the trauma bay, Ben took over for him, and Dr. Patel reached out a hand to stop him. "I've got this Will," she said, blocking his way as she squeezed his forearm before pulling the curtain closed.

"You can't stay here, Will," Ginger said, hooking her arm through his and turning him toward the nearby conference room. "As her family arrives, I'll bring them to you in here."

Feeling grateful for the privacy this would give the family, Will followed her into the very room where he had sat so many times for staff meetings.

"Is she married?" Ginger asked.

Will shook his head. "No, her husband died a few years ago."

"Does she have a medical power of attorney?"

"I don't think so."

"I'm just trying to figure out who we can talk to about her condition."

"Her parents will be here shortly, and I know she recently signed a HIPPA form for some testing at Hopewell Atlantic where she named her sister, Amy … and me."

"She's more than a friend then?"

Will could feel her gentle scrutiny as he nodded. "I'm going to marry her."

"Oh Will, I'm so sorry," Ginger said, reaching out a hand to touch his shoulder. "Sit tight. I'll be back when we know more."

Will sank into a chair at the conference table, leaning forward with his head in his hands. He could still see the look of terror in Cherie's eyes as she fell, her hand reaching for him but with Molly in his arms he could do nothing to help her. Behind closed lids, his eyes stung with unshed tears. She had risked her life to save Molly, and now Cherie might lose her own. No, he shook his head, forcefully pushing that thought away. Cherie's family would be here soon, and he needed to be optimistic for them. And the girls? What must be happening to them right now?

The door opened and John rushed in followed by Jake.

"Anything yet?" John asked.

"They're still examining her," Will responded, getting to his feet. "Who has the girls?"

"Amy took all the kids back to our house, and your niece offered to go with her and help. Joe and Judith are right behind us. Your sister was following Paster Michaels over here."

"Any change on the way in?" Jake asked. "Looked like she wasn't even responsive to pain."

Startled by that insight, Will studied Cherie's brother. Not many people outside the medical profession would understand the use of supraorbital pressure to check for pain. "She is still deeply unconscious, at least for now." He turned to John. "I want to thank you. You knew just what I needed you to do."

"I've done hundreds of medical calls in my career, but I was as scared as I have ever been on that one," John admitted, running a hand through his hair.

The door opened again and with the arrival of Judith and Joe followed by Gabby and Maddie, the room grew full. Judith rushed over to him.

Will saw the raw fear in her eyes, the sheer terror that was mounting with each minute that passed. He squeezed her hand. "No word yet, we should hear something soon."

Will glanced at the clock, 42 minutes since the accident. He knew exactly what they were doing in that trauma bay to save Cherie. So many times, in the last four years, he had done the same, the time flying by as they assessed and treated, all while the family waited in agony to hear the outcome of their work. By the time he was ready to speak to them, the ER staff had taken the family to a private waiting room to give them the privacy they would need to hear his words, often difficult words. Frantically, Will looked up at the family gathered in the conference room. Was that what they were doing here?

Maddie's hand settled on his back; her words whispered close to his ear. "Don't give into it, Will, that panic that is raging inside you right now. Trust in God."

"I can't find it, Maddie, the faith that Cherie believes in with her whole heart. I can't find the words to pray," he answered softly.

"Then do it for Cherie while she can't do it for herself. Stand in that gap of faith -- that place that you can't seem to cross -- and call out to the God she loves on her behalf."

Will turned his head to meet her gaze. "Even if I don't believe it myself? Why would God listen to me now when I've barely given him a second thought for most of my life?"

"Because He listens to all of us, because He loves Cherie like you do … no, more than you do."

Will shook his head, tears welling up in his eyes. "That's not possible. I love Cherie with my whole heart."

"I know you do, and as hard as this is to fathom, God loves her more. He created her, He loved her then and He loves her now. Trust Him."

A knock sounded on the door before Dr. Patel stepped into the room. After introducing herself to everyone, Anika asked. "Is Amy here?"

On his feet now, Will shook his head. "No, she's taking care of Cherie's children."

"Then you are the one I need to talk to," Dr. Patel said. "We contacted Hopewell Atlantic, and they sent over a copy of the HIPPA form Cherie signed a few weeks ago. Can we speak outside?"

Will glanced around the room. "No, we can all hear it together. These are Cherie's parents and some of the rest of her family."

Dr. Patel nodded, addressing the group. "The injuries Cherie sustained from the fall are not limited to one body system. Multiple system trauma," she said, looking over at Will, "makes our job more difficult. But our priority is surgery to address a subdural hematoma, a collection of blood pressing on Cherie's brain that is growing larger. The neurosurgery team has evaluated the CAT scan, and they are taking her to surgery as we speak."

Will closed his eyes in pain, knowing the situation must be life-threatening if they were going to the OR without obtaining consent from the family. He glanced at the clock: 56 minutes.

"We were able to stabilize her collapsed lung by placing a chest tube," Anika continued. "She also sustained a clavicle fracture and a broken bone in her left arm."

Will knew Dr. Patel was doing the very thing he had done with so many families of trauma patients, choosing words that would make them aware of the serious nature of the injuries but wouldn't scare them, leaving some room for hope.

"We did a full assessment and found no bleeding in her abdomen or any additional fractures," Anika continued. "According to the paramedics on scene, the ground was softer than they expected due to the rain and that has made a difference in her injury pattern. She appears to have taken the brunt of the fall to her upper back and head. The x-ray and CAT scan show no spinal fractures which is a blessing given the mechanism of her injury."

Anika met Will's gaze with a professional nod, having assuaged one of his biggest fears.

"Who is the in-house neurosurgeon tonight?" Will asked.

"Dr. Garrison," Anika Patel said with the first break in her professional demeanor.

A wave of relief flooded through Will at the name of the vice-chair of the neurosurgery department. Cherie was in the best hands they had here at Mercy.

"Thank you, Anika," Will said, stepping over to her, and seeing the angst she felt having delivered this news to a colleague and friend. "I'm so glad you were here tonight. I know you don't usually work weekends."

"I took Matt Hampton's shift so he could go to a family party. Glad I did." She reached out a hand, squeezing his arm. "The medics told me they had a hard time with the airway in the field, and you were the one who intubated her."

"I did. Good thing I learned from the best."

Anika hugged him quickly. "Hold a good thought, Will. Cherie's in great hands."

After she left, Will turned back to the family and found them all gathered around the table.

Pastor Michaels held out a hand to him. "We didn't want to start without you."

Will nodded, knowing this was what they needed. He stepped up to the table and joined hands with Maddie and Gabby completing the circle before they all bowed their heads. He had done this many times with the families of his patients, and then, as now, he felt like an outsider in this circle of faith.

Pastor Michaels' rich alto voice broke the silence.

"Heavenly Father, we stand here tonight and ask for your divine intervention in the healing of your precious child, Cherie. We beseech you to take control of that operating room and to guide the hands of the surgeon, the anesthesia team, the nurses, and technicians, to bring about healing in Cherie's body and to safeguard her mind."

Will nodded his agreement. Getting through the surgery was just the first step of what would be a long recovery.

"We know that where two or three are gathered in your name," Gabby continued softly, "you are there in their midst. We ask that you restore Cherie to full health without deficit of any kind, that she may be able to come home to those who love her very soon. And we ask that you help us to offer comfort and love to her precious children who have witnessed what happened to their mother."

Tears stung Will's eyes at the mention of Cherie's daughters, the girls she loved more than life itself.

"You know we are scared, Lord, terrified to our very core for this woman we love, but you can do more than we can ask or imagine, and with thanksgiving in our hearts for what you are about to do, we leave this in your hands, in Jesus' name. Amen."

She paused then asked, "Does anyone else have anything they would like to pray for?"

Around the table silence lingered for a moment until one by one the family started to add their heartfelt pleas, voices raised to a God they all believed in. Hearing their faith, Will wished he could find it in himself, but he could not.

Joe cleared his throat the last to speak, clearly trying to make his words heard despite his distress. "And Father, one final prayer," he said, the tenor of his words growing stronger. "We want to thank you for Will, for his swift action after the accident, and his ability to place that tube and save Cherie's life. And Lord, I want to thank you for placing this man in my daughter's life. He has brought the gleam back to her eyes and the dreams back to her future. He has opened her heart to love again, and for that great gift and all you are about to do to bring that future about, I thank you. Amen."

The group voiced a joined Amen as Will covered his face with his hands, his shoulders shaking as he finally gave in to his tears.

Chapter Eighteen

Close to eleven and still they waited. John had gone home to help Amy and Kylie get the kids to bed. Maddie had lingered, not wanting to leave Will until an hour ago when he had given her the keys to his condo and directions to Amy's house so she could pick up Kylie. He had promised to call if he heard anything. Which left Cherie's parents and Jake. Will knew that Judith would never consider going home until they heard from the neurosurgeon about Cherie's condition.

The surgical waiting area, spacious and open, was empty at this time of night. Will retrieved a bottle of water from the vending machine, twisted the cap and took a long sip.

"This is taking a long time," Jake said, stepping up next to Will, his eyes on his parents huddled together by the window. "Shouldn't they be done by now if it was just an evacuation of a hematoma?"

Will glanced over at him. "Neurosurgery is a tricky business. You never know exactly what you're going to find until you get in there. Longer isn't necessarily bad as long as they relieve the pressure."

"Are they still using burr holes or is it a full craniotomy?"

Will studied Jake, wondering where a church groundskeeper had gained that insight into the history of neurosurgery. "Something you're not telling me, Jake?"

He glanced over at his parents. "I was keeping it to myself until I finished my training, but I've been studying to be a paramedic for the last year. I've been on the receiving end of their care, and I know what they do saves a lot of lives."

Silently, Will debated speaking the obvious, but then plunged ahead. "With that training you know Cherie will no longer be an eligible donor?"

"I don't care about any of that," Jake replied, his tone strident as he tried to keep his voice low in the quiet waiting area. "It never felt right to me, you know that. All I want right now is for Cherie to come through this surgery and go home to her girls. Whatever happens to me doesn't matter."

Will could hear the sincerity in his tone and regretted bringing up the transplant, though he was honest enough to admit he had wanted to see Jake's reaction. Having done so, Will felt not relief but shame.

Will spotted Dr. Garrison covering the distance down the long hallway from the OR to the waiting area. A tall man in his late forties, he tossed his surgical cap in the trash revealing a full head of gray hair flattened by the cap he'd worn for hours of surgery. Will could see his fatigue in his shortened stride and pale coloring. Between his hair and the pallor of his skin, he looked like a ghost moving toward them as Will felt a cold shiver shoot up his spine. He tried to read the man's carefully neutral expression, but gave up, knowing he was about to hear the outcome of the surgery from the man who had brought it about.

"Will, let's sit down," Dr. Garrison said with a light touch to his shoulder.

"I'm going to wait with Mom and Dad," Jake said, giving them some space.

Will turned all his attention to the surgeon who led the way to a private waiting room. "How is she?"

Garrison took a seat across from Will getting right to the point. "We were able to evacuate the hematoma. Identifying the source of the bleeding took some time and establishing hemostasis longer still. We are keeping her sedated and allowing the brain swelling to resolve which may take several days."

"So, she's in a medically induced coma," Will said, having expected this but still fighting his disappointment.

"Yes, we will monitor her intracranial pressure and hope to withdraw the sedation in the next two days. We won't know anything about her long-term prognosis until then. As you know, the course of recovery for patients with traumatic brain injury is as individual as they are."

"But she's stable?" Will asked, sensing concern and exhaustion in the surgeon's demeanor.

"She is," Garrison replied. "We had a period during the surgery when her vital signs fluctuated but getting control of the bleeding stabilized the rest."

"Transfusion?"

"Two units."

Which explained the lengthy surgical time, Will thought, his anxiety growing. He recalled sitting in the Hopewell Atlantic cafeteria with Cherie and telling her he wanted to be the family member who got to hear the answers. It had all seemed so abstract then; he'd had no idea the reality would be so gut-wrenching. "Can I see her?"

"Yes, of course, though I will ask you to wait until they transfer her from the recovery room to the ICU."

"Cherie's parents are waiting outside. When can they see her?"

"Let's just have you for tonight and tomorrow morning her parents can come to the ICU."

"Thank you, Dr. Garrison," Will said, getting to his feet, knowing he needed to talk with Judith and Joe. And Jake.

"Will, you can call me Keith."

Looking up, Will met his gaze. "I'm glad you were there tonight, Keith."

"I'm very glad as well."

A chill of pure fear shook Will's shoulders. Had it been that bad? He knew most neurosurgeons thought highly of their own skill level, but the subtle inference that the outcome of the surgery might have been different in lesser hands was unmistakable.

Garrison reached into the breast pocket of his scrubs and handed Will his card. "This is my personal cell number. Call me if you have any questions."

"Thank you. I'll do that."

"I heard Cherie is your fiancée."

"I'm wishing now I had made that more official than just a conversation, but yes."

"She's young, Will, with a strong heart. She can pull through this," Keith added. "But a little prayer wouldn't hurt, if you're so inclined."

Surprised, Will studied the surgeon. "I don't think I have ever met a neurosurgeon who believes in prayer."

"You'd be surprised," Keith replied with a weary smile as they turned toward the door. "As a surgeon, you can either stare at the brain every day and think of it as just another organ in need of fixing or you can marvel at how this collection of cells produces conscious thoughts and feelings. The complexity of the brain is like the harmonics of music, unexplainable in its origin and perfect in its function. I'm not ready to rule out the possibility of a great designer for either one." He extended his hand to Will in parting. "It was my pleasure and privilege to help Cherie. I'll talk to you tomorrow."

Watching him walk away, Will marveled that of all the neurosurgeons on staff at Mercy, Cherie had drawn by pure happenstance the one who believed as she did. Keith Garrison believed not only in a God who created, but also in a God who cares, who hears and answers prayer.

Crossing the waiting area to speak to Cherie's family, he managed a smile, and instantly saw the relief on their faces. He remembered what Cherie had told him about waiting to hear the news about Molly the night of the fire, that every moment had been an agony of fear. He wasn't putting her parents through that one second longer than he had to. Cherie was alive and stable. Their prayers had been answered and a major hurdle spanned. What was left was the healing and the waiting.

* * *

Will pulled a chair up to the ICU bed and gently captured Cherie's hand. After nearly twelve hours of terror, the chance to touch her was irresistible. He wasn't afraid of all the IV's, the arterial line, and the monitoring leads. If anything, they gave him comfort. The steady wheezing of the ventilator's bellows breathing for Cherie. The regular rhythm of the cardiac monitor on the screen above the bed. The oxygen saturation monitor with its steady audible beep, letting him know all was stable and Cherie was alive.

Will lifted his eyes to her face, the endotracheal tube distorting the side of her mouth. Reaching out, he gently ran one finger up her forehead, finally coming up against the white kerlix dressing that covered her hair. His hand cupped the side of her head, his gaze lingering on the stillness of her face.

In the past few weeks as the details of the transplant were finalized, he had seen so many emotions play across her features. Everyday moments that produced expressions of contentment, like the evening he had looked up from reading Carey and Sarah a story to find Cherie leaning against the door frame, her mouth lifted in a soft smile. He had watched annoyance furrow her brow as Molly stalled for time before bed or Carey went from finger painting at the table to climbing down from the chair and leaving a trail of purple and pink on every surface in her wake. What Will had discovered in the last few weeks was the joy and hard work of taking care of three children, trying to keep them safe, entertained and thriving. He bent his head and kissed the back of Cherie's hand then pillowed his head on his folded arms, turning to watch her.

Somewhere inside this medically induced stillness was the vibrant, intelligent woman he had come to cherish. Will studied the placid nature of Cherie's unconscious features so different from natural sleep. He had seen her drift off while watching a movie together, and even in sleep her features retained a semblance of their waking state. The slight grimace as she turned her head to find a more comfortable position, the soft regular exhale that was almost a snore, and the relaxation of her features as he covered her with her favorite blanket.

In forty-eight hours, the medical team would withdraw the drugs keeping her still and her conscious mind would rise to the surface. She would open her eyes and tell him she loved him. Will closed his eyes, compelling himself to believe it. He refused to even consider any other outcome but that the medical profession he had given his life to, could now save the woman he loved. And with that firmly established in his mind, sheer exhaustion won out and he slept.

* * *

He woke to the gentle shake of his shoulder and looked up to find Judith, her eyes puffy and bloodshot, staring down at him.

"What time is it?" Will asked, sitting up in the chair and feeling the strain in his back.

"Just after eight. What time did they let you in last night?" Judith asked.

"Around 4:00, after the ICU staff got her situated."

Joe rolled his wheelchair up to the foot of the bed, his gaze riveted to his daughter's face. "You said last night we won't know anything about when she'll wake up until at least tomorrow?"

Will heard the slight break in his voice. "Yes, but Cherie's vital signs are stable, she's not in any pain and her body is getting a chance to heal. I know it feels like a holding pattern and you want answers ..."

"We just want her to wake up and if this is what she needs right now, we can wait," Joe said simply.

"We went by to have breakfast with the girls, and Carey's been asking for you," Judith said, her hand flitting over the blanket and then finally settling on the bed railing.

"While you're here, I'm going to head over to Amy's and see them. How are they?"

"Scared. Asking a lot of questions we don't have the answers to. Missing their mom, mostly," Joe answered.

Judith clasped her hands under her chin, her eyes brimming. "I don't even know where I can touch her."

Will got to his feet, realizing that the equipment he found so reassuring was terrifying to Cherie's parents, especially the intracranial pressure monitor poking out of the dressing on her head.

"Judith, come sit here," Will said, drawing her over to the chair he had vacated. "You can hold her hand just steer clear of the IV lines."

Judith sank onto the seat, tears spilling down her cheeks as she touched her daughter's hand. "How can this be happening? Hasn't she been through enough?"

Will squeezed her shoulder. This strong, assertive woman looked broken and frail, her hair unbrushed, her eyes puffy and devoid of makeup. He had no answers to give her, nothing he could say would make this time of waiting easier. Cherie would have told them to pray, but Will could no more say the words than he could make their beautiful daughter whole again. Having no answers to Judith's questions or his own, Will defaulted to the clinical. "The ICU staff are only going to let you stay for fifteen minutes, but you can go to the family waiting area and come back in later."

"We'll be fine, Will. We just need a few minutes with her," Joe said, gently resting a hand on Cherie's leg. "Go and see the girls. They need you."

Will nodded, knowing these loving parents needed this time just as he had last night. In the doorway, he glanced back as Joe bent his head and kissed his daughter's covered feet. And much as he wanted to stay with Cherie, he knew he was needed elsewhere.

* * *

"Doc Finn," Carey shouted. She ran to him at full speed and Will dropped into a squat, her sturdy little body colliding with his chest as she wrapped her arms around his neck and held on tight.

"How is she?" Amy asked, holding Sarah's hand in hers. "We've been best pals all morning just waiting to hear."

"When's mommy coming home?" Sarah asked, looking at Will.

"Your mommy needs some time to rest before she can come home," Will said, sitting on the floor with Carey in his lap. "How's Molly?"

Amy followed suit, holding Sarah as the four of them sat face to face. "She's not talking, not even to Mark."

"She doesn't want to talk 'cuz Mommy fell," Sarah said, staring at Will. "But you helped her."

Will nodded. "I did, and then we took your mom to the hospital and she's sleeping now so her body can start to feel better."

"See her?" Carey asked, turning her face up to Will, her eyes wide and trusting. Will swallowed hard, trying to find his voice.

"The hospital doesn't allow children to visit," Amy answered for him. "We may have to wait a few days until your mom is ready to come home."

"How many days?" Molly stepped into view around the wall dividing the family room from the entryway.

Will looked up to find Molly staring directly at him with a look on her young face that demanded the truth. He chose his words carefully. "We don't know exactly how many days she will have to stay in the hospital, not yet."

"Did she have a surgery?" Molly asked. "Like in those medical shows on TV?"

"Yes, she did, to clean out the head wound so it could start to heal." Will shifted his position, sensing what was coming.

"Did they cut her hair off?"

"They had to cut some of it, yes."

"Can I see her on Facetime?" Molly asked, her lower lip beginning to quiver, her eyes full, as tears started to roll down her cheeks.

"When she wakes up, we could do that," Will said, handing Carey to Amy and getting to his feet, picturing Cherie as he had just left her.

"She's dead, isn't she? Like my dad," Molly whispered fiercely, her eyes wide with fear before she spun and ran from the room.

"I've got her," Will said, over his shoulder as he raced after Cherie's distraught daughter.

He saw the bedroom door slam shut and drew in a deep breath reaching for the doorknob. If he was a praying man this would be the time for it, and knowing he was completely out of his depth, he whispered under his breath, "I need a little help here." It wasn't a prayer so much as a statement of fact as he opened the door to find Molly curled up on the twin bed, her shoulders heaving with wrenching sobs.

He sat down beside her. "She's not dead, Molly. I promise you that. When I left the hospital to come here, she was sleeping, and your Grandy and Pop were right there with her."

"It's all my fault," she sobbed, crying even harder. "She fell because of me!" Molly spun to face him, her face puffy and red, her cheeks wet with tears, her nose running. "I saw your face. You wanted to help her, but you couldn't because you were holding me."

Which was the truth, Will thought, knowing at the same time he would never say it aloud. The words came to him in a flash of insight. "I love your mom, you know that, right?"

Molly nodded.

"And you also know how much your mom loves you. You are everything to her, Molly. Her whole world. You and your sisters. She gave you to me, so I could keep you safe, and that's what I did, because she loves you that much." Will reached over and wiped her face with the sleeve of his shirt. "She's going to be okay, Molly. The doctors are going to help her get better."

"And you, too?"

"Me, too. I'm going to be there every day, helping your mom so she can come home to you and to me."

"And then you're going to marry her, right?"

"Yes. Are you okay with that?"

"She smiles and laughs a lot more now that you're around." Molly nodded, her face still solemn but no longer covered with tears. "Would that make you, my father?"

Will met Molly's lifted gaze. "No one can ever replace your father, Molly, and I'm not trying to do that, so when your mom and I get married you can call me whatever you like. Doc Finn would still work."

Molly studied him for a moment, her brow furrowed before coming to a decision. "I think I'm going to want to call you … Dad."

Will felt his heart break at her words, and he only hoped someday very soon that would be true.

* * *

Will opened the door of his condo to the smell of bacon and toast. In his worries about Cherie, he had almost forgotten he had given his keys to Maddie last night. She appeared in the kitchen archway, drying her hands on a dish towel, her eyes wide with expectation and a touch of fear. Beyond her shoulder, Will saw Kylie get to her feet.

"Amy called. She said you were headed home to change," Maddie said, closing the distance between them and giving him a quick hug. "I know you want to get right back to the hospital, but you need to eat something before you do."

Will opened his mouth to protest before his stomach, reacting to the familiar aromas, reminded him he hadn't eaten anything since yesterday morning. He could sit for five minutes. "It's good to have a big sister looking out for me." He wrapped his arms around her, holding her close for a moment and drawing from her the strength he needed to bolster his own.

He followed her to the kitchen table as Kylie poured a cup of coffee for him.

"I woke up to your text this morning," Maddie said, producing from the oven a warm plate filled with scrambled eggs, bacon, and toast. "How was she when you left?"

She set it in front of him as he took a seat and reached for the coffee, a caffeine lifeline he would need to make it through the day. "She's stable. Judith and Joe are there now. I'm headed back as soon as I change." He glanced down at the dress shirt he wore, the front stiff with dirt from lying on the wet ground while placing the tube Cherie needed to breathe. Was it only yesterday? It seemed like so long ago now.

He didn't think he could manage more than a few mouthfuls of the meal set before him, but the buttery eggs and crisp bacon went down easily along with a bowl of mixed fruit Maddie set at his side.

"I know you're going to be spending all your time with Cherie, and we don't want to be in the way, so Kylie and I are going to head home this morning," Maddie said, smiling as she watched his appetite win out over his anxiety. "But if you need me, I can be back in just a few hours."

"I appreciate the offer. I'll call you if I need to take you up on it," Will answered, turning his attention to Kylie. "I want to thank you for helping Amy with the girls and for taking care of Carey yesterday. When I looked up and saw she was in good hands, that was one less thing I needed to worry about."

"I'm glad I could help, Uncle Will," Kylie replied, the maturity in her gaze reminding Will her family had had their own recent struggles.

"You are good under pressure. Kylie. Maybe you should consider a career in medicine."

She smiled at him. "Already giving that some thought."

Will caught the look of pride on Maddie's face as he finished his coffee and got to his feet. "I'm just going to grab a quick shower. Maddie, thank you for this. I didn't think I was hungry, but clearly my body knows what it needs even if my mind is too preoccupied to care."

Standing under a warm shower moments later, he used the shampoo on his head for the rest of his body making quick work of getting clean. Letting the powerful shower head rinse the soap from his hair, he felt so grateful for Maddie. Having her here had made this whole nightmare just a bit easier, and though he wouldn't ask her to stay, he knew he would be calling to give her regular updates. He hadn't even known how much he missed having a family until Maddie had appeared in his life again. Out of nowhere, so random, and yet she was here when he needed her. Will marveled at the timing, so thankful he didn't have to do this alone.

By the time he returned wearing jeans and a sweatshirt, his hair still wet, the kitchen was pristine, and Kylie was putting their bags in the car.

"Maddie, thank you," Will said, giving voice to his thoughts. "I can't tell you how much it meant to have you there with me last night. I love Cherie's family, but last night I needed mine." He took her hands in his. "I'm just so grateful you are in my life right now."

"I wondered why, after all these years, you kept coming to mind," Maddie said, looking up at him. "And then I finally stopped ignoring the obvious and just called you. I didn't know why either, until now. God knew what you would need in this moment, and He started providing it months ago."

"I'm having a very hard time believing in God right now," Will said, the tenor of his voice shifting from gratitude to the darker tones of bitterness. "I listened to all of you praying last night, and I was left with only one thought: how could God let this happen to her?"

Maddie squeezed his hand, her words soft as she drew him over to the table and sat down. "I can't tell you why accidents happen. No one on this earth can explain it in any way that makes sense, but I know that from the moment Cherie fell, she has been in God's hands."

Will took a seat facing her. "That might be wishful thinking, Maddie. I don't want to belittle your belief but ..."

"Will, believe me when I tell you I was right where you are two years ago, filled with pain and rage. Angry at God for a life-threatening diagnosis, guilty at my own behavior. I felt lost and abandoned until God sent my own husband to save me."

Will listened, not knowing what to say. He had to admit Maddie was very different from the college kid he remembered as more concerned with her hair and makeup then she was the existential issues they were discussing now. Clearly, she had matured in the intervening years, but the change in her felt like something else. Like faith.

"You sound like Cherie." Will ran a hand through his wet hair. "She speaks so easily about the God who loves her, but this doesn't feel like love to me. How can this be part of God's plan?"

"God didn't cause this to happen ..." Maddie began.

"But He didn't stop it either," Will cut in.

Maddie held onto his hands, leaning forward, their knees touching. "That's true, but there's a difference between actively making something happen and intervening afterward to ease the consequences."

"Kind of splitting hairs, aren't you?" Will countered, shaking his head. "But even if it's true, and this is all some terrible accident, and that railing was just weak and going to give way, why did it have to happen when Molly was standing there. Why not earlier or later?"

"When someone else was standing there, you mean? So, it's okay if it happened to someone else, just not to your family?" Maddie said softly.

Will met her gaze. "Okay, I know that sounds selfish and awful."

"Let's just say it was someone else. What if that person didn't believe in God and didn't have a dozen family members praying for them from the moment it happened. What if it happened to someone older, too frail to survive the fall?" Maddie paused, letting that thought linger. "Cherie acted to save her child. Call it instinct, call it maternal love, but she chose to put her life at risk to save Molly, and I believe with all my heart that God knew she would do that, and He had been laying the groundwork to deal with the aftermath."

"Like some cosmic confluence of events? Seems like a stretch," Will said.

"I don't know how these rescues usually go but didn't it seem like everything happened quickly? The police arrived so fast and the medics, too. Does it usually happen that way? Or was it somewhere in God's providence that the paramedics would be just a minute away when we needed them."

Will remembered his relief when he'd seen them appear around the side of the building carrying the very equipment he needed to help Cherie.

"Even meeting you, Will. Without you there, it might have taken much longer to get that tube in the right place."

Will shuddered, a tremor of fear making his shoulders quiver. Any delay at that point in the rescue would have cost Cherie her life. That hematoma was getting bigger and in a confined space like the skull, the pressure could have created a brain herniation and Cherie would have died. He wasn't conceding the point, but Maddie was right about the timing; it had been quick.

"I need to get back to the hospital," Will said, getting to his feet.

"Of course, let's walk out together," Maddie said, scooping up the keys in the middle of the table and handing them to him. "Don't forget these."

Will pocketed the keys and still holding on to Maddie's hand, they walked out to the cars. He gave Kylie a quick hug before watching her climb into the driver's side of the SUV.

Turning to Maddie, he said, "Thank you for breakfast. I am listening, Maddie, but right now I don't feel like I have the strength to deal with all of this and God, too."

"I get it, I do, but I believe something good can come out of this horror you are living through right now. I am living proof that dawn follows the darkness." Stretching to her full height, she kissed his cheek. "Take care, little brother, I'll call you later today."

Will watched as they drove off, feeling as alone as he'd ever felt in his life.

* * *

Maddie turned in the passenger seat, catching a last glimpse of Will. The sight of him, standing alone in the driveway, made her eyes fill with tears.

"We could have stayed, Mom," Kylie said, breaking into her thoughts. "Classes in June are a joke. I wouldn't be missing much."

"Just the review for finals." Maddie wiped her eyes with the heel of her hand. "Besides, I think your Uncle Will needs his space now, but we're going to keep praying for him and for Cherie and the girls."

"Uncle Will doesn't believe in God, does he?"

"Your Uncle Will believes in medicine and in himself. And right now, neither one can fix this for him."

"So, what would it hurt to pray then?" Kylie asked.

"A very logical question from a girl who already believes," Maddie said with a smile.

Kylie checked the rearview mirror before changing lanes. "When God is all you have, you find out God is all you need."

"Sounds like a bumper sticker. Where did you see that?" Maddie asked, wondering where her daughter had found the insight.

Kylie shook her head, her eyes on the road. "I didn't see it, Mom, I lived it."

Startled Maddie turned to study her daughter's serious profile. "When I was sick, you mean?"

Kyie nodded. "People make it so hard. Why not just ask for the thing you want?" Kylie shrugged her shoulders with a soft smile. "Though I guess I didn't really believe it either until I saw God answer the one prayer I'd been praying for years."

"Care to share?" Maddie asked, intrigued but not really expecting a straight answer.

"The weird thing was cancer sounded like the worst thing ever, but then it was the answer," Kylie mused.

"To what?"

"To you and Dad loving each other again."

Speechless, Maddie simply stared at her beautiful daughter.

"You just have to keep asking for what you want," Kylie nodded. "Can we stop for a latte?"

227

Chapter Nineteen

On Wednesday morning, Will stood in the ICU bay and watched the nurse shut off the infusions keeping Cherie sedated. Resuming his seat at her side, he reached for her hand and began the wait. For a patient like Cherie with traumatic brain injury, the return to consciousness was not simply a matter of withdrawing the cocktail of medications that had kept her still. So much depended on the extent of injury to the brain and the amount of time the neurons did not receive their full complement of oxygen due to pressure and impaired circulation.

As Cherie's family came and went throughout the day, Will stepped outside in keeping with the ICU policy on having no more than two visitors at a time. During one of these downtimes yesterday, he had been able to arrange dialysis for Jake here at Mercy keeping him on his Tuesday, Thursday, Saturday schedule. After each visit as Cherie's family returned to the waiting area, Will would then resume his place at her side, desperately hoping something would have changed in response to these visits from the people Cherie loved. But as the day gave way to evening with no change in her condition, Will could feel his hope giving way to dread.

Shortly after 8:00 p.m., after sending everyone home to get some food and sleep, Will returned to the ICU to find Dr. Patel waiting for him.

"They're going to do a breathing trial tomorrow," Will said, stepping up next to her at the foot of the bed.

"They need to get her off the vent if they can. Pulmonary fibrosis is a real concern with long term ventilator use," Anika said, turning to Will. "The nurses tell me you've been sleeping here. You know as well as I do that there's no way of knowing when Cherie will come out of this."

"And I want to be here when she does."

"Being here 24/7 won't make that happen any faster, and the hard work starts when she wakes up. Go home, Will."

"Good advice. How's the ER?" Will said, trying to redirect her focus.

"As busy as ever. We'll be glad to have you back when you're ready."

"And I'll be glad to be back when this is over," Will said, waving a hand at the monitors, pumps, and drains. "Turns out I'm not very good at waiting."

"None of us are," Anika said, placing a hand on his shoulder. "We want to give the answers, not wait for someone else to give them to us. I'll check in tomorrow."

Will took his seat resuming his vigil, his gaze resting on Cherie's still countenance. Without her laughter, her quick wit and gentle smile, Will realized he was starting to think of her as a patient. The shift was a subtle one, and likely one only another healthcare worker would understand. He found his attention focused on the physical findings of monitors and vital signs. As a new resident, it had served him well, helping him maintain an emotional distance from the tragedy his patients were facing. If he got lost in their emotions, he would never be able to do his job. Yet, he still needed to treat each patient as an individual, to never lose sight of the fact the person in front of him was more than just an injury or a disease process. Like a tight rope walker at the circus, it was necessary to find the balance if you were to do the job well.

As each hour passed without Cherie waking, Will could feel the clinical data taking over his thoughts as he retreated from the emotions hiding behind the medically mundane. He wasn't ready to stare down the terror, to even allow a whisper of panic to creep into his thoughts. Because if he truly focused on Cherie and allowed himself to linger on her overflowing love for her children, on the memories of her warm smile looking up at him, then he would be useless. To Cherie. To her parents. To her beautiful daughters.

Will shifted his gaze from the ICP monitor to Cherie's face. The exterior was still the same, still lovely, but where was the rest? He had waited a lifetime to find someone he could love with all his heart and hadn't even known what that truly meant until he met Cherie. And here she was, still beautiful but ... gone. Where was Cherie right now, her consciousness no longer suppressed by drugs? And was she ever coming back?

Will could feel the panic rising from his gut to squeeze the breath from his chest, the tremor in his shoulders igniting a fire in his brain. His fingers curled into a fist around the coarse cotton blanket in blinding rage, grasping for someone, anyone to blame. And finding only one outlet.

"What kind of a God are you?" he whispered, his tone thick with wrath. "How could you let this happen to her?"

* * *

Will found Judith and Joe in the waiting room the next morning talking with Amy and Jake. John was getting all the kids off to school this morning, reestablishing their routine to occupy this time of waiting. At least he finally had some good news to share, Will thought, watching them surge to their feet as he came through the door.

"The breathing trial went well," Will said. "They were able to pull the endotracheal tube. Cherie's breathing on her own."

"Is she awake?" Judith asked.

Will shook his head. "No, she is still in a coma, but the fact she is breathing spontaneously is a good sign. Her brain is healing. Hopefully, it won't be much longer before she regains consciousness but as we talked about yesterday, each patient's course of reemergence from coma is different."

"And we won't know anything about her long-term prognosis until she does," Jake said.

Will met his gaze. "That's right."

Jake had been placed back on the transplant list as of Monday. Now without a living donor, he awaited a match from a deceased donor, a brain-dead victim of an injury or stroke whose family chose to donate their organs. The average wait time in the United States for a kidney was 5 years and for some, depending on blood type and other factors, it could be much longer. Many of those would die of complications from their end-stage renal disease before a donor was found.

"Cherie's intracranial pressure is normal, and they will most likely remove the ICP monitor tomorrow as well. She's making progress."

"Thank God," Joe said, casting an assessing glance at Will's weary smile and wrinkled scrubs. "Will, you need to go home. You've been here with Cherie for the last four days."

Will glanced down at the scrubs he hadn't bothered to change since relegating his jeans and sweatshirt to his locker. "I'm headed home this morning while you are all here with Cherie. A shower sounds like a great idea."

"Will they keep her here in the ICU?" Judith asked.

"Yes, for now," Will answered, knowing the ICU's limited bed space might be a problem if sicker patients needed their specialized care. Technically, Cherie was stable physically, healing from her craniotomy, her pneumothorax resolved. If her condition remained the same, they would have to transfer her to a regular floor.

Will didn't want to consider anything beyond that. Cherie was going to regain consciousness soon. She was young and healthy before the fall, and she was coming back to him. He had to believe that, refused to even consider the alternative as he headed home.

Until the alternative became his reality.

* * *

Will stepped off the elevator, nodding at the nursing staff he had come to know well in the last two weeks. Cherie had been transferred to this specialized floor ten days after her initial surgery. The staff here had extensive experience dealing with patients in coma.

A week after Cherie's transfer and with no significant change in her condition, Will had returned to work. He spent his days in the ER and his nights in the recliner next to Cherie's hospital bed, holding her hand as she slept. His only break from the hospital was to visit the girls every few days at Judith and Joe's where they were now living. Molly and Sarah were quiet, sometimes tearful, and Carey often clung to Will with a desperation that broke his heart. They wanted their mom to come home, couldn't understand why that wasn't happening, and Will couldn't explain to them what he could not understand himself.

Today the emergency room had been remarkably quiet, odd for a Wednesday, and with only a few hours left on his shift, Dr. Patel had sent him home to sleep. He was going to sleep. Just not at home.

Coming through the door, he found Cherie much as he had left her before starting his shift this morning. Now she lay on her left side, having been repositioned by the nursing staff, her face turned to the late afternoon light that shone through the window. Will stopped at the foot of the bed, arrested by the pallor of her skin and her beautiful face devoid of any expression. If he hadn't seen the even rise and fall of her breathing, he might have thought she was gone.

"Will?"

Startled, he spun to find Dr. Garrison standing in the doorway, wearing green scrubs and a white lab coat, his gray hair neatly combed. "Still no change?"

Will shook his head.

"My team has been following Cherie's recovery since her transfer from the ICU," Garrison said.

Will watched the surgeon carefully choosing his next words. Will had done the same thing often enough to recognize the pregnant pause. "Does her family know that at this point she's unlikely to have any meaningful recovery?"

Will flinched, hearing the stark prognosis he had chosen to ignore spoken so plainly. "No, not definitively. I wanted to wait until we were outside the 4-week window."

"Coming up on that in a few days," Garrison said, his tone quiet and kind.

"I was hoping ..." Will's words fell away, his throat suddenly so tight he couldn't move enough air to make another sound. Confronted by the surgeon who had saved Cherie's life, Will felt the walls he had erected to protect himself begin to crumble under the pressure of elapsing time.

"You might want to start preparing them. I read the note from case management in her chart. She's going to need a long-term placement soon."

Will shook his head, barely able to imagine what telling Cherie's parents about her prognosis would do to them, to all of them. "They know her condition is serious, but they're praying for a miracle."

"Have you been praying for her?" Keith asked, advancing into the room to stand beside Will.

"She has dozens of people praying for her. Her family. Her church. They held a candlelight vigil last night with people staying all night to pray for her."

"But not you. Why?"

"Because I can't believe in a God who steals a mother from her children and a child from her parents," Will answered, his tone caustic.

"You're angry."

"Angry doesn't even begin to cover it." The words poured from Will's soul like a dam breaking free. "I turned my whole life upside down to join this profession, so I could save families from this kind of agony, and now I can't save the one person who matters most to me, the woman I love with every breath of my being."

"So, are you too angry or too proud to pray?" Keith asked quietly.

Will felt the surgeon's words blow like a tempest through his soul, snatching all the rage and sending it skyward, leaving nothing behind but raw, searing pain. The question echoed in his ears as if from a distance as Keith laid a hand on his shoulder.

"I get it, Will, I do. I was right where you are, nine years ago, when I lost my son to cancer. Eighteen months old, the light of my life, and I couldn't pray for him. It seemed like foolishness to me, and even as desperate as I was, I couldn't bring myself to call out to a god I didn't believe in to save my son. I don't know what would have happened if I had, maybe the outcome would have been the same, but at the very least I would have known I did everything in my power to save him." Keith drew in a deep breath, his audible exhalation filled with pain and remorse. "Don't make the same mistake, Will."

Drawn from his own concerns by the angst in the surgeon's voice, Will turned. "I'm sorry."

"It's a regret I can't shake." His hand squeezed Will's shoulder before he turned toward the door. "Sharing it is all I can do now."

Will watched the surgeon leave as quietly as he had come, a chill working its way across his shoulders and settling at the base of his skull. He knew Keith's heartfelt confession deserved more consideration. It came from a core of deep regret, and Will doubted Garrison shared it often.

Rounding the bed, Will stared at the afternoon light playing across Cherie's still features. Bending down he pressed his lips to her forehead, seeking to draw from her the belief he could not find in himself.

He didn't think it was foolish to believe in God. He understood many people drew comfort from their belief, but he just didn't think it was real. He didn't think God reached into the lives of people on earth and changed the outcomes. The God of his upbringing was the only touchstone he had as a reference, and that God was one of distance and wrath, the 'gotcha' God who chastised wrongdoing with retribution. As an adult he recognized the childlike nature of that thinking, but there was a part of him that couldn't get past it, because he had no other benchmark.

Until he met Cherie.

She spoke with love of a God of relationship, there with her in the darkest moments of her life, not drawing her out of the darkness but staying there with her. A God intimately involved with every utterance of pain and anguish, who could take her anger and not penalize her for it. How could the God he remembered have anything in common with the God Cherie described with such reverence.

Will pushed the hair back from Cherie's forehead, the texture silky, slipping through his fingers. Amy and Judith had been here earlier and had washed her hair. Will wasn't sure how they had managed it, but their love had won out over the logistics.

He could pray for Cherie, he thought, just as Maddie and Keith had suggested. He could stand in the gap and pray for her when she couldn't do it herself. But Will knew it would be an empty gesture without the one element Cherie had been trying to help him find since they met. Faith.

Without faith, prayer was just a desperate ask. And if you didn't believe in the one you were asking, it was nothing more than a field goal kicked form the fifty yard-line with nowhere to land.

He couldn't just summon up faith because he needed it. Faith came from a place of certainty, of believing, like Cherie, in what you could not see, and Will knew in his heart he had none. He only believed in things he could see and touch and feel.

And God was nowhere to be seen in any of this horror. The fall. The surgery. The endless waiting for recovery. Will shot to his feet, his anger resurfacing in a wave of rage that made his pulse race, his breathing ragged. This couldn't be how it ended, in some celestial stalemate with a God he didn't believe in. He felt the heat rise in his face, recalling the words spoken just moments ago that seemed to linger in the still room.

Are you too angry or too proud to pray?

His gut clenched in pain, his stomach roiling. Was he still making excuses because he was too proud, too stubborn to pray? Was his lack of faith just another excuse? The thought landed like a one-two punch to the gut. Saliva filled his mouth as his stomach heaved.

He rounded the bed and shoved open the bathroom door, hearing it bang against the wall and then swing inward. Bracing his arms on the sink, he retched, but having eaten nothing since early this morning, he was left dry-heaving, waiting for the wave to pass. His forehead drenched in sweat, he spit into the sink, feeling the nausea begin to subside. He turned the cold tap on full and cupped his hands to splash his face, the bracing cold a welcome relief. With the chill on his skin, he could feel his anger receding, but one thought clear and simple remained. A challenge he knew he had no right to ask. Yet, he did.

"If you are here with us, then show me," Will said as he raised his dripping face and met his own gaze in the mirror above the sink.

He waited, standing to his full height, and reaching for a paper towel. He closed his eyes and brought the crisp paper to his face, a series of images flashing through his mind.

The young woman covered in blood, and the tube he had been unable to place.

The medics rounding the corner of the restaurant with their life-saving equipment within minutes of Cherie falling.

The wet ground beneath his belly as he held the endotracheal tube over Cherie's mouth.

Dr. Patel pulling the curtain closed and leading the team in the ER.

Dr. Garrison, weary and rumpled, throwing his surgical cap in the trash as he made his way down the hallway after so many hours of surgery.

The speed with which Cherie was able to be extubated and breathe on her own.

The final image was one from weeks ago, the night he had lost two patients in one shift. That night he had held Cherie in his arms for the first time as she offered comfort for his guilt and grief, driving the darkness of his failures from his soul. She had called faith a warm blanket people wrap around themselves, not because they have to, but because they want to, making faith a result of choice, not need. He could almost hear her words now. 'Blest are they who have not seen but still believe', she'd told him revealing her story of finding God in the darkest moments of her loss and how she had clung to Him in desperation. Well, he was equally as desperate now.

Will turned from the mirror and took a step toward the door. Those who knew more than he did were telling him Cherie might never have any meaningful recovery. He had nowhere else to go. Could he make the choice Cherie had talked about, with all his lingering doubts, could he make a choice to believe?

Slowly, Will sank to his knees.

"I can't do this alone, not anymore," he whispered, the floor cold through the thin cotton of his scrubs. "I am desperate, filled with anger and … pride. I have nothing to offer you but the tiniest sliver of faith, more a choice than a feeling. But I see it now. The timing. The perfect people there at the right time to save her. Even me. I don't understand why it had to happen in the first place, but I see you now, just like Maddie said, in what happened after. I don't deserve your help. I've never looked to you for anything or offered a prayer in thanks for all I've been given and for that and my pride, I'm sorry."

"Cherie loves you, Lord," Will continued, bending his head and though he'd thought the name would stick in his throat, it came out as easily as all the rest. "You know I love her with my whole heart, so I am asking you to save her, to restore her to consciousness and health, to bring her back to her little girls and to me." He paused, tears filling his eyes. "I will leave her if you need me to or love her my entire life if you let me, whatever you want, but please save her. I don't remember much about how to pray, but I do remember they all end the same way, in Jesus' name, Amen."

Will couldn't move, didn't want to. His anger was gone and in its place was … stillness. And all he wanted to do was rest in it.

He heard the door open and lifted his gaze. Through the opening between the bathroom door and the wall, he heard the squeak of footsteps. Expecting to see one of the nurses, Will began to get to his feet, but grew still, remaining on his knees as he watched Jake approach the bed where Cherie lay.

Jake stood for a moment simply watching his sister's slow even breathing. Then he reached out and laid his hands, one on her shoulder and the other on her forehead. Closing his eyes, he lifted his face upward, his lips still. Cherie looked so small in the bed, a sharp contrast to her brother whose wide shoulders and stance spoke of a confidence in prayer so different from Will's own. Opening his eyes, Jake slowly bent down and kissed Cherie's cheek. He lingered for only a moment longer, but before Will could get to his feet, Jake was gone.

Will pulled open the door, wondering why Jake hadn't stayed longer. He'd driven an awfully long way to stay for less than five minutes. Distracted by his thoughts, Will saw the movement thinking it was a flicker of shadow from a cloud passing in front of the sun. But instinctively registering the difference, he waited, holding his breath, and willing it to happen again. He could have been mistaken. The blanket lifted ever so slightly. He exhaled sharply, the thrill of possibility sending a shiver of anticipation up his spine. In quick strides, he covered the distance to the bed and pulled back the covering over Cherie's feet. Will watched her toes move, first one foot and then the other. A grin split his face as the tears rolled down his cheeks.

He hurried to the other side of the bed, his gaze riveted on her eyes, knowing that often the first sign of reemergence from coma was eye opening. Beneath her closed lids, he could see her eyes moving before they blinked open slowly, seemingly unable to focus. Confusion in the post coma state was not unusual. Will didn't want to scare her or increase her confusion, so he kept it simple. Just her name.

"Cherie?" he said softly.

Her eyes tracked toward his voice and Will swiped a hand across his eyes to clear his vision.

"Will." One word. One simple word of recognition and hope, before her eyes fluttered closed.

'Blest are they who have not seen but still believe,' Cherie had told him, and now Will recalled the rest. 'Well, I wasn't one of those, but I do believe.'

Me too, Will thought, lifting his eyes upward and feeling like his heart would explode in his chest, offering up the first prayer of gratitude he had ever prayed. "Thank you."

Chapter Twenty

Will helped Cherie from the car, wrapping an arm around her as they walked up the path to her parents' house. After two weeks of intense rehab, Cherie didn't need his help to walk any longer, but Will relished the simple pleasure of walking beside her, his arm around her waist.

Cherie turned her head to look at him. "I can't wait to hold the girls; I've missed them so much!"

"They were so excited last night; they didn't fall asleep until after ten. Sarah said it was like waiting for Santa Claus only better."

"Good to know I rank higher than the big guy with the presents," Cherie laughed, her gaze fixed on the front door. "I haven't lived with my parents since I was in college. This is going to take a little getting used to."

"It's only for a few weeks until you build up your strength," Will said, dropping a kiss on her head. "I don't think you're quite ready for full-time parenting yet, do you?"

Cherie shook her head. "I was barely able to juggle all that before the fall, and now I need more naptime than Carey."

The front door flew open.

"Mommy!" The three girls squealed with one voice as they pushed open the screen door. Clearly Molly remembered what they had talked about last night, Will noted as she held out a hand to restrain her sisters.

Cherie sank down on the top step, holding out her arms as Carey climbed into her lap and Molly and Sarah flanked her on either side, sitting as close to her as they could get. Watching them together, all laughing and talking at the same time, Will knew there were so many people to thank for this remarkable reunion. His gaze lifted to the rest of Cherie's family gathered in the doorway, giving the girls this time with their mom.

Inside moments later, the mood was one of pure joy with smiles and hugs, gentle tears, and words of wonder. He and Cherie had spent the last two weeks working tirelessly to repeat the exercises prescribed by the physical and occupational therapy teams, and all so she would be ready for this moment, to come home to her family. And even with all that time together, Will still felt reluctant to leave her side.

Pastor Michaels joined the group shortly after their arrival, her joyful spirit adding a new layer of gratitude to the day. She gently embraced Cherie, keeping her enthusiasm in her words, not her hugs. "Welcome back, my friend. It is so good to see you."

"Thank you for the prayer," Cherie smiled. "And the all-night vigil."

"I was blown away by that myself, a truly spontaneous outpouring of prayer after the evening bible study," Gabby said. "So many felt the need to intercede for you and your family. And when word got out via text even more people joined them. The veterans' group. The parents of your students. The women you have worked with in ministry. It was quite a sight."

"And you loved every minute of it."

Gabby's features grew still, her gaze focused on Cherie like she was the only one in the room. "I was awestruck. I didn't have to ask them to pray, their faith led them to it, to speak as one voice and petition God for your full recovery. Now, here you are, whole and healing, and I am humbled at the faith of our community. How are you feeling?"

"Getting stronger every day."

Gabby squeezed her hand as a smile lit her face. "Has he told you yet?"

"Told me what?" Cherie asked, glancing over at Will, who knew what was coming but had managed to keep it to himself. The story was not his to tell.

"Jake. Has he told you about the match?" Gabby raised her arm and waved him over.

Jake crossed the room to join them.

"Sorry, I think I blew the surprise," Gabby said. "Couldn't keep it in a minute longer."

"I know the feeling," Jake said, turning to Cherie. "The donor drive at your church produced a match for me, an altruistic donor."

"Oh Jake, that's wonderful," Cherie said, reaching for his hand.

"Not the best part though," Gabby inserted.

Jake laughed at her enthusiasm. "The young woman who matched me wanted to make her gift have the largest impact possible. She could give her kidney directly to me and that would be one life changed forever by her generosity, but the transplant team had something bigger in mind and when they asked her, she agreed."

"It's called a compatible share program," Will said, stepping up next to Cherie. "There are many people on the transplant list with family members willing to donate but who don't match. So, using the data in the system UNOS creates compatible pairings in a chain of donation where those willing to donate give to someone else's family member and then theirs in turn receives a compatible kidney."

"In this case, the chain is ten pairs long," Jake said, a hint of awe coloring his tone. "Ten people will receive a new kidney and all because one young woman stepped forward willing to donate to a perfect stranger."

"And this all happened because you had the idea to do a donor drive at the church," Cherie said, looking over at Gabby.

"Now whose idea was it?" she asked with a smile. "I guess I could take the credit, but I think there was always a bigger plan here."

Jake reached for Cherie's hand, meeting her gaze as the two stood face to face. "When your generous gift to me was no longer an option, I think God created a bigger opportunity to help more people. But the most important part, what I keep coming back to, is that without my diagnosis and your willingness to consider being my donor, we might never have found our way back to each other, to this place that has made our family whole again." Jake glanced over at Judith, smiling as she handed Joe a bowl of potato salad from the refrigerator.

With a booming voice, Joe called, "Time to eat! But first can we say grace? Pastor Michaels, can you do the honors?"

"With pleasure," Gabby said as the family gathered around the kitchen island. "I'm going to keep this short and sweet because these little girls need to eat, and so do I."

Gabby stretched out her hands, palms open. "Thank you, Lord, for the joy, the healing, the forgiveness, and the food, all given by your hand to those you love. We are humbled by your abundant generosity, Amen."

Will lingered in the kitchen after getting Cherie and the girls settled at the table on the deck.

Beside him, Jake filled his plate with a large helping of salad and a piece of grilled chicken. "I can't wait to be able to eat mom's pickles and potato salad again."

Will turned to him, empty plate in hand, reminded how he had misjudged this man. "I saw what you did for Cherie that day in the hospital."

Jake met his gaze squarely. "It's called the laying on of hands. It's been a part of the Christian church since its inception."

"You saved her, Jake," Will said, his throat tight.

"Not just me, Will. So many people were praying for her. I was just the final step."

"But you healed her."

"I didn't heal her," Jake said, setting his plate aside and placing a hand on Will's shoulder. "God did. He sent me there as clearly as if He'd called me on my cell phone. I woke up that morning and I knew I had to get to the hospital and pray for Cherie right there in her room." He leaned back against the counter. "Funny thing was, I was trying to get there all day but one thing after another just kept getting in my way. A last-minute call about a job interview. A scheduling glitch with my paramedic exam. It was weird, like God was waiting for something."

Will closed his eyes for a moment. "He was waiting for me. Waiting for me to choose faith over my own pride. I think He wanted to show me the power of a prayer offered in faith, even if that faith is no bigger than a speck of dust."

"So maybe you were the one who healed her."

"Too big a job for me. Just one of many, like you said." Will paused, then asked the question he had been pondering since the day it happened. "Is that the first time you've done that? The laying on of hands?"

Jake stilled; the answer apparent before he said the words. "No, once before, when Neil had a heart attack at the restaurant. It's one of the reasons I started my paramedic training. You can help people either way, I think."

"So, this wasn't an isolated event then?"

Jake looked up at him. "I think that God intervenes more than we even realize. We call it coincidence or timing or luck when it's someone else entirely."

"I don't know if I can wrap my head around that."

"Me either," Jake said. "But sometimes it's as simple as asking for what you need."

"Doesn't explain all the unanswered prayers though, does it?" Will said, a remnant of the skeptic stirring inside him.

"It doesn't, you're right. But I'm going to keep on asking, keep on trusting. I've been on the other side, and I'd rather live with God than without Him. How about you?"

Will glanced out the window and watched Cherie laugh at whatever story Molly was telling her. "I think you might be right about that."

Epilogue

Cherie couldn't imagine a more perfect end to the summer than Labor Day weekend with Will and the girls in New Hampshire. Standing on the dock, Cherie savored the quiet beauty. Will had been right. Maddie's home on the lake was the perfect place to spend this holiday weekend.

Late afternoon sun created prisms of light on the water's surface as a warm breeze stirred up tiny undulating waves. Glancing back toward the house, she could see Kylie herding the girls into the house to change for dinner, their faces sun-kissed and their giggles floating across the lawn. Cherie had offered to help Maddie with the dinner preparations but had been cheerfully shooed out of the kitchen. Not that she minded really. The breeze caught the edges of her yellow sundress as Cherie closed her eyes, lifting her face to the sky, the sun warm on her skin.

"Perfect, isn't it?" Will said from behind her.

"It is now," Cherie answered, glancing over her shoulder. He wore a blue dress shirt and pressed khakis, his feet bare. "Very handsome."

"I saw the dresses you laid out for the girls; just matching the mood." Will closed the distance between them and wrapped his arms around her.

"I can't believe the summer is over," Cherie said quietly, tipping her head back and resting it against his shoulder, trying to put into words a thought she was just starting to get a handle on herself. "It feels funny after all that's happened to be stepping back into the same routine. Don't get me wrong, I am so thankful to be alive, healthy, and here with you and the girls. Sitting in church today with you beside me I was overflowing with gratitude for all of it." She paused. "But I don't think I want to go back. I'm different now, we're different now. Does that make sense?"

"Yes, it does," Will said, his words warm in her ear. "What does that look like?"

Cherie turned to him, her hands resting on his chest, the idea that she had been keeping to herself just waiting to be heard. "I think I want to change careers, Will."

He smiled broadly, clearly understanding the impulse. "What do you want to do?"

"You may think this is crazy …"

"After the last few months, my meter when it comes to crazy is way out there, so what's your dream, Cherie?"

"I want to be a transplant coordinator," Cherie said, watching his face to gauge his reaction.

Will didn't hesitate, his lips turned upward in a wide smile. "Makes perfect sense to me. After seeing how the transplant has changed Jake's life, you've got a real-life perspective to bring to the job."

"He really is doing amazingly well, isn't he? I would love to be a part of the team that makes that happen." Cherie paused, giving voice to the obstacles in her path. "I know I need to go back to school to do it, and with the kids and my job it's going to take time to get there …"

"But if this is what you want to do, we can work all that out," Will said, considering a moment before offering a thought. "It might not take as long as you think if you go back to school full time?"

"I wish I could, but I can't afford to do that," Cherie said with a wistful sigh. "I still need to pay rent and take care of the girls."

"I can see we're going to have to up end everything to take care of that." Taking a step back, Will held her gaze. "Remember when I told you that you would know beyond a shadow of a doubt …"

Cherie's eyes widened, her pulse beginning to race as she watched Will reach into his breast pocket. "We're doing this now?"

"Yes, we are." He withdrew an exquisite ring, the center diamond sparkling in the light as he held it in his hand. "Just to be perfectly clear, I am proposing to you, Cherie. Ready?"

She nodded, transfixed by the perfection of the moment and the love she felt for his man who had changed her life, who had already demonstrated in full what it meant to stand firm in sickness and in health. "You're not going to get down on one knee, are you?"

Will smiled softly. "Only if you want me to."

"I'd prefer you stay right here with me," Cherie said, her eyes brimming as she held out a hand to him.

Will's eyes were as shiny as hers as he took her hand and lifted it between them. His gaze never wavered, his words clear and resounding. "Cherie Hollister, you are the love of my life, a love I never could have even imagined until the day I met you. And having come so close to watching it slip away from us and now being blest with the chance to spend a lifetime together, I am asking you formally and reverently, will you marry me?"

Cherie held his gaze as tears rolled down her cheeks, her chest tight with the intensity of her love for him. "Yes, Will Finnegan, I will marry you, and I have one question for you." She paused, a grin of sheer joy overtaking her face. "Can we do it really soon?"

Slipping the ring on her finger, Will stepped in closer, her hand resting between them. "You don't want a big wedding?"

Cherie shook her head. "Time is too precious. I knew that before, but it is infinitely clearer to me now. I don't want to wait a minute longer to be your wife."

She could see the impact of her words as his features grew still, a look of awe and wonder in his eyes. "I love the sound of that word on your lips. Wife. My Wife."

Both with the same thought, Will bent his head to kiss her as she rose on her toes to meet him.

A perfect kiss, as exquisite as the ring and as sweet as the laughter that suddenly surrounded them.

"We're getting married, aren't we?" Sarah said, wrapping her arms around both their legs.

"Soon?" Molly asked, her hair falling away from her face as she smiled up at them.

"Very soon," Will answered, lifting Carey up before she got trampled in the moment.

"Morrow?" Carey asked, glancing back and forth and mimicking the smiles she saw on all their faces.

"How about two weeks?" he asked Cherie over the heads of their girls. "Your mother will never forgive us if we do this without her."

"I think I can wait that long," Cherie answered, "but just barely. You do know you may never have another quiet moment in your life."

"I'm counting on that," Will grinned.

THE END

Acknowledgments

Writing a novel is a solitary endeavor, at least at first but there comes a day when the sentences are completed, the story finished, and it is time to put your words in the hands of a team that can make it better, a team you trust to be honest and encouraging all at the same time. Thank you to Kelly Anderson, Allison Anderson, and Mary Ellen Sullivan who read the first draft of *In This Lifetime* and gave valuable feedback that helped tighten the story and further the character development.

Many thanks to Katie Szucs MSN, APN Clinical Manager, Living Donor Institute Renal and Pancreas Transplant Division at Cooperman Barnabas Medical Center, for sitting down with me and answering all my questions about living donor transplant surgery. Thank you also to Melissa Gato MSN, RN, CEN and Jennifer Viray RN for their help with the medical details. Transplant centers across the country vary somewhat in terms of their internal policies and procedures, and I have taken some literary license in the timing of events and testing to facilitate the story, but valuable life-saving work is accomplished all across the country, every day, by transplant teams like ours at RWJBarnabas Health.

To those who gave generously of their time and talents to help me at various steps on the road to publication I would like to thank: Elizabeth Fitzpatrick, George Barry, Fr. Brian Sullivan, Dennis Corcoran, Erin Ranft, and Pamela Abell. A very special shout out and thank you to my cousin, Jodi Daley for putting together the promotional video, a task well beyond my skill set.

My thanks to Kharis Publishing for finding the manuscript synopsis I posted on Christian Book Proposals and then asking me to submit a proposal. The team at Kharis has made this return to the world of publishing a joy in my life.

A special thank you to those who have encouraged me over the years and who have rejoiced with me in the culmination of this dream: Meredith Stehle, Michael Anderson, and Grace Hoefig. I wish my sister Heather-Jo Taferner had lived to see this moment. She read and edited so much of my earlier work, when I was still learning to be a writer. I know she's smiling down from heaven as this book goes out into the world.

And one final thank you, to my husband and best friend, Rodd, for the family we have created together, for sharing the victories, helping me through the sorrows and feeding me lavishly all along the way. God has truly blest us!

About
Kharis Publishing:

Kharis Publishing, an imprint of Kharis Media LLC, is a leading Christian and inspirational book publisher based in Aurora, Chicago metropolitan area, Illinois. Kharis' dual mission is to give voice to under-represented writers (including women and first-time authors) and equip orphans in developing countries with literacy tools. That is why, for each book sold, the publisher channels some of the proceeds into providing books and computers for orphanages in developing countries so that these kids may learn to read, dream, and grow. For a limited time, Kharis Publishing is accepting unsolicited queries for nonfiction (Christian, self-help, memoirs, business, health and wellness) from qualified leaders, professionals, pastors, and ministers. Learn more at: https://kharispublishing.com/

9 781637 462638